MW01110176

CHRISTIAN LIGHT EDUCATION
Reading Series

The Road Less Traveled

Seventh Grade Reader

Compiled by Tim Kennedy

 **CHRISTIAN LIGHT EDUCATION**
A division of **Christian Light Publications**
Harrisonburg, Virginia 22802   (540) 434-0750   www.clp.org/cle

CHRISTIAN LIGHT
Reading Series

THE ROAD LESS TRAVELED
Christian Light Education, a division of
Christian Light Publications, Harrisonburg, VA 22802
©2004 Christian Light Publications, Inc.
All Rights Reserved.

Printed in China

Sixth Printing, 2018

ISBN: 978-0-87813-852-4

Table *of* Contents

705   Stooping Gracefully

The Road Not Taken

Two roads diverged in a yellow wood,
And sorry I could not travel both
And be one traveler, long I stood
And looked down one as far as I could
To where it bent in the undergrowth;

Then took the other, as just as fair,
And having perhaps the better claim,
Because it was grassy and wanted wear;
Though as for that the passing there
Had worn them really about the same,

And both that morning equally lay
In leaves no step had trodden black.
Oh, I kept the first for another day!
Yet knowing how way leads on to way,
I doubted if I should ever come back.

I shall be telling this with a sigh
Somewhere ages and ages hence:
Two roads diverged in a wood, and I—
I took the one less traveled by,
And that has made all the difference.

– Robert Frost

Deciphering
Nature's Parables

The Mahogany Fox

Samuel Scoville, Jr.

He began life as a red cub. As he grew older, his coat became darker until it was the exact shade of a well-polished mahogany table and gained him his name. By the time Old Mahogany had reached his full growth, he was the largest, the handsomest, and the wiliest fox in all that hill country of Litchfield County, Connecticut.

In his fifth year the three best fox hunters of Cornwall conspired against him. Myron Dean, off the Barrack; Rashe Howe, down from the Cobble; and Mark Hurlburt, out of the Hollow, agreed to pool their packs and hunt him down.

"Let Mark start off tomorrow morning with his young dogs," said Myron, when they met at the village store. " 'Bout the middle o' the morning Rashe here can spell him. In the afternoon, if he's still goin', I'll turn my old dogs loose."

"He'll be goin' all right," returned Rashe. "I don't believe there's a dog livin' that can run him down."

"Well, that's right," returned Myron, "but perhaps fifteen of 'em can."

The next day, early in the morning, the great fox left his den in the side of Rattlesnake Mountain. The deep mahogany of his back showed glints of gold; his long slim legs were coal black, and his flanks and thighs a blending of tawny pinks, russets, and ebony, while his brush[1] seemed tipped with snow.

On the hillside, where the pale-rose sedges waved in the wind, he suddenly stopped and the next moment pounced upon a tuft of grass that had moved ever so slightly. Thrusting his slim muzzle down between his forepaws, the great fox gripped and swallowed in a couple of gulps a round-bodied, short-tailed meadow mouse. Before he left the hill, he had caught and eaten six more and finished his breakfast by drinking

2   1   brush: tail

sparingly from a little brook whose shadowed surface showed like a twisted strip of watered silk against the snow.

A little later and Old Mahogany was well satisfied that he had not eaten more heavily, as he heard from the bare crest of the Cobble the bell-like notes of Rashe Howe's dappled black-and-yellow fox hounds.

For an instant the trim figure stood tense, like a statue of speed. Then he was gone—and only a flash of red against the melting drifts at the far end of the valley showed where.

As the hounds quartered[2] the valley, they came upon the fresh tracks of the great fox, and the hillsides echoed with their baying.

A mile ahead, circling Rattlesnake Mountain, the fox moved with a long easy stride that ate up the ground like fire. Through thickets and second-growth timber he ran straight and true, with the clamor of the pack sounding louder behind him, until he reached the middle of a great sandbank that stretched for some distance along the mountainside. The loose, dry sand completely covered both his tracks and his scent.

For two hundred yards he made his way along the slanting sand until he came to where a white ash grew horizontally from the side of the hill about six feet above his head. For an instant the fox stopped and eyed the tree above him. Then, with a tremendous bound, he hooked his forepaws over it, scrambled up on the trunk, and the next moment had disappeared in a thicket on the slope of the mountain.

A little later the pack burst out of the valley in full cry. At the sandbank they lost the scent, separated, ran along both edges of the bank, and circled each end without finding any sign of the fox's tracks. Again and again the well-trained dogs hunted back and forth, trying vainly to locate the spot where the fox had left the bank. At last their leader, a crafty **veteran**, happened to run out a few feet on the ash tree. Instantly he caught the lost scent, and the next second his loud bay brought the other hounds to the spot.

For half the length of the trunk the fox tracks showed in the snow. Then they disappeared. It was plain to the pack what had happened. The fox had leaped from the tree trunk and landed somewhere in the surrounding thickets. Instantly every hound was nosing and sniffing his

---

2 quarter: to crisscross in many directions

way through masses of close-set bushes until suddenly one of them gave tongue—and the chase was on again.

All this delay, however, had given the fugitive a long start; and by the time his pursuers were on his trail, he had crossed the mountain. On its farther side he came out on a concrete state road that connected two of the larger towns of that northern country. Down its long stretch the fox moved leisurely, his wise face wrinkled deeply as if he were planning some new stratagem.[3] Then, as he heard again the baying of the pack from the crest of the mountain behind him, he increased his pace, only to leave the road with a bound and crouch in a thicket as he saw a car approaching.

It was only the battered sedan in which Bunker Rogers was bringing back a load of groceries from Cornwall Bridge, but to the hunted animal it was refuge and escape. With a quick spring he landed on the spare tire at the rear of the car and, crouching there, doubled back on his trail without leaving track or trace of his going.

Undoubtedly the Red One had expected to be far away in an opposite direction to the trail that the hounds were following long before they reached the road. If so, he had miscalculated their speed, for the car met them racing along hot on the fresh scent. Old Bunker sounded his horn, and the pack reluctantly divided to allow the car to pass. If but one of them had looked back, he would have seen, not six feet away, Old Mahogany clinging to the spare tire.

As he whirled past his enemies, unseen, the Red One's tongue lolled out; and if ever a fox grinned, that one did.

It was Mark Hurlburt who prevented Old Mahogany from making a clean getaway. Mark was a great believer in Irish terriers, and in a flivver[4] of ancient vintage overflowing with tawny little dogs, he had been patrolling the road a few miles farther on, convinced that sooner or later the fox would follow the highway.

When at last he met and passed Bunker's car, his terriers began to yelp frantically. Looking back, Mark saw a mass of dark red fur at the rear of the speeding sedan; but by the time he had stopped and turned around, the other car was nearly out of sight.

---

3 stratagem: a trick to deceive an enemy
4 flivver: an old or cheap car

Then began an unusual fox chase. Rattling along in his old flivver, Mark tooted his horn incessantly, while beside him the terriers barked and howled at the top of their shrill voices. For a time the fox gained on the pack. Gradually, however, running at full speed, the flivver began to overtake the sedan, and before long Mark could plainly see the fox clinging to the spare tire and grinning defiance at him.

At last the **tumult** of toots and barks penetrated even Bunker's deaf ears, and he stopped his car, while the fox leaped down from his perch and disappeared in the brush. With some difficulty Mark managed to unleash his tugging terriers, and in another moment they were hot on Old Mahogany's trail as he headed toward the Hollow, the largest valley in Cornwall Township.

All that morning the fox had run without stop or pause, save for the short ride, and the pace had begun to tell—otherwise the terriers could never have kept so close to him. They were in sight as he reached the slow, deep brook that wound its way through the Hollow, and they were still nearer, when directly ahead of him sounded the baying of the Howe hounds, that had raced back along the road and crossed the Hollow when they heard the yelps of the terriers.

Then it was that the Red One, with a pack behind him and a pack before, and his strength half gone, fell back upon the craft that had saved his life so many times before.

Hollow Brook was a good thirty feet wide and filled with floating ice. At one point a broken tree trunk spanned about a third of its width and along that the fox made his way until he reached the end of the stub. From there it might have been possible for him to reach the farther bank, but with such a slippery take-off, the chances were all against him.

Old Mahogany, however, had not the least intention of risking that jump. Turning in his tracks, he went back along the slanting trunk until he reached the bank and then broke his trail by a tremendous bound into a nearby thicket, whence he made his way up the mountainside to the highway again. Hardly was he out of sight when both packs came into view from either end of the valley and met at the brook. The terriers reached the tree trunk first. Following the hot scent along the stub, the **staunch** little dogs made their way to its end and from there plunged into the icy water and swam to the farther shore.

The hounds were hard on their heels. By a tremendous jump the leader just managed to make the opposite bank, but the force of his spring broke the decayed trunk and plunged the rest of the pack into the brook. The next minute they had joined the dripping terriers on the farther bank and were casting back and forth trying to find some trace of the vanished fox.

The leader of the hounds, after he had quartered the whole bank without picking up a scent, decided that both packs had been deceived by the unscrupulous fox. With a melancholy bay he plunged into the freezing water and swam back to the other bank, followed by the hounds and terriers alike. There they soon picked up the trail again, but the time lost had given the hunted animal a long lead.

In the meantime, Old Mahogany was trotting along the state road, perhaps hoping for another ride such as had almost baffled his pursuers a few hours before. No such good luck was his this time, for the highway stretched away before him, deserted and untraveled, nor was it long before he heard again down the wind the baying of the hounds.

At the sound the fox turned into an abandoned road that crossed the tracks of a little branch railway leading to some quarries. The long chase since early morning had begun to wear down even his iron endurance. The brush, which had flaunted[5] high all day like a dark red plume, drooped; and the long easy bounds that had taken him so far and fast had shortened by the time the trestle bridge spanning Deep River like a vast cobweb was in sight.

The baying of the packs sounded much nearer. All at once around a bend in the road appeared the hounds in front and the terriers strung out behind. As they came in sight, from far down the track came the whistle of an approaching train. At the sound the red fox ran more and more slowly until, by the time he had reached the path that spiraled up to the trestle, he was leading his pursuers by a scant hundred yards.

As the packs rushed up the path and reached the trestle, they found the fox plodding along the ties with drooping brush and lowered head. Every dog gave tongue and dashed after him.

Suddenly there was another whistle, and around the bend came the train. Before the pack even realized their danger, the engine had reached

_____

5 flaunt: to wave proudly

the trestle and was rushing toward them. At the sight, the mahogany fox came to life and with a quick bound sprang from the middle of the track to a series of beams not six inches wide that joined the end of the ties at the edge of the trestle.

Fifty feet below was the black river; yet he ran unconcernedly at full speed toward the approaching train. Then, when it seemed as though he had but a few seconds to live—the fox disappeared!

Long ago Old Mahogany had learned that in the middle of that great span a tie had been taken out, leaving an entrance to a winding set of steps for workmen on the bridge.

As the engineer saw the dogs just ahead, he set his brakes, while the pack turned and fled for their lives. Even so, the engine would have run them down if it had not been for the leader of Rashe Howe's pack. Seeing that he was about to be overtaken, he instantly leaped out into space, to land in a great snowdrift by the edge of the river, immediately followed by the rest of the pack until the air was full of leaping, yelping dogs. All escaped with their lives but were too shaken to do any more fox hunting that day.

As the train came to a full stop at the far side of the trestle, Mark's car rattled up the steep grade to the track.

" 'Twarn't your fault," the old man bellowed to the engineer. " 'Twas that red fox . . . who nearly killed off two o' the best packs of huntin' dogs in this county. There he goes now," he shrieked a second later.

Sure enough, loping leisurely across the railway bridge was the fox, who had popped up as soon as the train passed above him.

"You ain't got away yet," muttered Mark. "Myron Dean's on the river road with his pack, an' he'll give you the run o' your life."

As he spoke, he fired both barrels of the shotgun that he carried, the agreed signal of the approach of the fox. So as Old Mahogany trotted along the narrow road that followed the farther side of the river, he heard a car approaching; and even as he plunged into the nearest thicket, Myron Dean pulled up beside the trestle and unloaded his pack.

For generations the black packs of the Barrack had been celebrated throughout Litchfield County. Other hunters might experiment with brown and yellow and white, but for a hundred years the Dean family had bred their hounds black. The six that tugged at their leashes as Myron stopped his car had not a white spot on their ebony bodies; only their ears and a patch of their flanks were marked with tan.

Samuel Scoville, Jr. (1872-1950) was born in New York and graduated from Yale University in 1893. After graduation he worked to become a lawyer. Some of his books have been translated into other languages.

Released, the pack at once caught the fresh scent, and for an instant their blended voices rose in one high, **vibrant** note; then they settled down to the grim silence in which the dogs of the Barrack always hunted.

The spent day was all rose red and pearl, while the tiny ponds scattered among the trees gleamed like pools of blurred silver in the wistful light as the mahogany fox sped through the slowly darkening woods.

There was little time to try any more of his wiles. Once, indeed, he ran along the top rail of a fence in an old pasture, hoping to break his trail by springing to some overhanging bough, but he fell off from sheer weakness before he had gone many feet.

For a brief moment he rested and saw far below him the wide curve of the stream. Then, as he squeezed the snow water out of his brush, he heard an ominous *pad, pad* behind him, and six black shadows flashed out of a thicket not fifty yards away.

Calling upon the last of his speed, the Red One raced toward the river, through the umber[6] patches of withered fern, with the dark hounds at his heels. Even as he reached the bank, a great cake of rough ice floated past, a good twenty feet away. Without a pause the hunted animal leaped far out. If he missed, or if he failed to keep his footing, he was lost, for no land animal could have lived in the rush of that swollen stream.

As his body arched high above the black water, it seemed as though he would fall short; but like the crack jumper that he was, the fox shot forward and landed full and fair on the floating slab of ice. It swayed and sank for a moment beneath his weight; but clamping his blunt claws deep into the rough surface of the ice pan, he clung to it, and the next moment he was whirling down the stream.

For a time the black hounds ran along beside him. Then, as a cross-current swept the mass of ice toward the farther shore, they turned and

---

6 umber: a dark yellow-brown

raced back across the railroad trestle to take up the hunt again on the other side of the river.

As the floe grounded, Old Mahogany sprang ashore and dashed away with a great show of speed. As soon, however, as the pack was out of sight, he hurried back to the bank, leaped aboard the ice cake as it floated off, and started once more on another voyage.

By the time the pack had crossed on the trestle and raced down to where the fox had landed, he was out of sight downstream; and while the dogs tried in vain to puzzle out his trail, he leaped to an overhanging willow tree on the opposite bank, a mile away, and made his way ashore.

Convinced at last that he had tangled his trail past all unraveling, the Red One moved like a shadow through the thickets. There was a smoky red flare in the east, and a crimson rim showed among the black-violet shadows of the horizon as he loped up the slope of Coltsfoot Mountain. Slowly the moon climbed the sky and became a great shield of raw gold, which turned the dark to silver. In the still light the fox made his way to the edge of a little clearing where stood an abandoned haystack, one of his many hunting lodges.

Beneath it he had dug a long winding burrow, connected with a maze of tunnels driven here and there and everywhere through the soft, dry hay. In the very center of the stack, he had hollowed out a room in which was cached a brace of partridges, part of a covey dug out from under the snow a few weeks before. On these Old Mahogany feasted full, and then, curled up in a round ball with his soft nose and tired paws buried in his warm brush, he slept soundly, as a fox should sleep who has outrun, outlasted, and outwitted in one day the three best packs of hunting dogs in the state of Connecticut.

"I know all the fowls of the mountains: and the wild beasts of the field are mine." – Psalm 50:11

The Fox

John Burroughs

I see the hills lift themselves up cold and white against the sky. Presently, a fox barks away up the mountain, and I imagine that I see him sitting there, in his furs, upon the illuminated surface, and looking down in my direction. As I listen, a brother fox answers him from behind the woods in the valley. What a wild winter sound—wild and weird, up among the ghostly hills!

Since the wolf has ceased to howl upon these mountains and the panther to scream, there is nothing to be compared with it. So wild! I get up in the middle of the night to hear it. It is refreshing to the ear, and one delights to know that such untamed creatures are among us. At this season nature makes the most of every throb of life that can withstand her **severity**. How heartily she **endorses** this fox!

I go out in the morning after a fresh fall of snow and see where he has crossed the road. At one point he has leisurely passed within rifle-range of the house, evidently reconnoitering[1] the **premises** with an eye to the henroost. The snow is a great telltale.

That clear, sharp track—there is no mistaking it for the clumsy footprint of a little dog. All his wildness and **agility** are photographed in it. Here he has taken fright or suddenly recollected an engagement, and in long graceful leaps, barely touching the fence, has gone careering[2] up the hill as fleet as the wind.

The wild, buoyant

John Burroughs (1837-1921), an American naturalist, was born in New York and lived much of his life there in his log house, "Slabsides." He was widely known for his many essays on nature.

---

1 reconnoiter: to make a journey to inspect
2 career: to run quickly, wildly

creature—how beautiful he is! I had often, at a distance, seen the hounds drive him across the fields. But the thrill and excitement of meeting him in his wild freedom in the woods were unknown to me, till one cold winter day, when, drawn out by the baying of a hound, I stood near the summit of the mountain, waiting a renewal of the sound, that I might determine the course of the dog and choose my position.

Long and patiently I waited, till, chilled and benumbed and disappointed, I turned back and was descending the mountain when I heard a slight noise. I looked up and beheld a most superb fox, loping along with **inimitable** grace and ease, evidently undisturbed. Not pursued by the hound, he was so absorbed in his private meditations that he failed to see me, though I stood not ten yards distant, absolutely **transfixed** with amazement and admiration.

I took his measure at a glance—a large male, with dark legs and massive brush tipped with white—a most magnificent creature. So astonished and fascinated was I by his sudden appearance and matchless beauty, that not till I caught the last glimpse of him as he disappeared over a knoll did I awake to my duty as a sportsman and realize what an opportunity to distinguish myself I had unconsciously let slip.

I clutched my gun half angrily as if it were to blame and went home out of humor with myself and with all fox-kind. But I have since thought better of the experience, concluding that the sight of Reynard in his untamed grace and freedom was worth more to me than the excitement of the most successful chase.

Why Reynard? How did *Reynard* come to be a nickname for foxes? The story begins nearly one thousand years ago. In the Middle Ages, tales began to be told in which the characters were animals. Reynard the fox was the hero, overcoming strength—usually the bear or the wolf—by trickery and craftiness. By the 1200s in France, these tales were so popular that the word *renard* became the French word for "fox." You may have heard the tale of how the bear lost his tail, in which Reynard tricks the bear into ice fishing with his tail, the water freezes over, the bear pulls his tail off, "and that is why the bear, to this day, has only a stub of a tail."

"The eye that mocketh at his father, and despiseth to obey his mother, the ravens of the valley shall pick it out, and the young eagles shall eat it." – Proverbs 30:17

A Cry in the Night

William J. Long

This is a story, just as I saw it, of the little fawns that I found under the mossy log by the brook. There were two of them, and though they looked alike at first glance, I soon found out that there is just as much difference in fawns as there is in people. Eyes, faces, **dispositions**, characters—in all things they were unlike. One of them was wise, and the other foolish. The one was a follower, a learner; he never forgot the important lesson that he must follow the white flag. From the beginning the other followed only his own willful head and feet and discovered too late that obedience is life.

When she knew I had found them, the wise old mother took both fawns away and hid them deeper in the big woods. For days after the wonderful discovery, I looked for them in the early morning or the late afternoon, while the mother deer was away feeding along the streams. I searched the valley from one end to the other, hoping to find the little ones again and win their confidence. But they were not there. Then one day, I ran upon the deer and her fawns lying together under a fallen treetop, dozing in the heat of the day. They did not see me and were only scared into action as a branch gave way beneath my feet and let me down with a great crash. At the first crack they all jumped like Jack-in-a-box when you touch his spring. The mother put up her white flag—the snowy underside of her useful tail—and bounded away with a hoarse *Ka-a-a-h!* of warning.

One of the little ones followed her on the instant, jumping squarely in his mother's tracks, his own little white flag flying to guide any that might come after him. But the other fawn ran off zigzag and stopped in a moment to stare and whistle and stamp his tiny foot in an odd mixture of

12

curiosity and defiance. The mother had to circle back twice before he followed her at last, unwillingly.

When she jumped away, the white flag was straight up, flashing in the very face of her foolish fawn. It told him, as plainly as any language, that he must follow this sign if he would escape danger and avoid breaking his legs in the tangled underbrush.

The most wonderful part of a deer's education shows itself, not in his keen eyes or trumpet ears or in his finely trained nose, but in his feet, which seem to have eyes and nerves and brains packed into their hard shells.

Once only I found a fawn with untrained feet that had broken its leg; and once I heard of a wounded buck, driven to death by dogs, which had fallen in the same way never to rise again. These were rare cases. The marvel is that it does not happen to every deer that fear drives through the wilderness.

And that is another reason why the fawns must learn to obey a wiser head than their own. Until their little feet are educated, the mother must choose the way for them; and a wise young fawn will jump squarely in her tracks.

After the second discovery of the fawns, I used to go in the afternoon to a point on the lake near their hiding place and wait in my canoe for the mother to come out and show me where she had left her little ones. Then I would paddle away and, taking my direction from her trail as she came, hunt constantly for the fawns until I found them.

This I succeeded in doing only two or three times. The little ones were already wild. They had forgotten all about our first meeting, and when I showed myself or cracked a twig too near them, they would promptly bolt into the brush. One always ran straight away, his white flag flying to show that he remembered his lesson; the other went off zigzag, stopping at every angle of his run to look back and question me with his eyes and ears.

There was only one way in which such disobedience could end. I saw it plainly one afternoon when I came over a ridge, following a deer path on my way to the lake, and looked down into a long narrow valley.

Just below me a deer was feeding hungrily, only her hindquarters showing out of the underbrush. I watched her awhile, then dropped on all fours and began to creep toward her, to see how near I could get and what new trait I might discover. But at the first motion (I had stood at first like an old stump on the ridge) a fawn that had evidently been watching me all the time from his hiding place sprang into sight with a sharp whistle of warning.

The doe threw up her head, looking straight at me as if she had understood more from the signal than I thought possible. There was not an instant's hesitation or searching. Her eyes went directly to me. Then she jumped away, shooting up the opposite hill over the roots and rocks as if thrown by steel springs, blowing hoarsely at every jump, and followed in splendid style by her watchful little one.

At the first snort of danger, there was a rush in the underbrush near where she had stood, and the other fawn sprang into sight. I knew him instantly—the **heedless** one—and knew also that he had neglected too long the lesson of the white flag. He was confused and frightened now. He came darting up the deer path in the wrong direction, straight toward me, and was within two jumps of me before he noticed me.

At the startling discovery he stopped short, seeming to shrink smaller and smaller before my eyes. Then he edged sidewise to a great stump, hid himself among the roots, and stood stock-still. It was his first lesson—to hide and be still. But just as he needed it most, he had forgotten completely the second lesson—to follow the white flag.

We watched each other five full minutes, scarcely moving an eyelash.

Brave little chap, I like you, I thought, my heart going out to him as he stood there with his soft eyes and beautiful face, stamping his little foot. *But what,* my thoughts went on, *would have happened to you before now, had a bear lifted his head over the ridge?*

Thinking I would teach the fawn a lesson, I picked up a large stone and sent it crashing, jumping, tearing down the hillside straight at him. All his courage vanished like a flash. Up went his flag, and away he sprang over the logs and rocks of the hillside, where presently I heard his mother running in a great circle until she found him and led him out of danger.

Down at the lower end of the same deer path, where it stopped at the lake to let the wild things drink, was a little brook. I was there one night, about two weeks later, trying to catch some of the big trout for my next morning's breakfast.

I was standing very still by my fire, waiting for a trout to bite, when I heard cautious rustlings in the brush behind me. I turned instantly, and there were two glowing spots, the eyes of a deer, flashing out of the dark woods. A swift rustle, and two more coals glowed lower down, flashing with strange colors; and then two more; and I knew that the doe and her fawns were there, stopped and fascinated by the wonder of the firelight.

I knelt down quietly beside my fire, slipping on a great roll of birch bark, which blazed up brightly, filling the woods with light. There, under a spruce tree, where a dark shadow had been a moment before, stood the mother, her eyes all ablaze with the wonder of the light; now staring steadily into the fire; now starting nervously, with low questioning snorts.

A moment only it lasted. Then one fawn—I knew the heedless one, even in the firelight, by his face and by his dappled coat—came straight toward me. Stopping to stare with flashing eyes when the fire blazed up, he stamped his little foot at the shadows to show them that he was not afraid.

The mother called him anxiously. She grew uneasy. Trotting back and forth in a half circle, warning, calling, pleading. Then she bounded away, her white flag shining in the night to guide her little ones.

Suddenly the mother's cry changed; a danger note leaped into it; and again I heard the call to follow and the crash of brush as she leaped away. I remembered having seen a lynx, and as the quickest way of saving the foolish youngster, I kicked my fire to pieces and walked toward him. Then the little fellow bounded away straight up the deer path in the opposite direction from his mother.

Five minutes later I heard the mother calling a strange note in the direction he had taken. I went up the deer path quietly to investigate. At the top of the ridge I heard the fawn answering her and knew instantly that something had happened. He called continuously, a cry of distress.

The mother ran around him in a great circle, calling him to come, while he lay helpless in the same spot, telling her he could not and that she must come to him. So the cries went back and forth in the listening night.

And then came the crash of brush as the mother rushed away followed by the wise fawn, whom she must save, though she left the heedless one to the prowlers of the night.

It was clear enough what had happened. Running through the dark woods, his untrained feet had missed their landing, and he lay now under some brush, with a broken leg to remind him of the lesson he had neglected so long.

I was stealing along toward him, feeling my way among the trees in the darkness, stopping every moment to listen to his cry to guide me, when a heavy rustle came creeping down the hill and passed close by me. I knew that a bear had left the blueberry patch and was stalking the heedless fawn that was separated from his watchful mother in the dark. I regained the path silently—though the bear heeds nothing when his game is afoot—and ran back to my canoe for my rifle.

When I returned, the cries had ceased; the woods were all dark and silent. I went as swiftly as possible to the spot at which I had turned back. From there I went on cautiously. Soon I heard the crashing of the bear up the hill. He was carrying something that caught and swished loudly in the bushes as it passed. Finally the sounds vanished in a faint rustle, and the woods were still again.

All night long, from my tent over beyond an arm of the lake, I heard the mother calling at **intervals**. At daylight I went back to the place. I found without any trouble the spot where the fawn had fallen. The moss told mutely of his struggle, and a stain or two showed where the bear had grabbed him. The rest was a plain trail of crushed moss, bent grass, and stained leaves, and a tuft of soft hair here and there on the jagged ends of brush. So the trail hurried up the hill into a wild rough country where it was of no use to follow.

Deer

Such gentle things they are,
Stepping **discreetly** over the cropped turf;
Or moving noiselessly through the woods,
Their smooth flanks flecked with sunlight.
Their eyes are calm as forest pools,
Unguarded, calm, reflective:
The world is watched through sensitive nostrils.
And when the wind (unfelt by us)
Warns them of danger, suddenly they are gone.
The woods are empty. The barred sunlight
Strikes across trunks only and **stippled** leaves.

– Clive Sansom

"And he shall turn the heart of the fathers to the children, and the heart of the children to their fathers." – Malachi 4:6

First Hunt

Arthur Gordon

His father said, "All set, son?" and Jeremy nodded quickly, picking up his gun with awkward mittened hands. His father pushed open the door, and they went out into the freezing dawn together, leaving the snug security of the shack, the warmth of the kerosene stove, the companionable smells of bacon and coffee.

Not that Jeremy had eaten much breakfast. It had stuck in his throat, and his father, noticing this, had said, "Just a touch of duck fever, son; don't let it bother you." And he added, almost wistfully, "Wish I were fourteen again, getting ready to shoot my first duck."

They stood for a moment in front of the shack, breath white in the icy air. Ahead of them was only flatness—not a house, not a tree, nothing but the vast **expanse** of marsh and water and sky. Ordinarily Jeremy would have been pleased by the bleak arrangements of black and gray and silver that met his eye. Ordinarily he would have asked his father to wait while he fussed around with his camera, trying to record these impressions on film. But not this morning. This was the morning when he was to be **initiated** at last into the world of duck shooting.

This was the morning. And he was dreading it, had dreaded the whole idea ever since his father had bought him a gun, had taught him to shoot clay pigeons, had promised him a trip to this island in the bay where the point shooting was the finest in the state.

He dreaded it, but he was determined to go through with it. He loved his father, wanted more than anything in the world his approval and admiration. If only he could conduct himself properly this morning, he knew that he would get it.

Plodding now across the marshland, he remembered what his father had said to his mother after the first shotgun lesson: "You know, Martha,

18

Jeremy's got the makings of a fine wing shot. He's got **coordination** and timing. And—the kind of nerve it takes too."

They came into the blind, a narrow camouflaged pit facing the bay. In it was a bench, a shelf for shotgun shells, nothing else. Jeremy sat down tensely and waited while his father waded out with an armful of decoys. Light was pouring into the sky now. Far down the bay a string of ducks went by, etched against the sunrise. Watching them, Jeremy felt his stomach contract.

To ease the sense of dread that was oppressing him, he picked up his camera and took a picture of his father silhouetted blackly against the quicksilver water. Then it occurred to him that this might not be the thing to do. He put the camera hastily on the shelf in front of him and picked up his gun again.

His father came back and dropped down beside him, boots dripping, hands blue with cold.

"Better load up. Sometimes they're on top of you before you know it." He watched Jeremy break his gun, insert the shells, close it again. "I'll let you shoot first," he said, "and back you up if necessary."

He loaded his own gun, closed it with a metallic snap. "You know," he said happily, "I've been waiting a long time for this day. Just the two of us, out here on the marshes. We—"

He broke off, leaning forward, eyes narrowed. "There's a small flight now, headed this way. Four, no five. Blacks, I think. They'll come in from left to right, against the wind, if they give us a shot at all. Keep your head down. I'll give you the word."

Jeremy kept his head down. Behind them the sun had cleared the horizon, now flooding the marshes with tawny light. He could see everything with an almost unbearable clarity: his father's face, tense and eager, the faint white **rime** of frost on the gun barrels. His heart was thudding wildly. *No,* he prayed, *don't let them come. Make them stay away, please!*

But they kept coming. "Four blacks," his father said in a whisper. "One mallard. Keep still!"

Jeremy kept still. High above them, thin and sweet, he heard the pulsing whistle of wings as the flight went over, swung wide, began to circle.

"Get set," Jeremy's father breathed. "They're coming."

In they came, gliding down the sunlit aisles of space, heads raised alertly, wings set in a proud curve. The mallard was leading; light flashed from the **iridescent** feathers around his neck and glinted on his ruddy breast. Down dropped his bright orange feet, reaching for the steel-colored water. Closer, closer . . .

"Now!" cried Jeremy's father in an explosive roar. He was on his feet, gun ready. "Take him! Take the leader!"

Jeremy felt his body obey. He stood up, leaned into the gun the way his father had taught him. He felt the stock cold against his cheek, saw the twin muzzles rise. Under his finger the trigger curved, smooth and final and deadly.

In the same instant, the ducks saw the gunners and flared wildly. Up went the mallard as if jerked by an invisible string. For a fraction of a second he hung there, poised against the wind and sun, balanced between life and death. *Now,* said something sharply in Jeremy's brain, *now!* And he waited for the slam of the explosion.

But it didn't come. Up went the mallard, higher still, until suddenly he tipped a wing, caught the full force of the wind, and whirled away, out of range, out of danger, out of sight.

There was no sound then, except the faint rustle of the grasses. Jeremy stood there, gripping his gun.

"Well," his father said at last, "what happened?"

Jeremy did not answer. His lips trembled.

His father said in the same controlled voice, "Why didn't you shoot?"

Jeremy thumbed back the safety catch. He stood the gun carefully in the corner of the blind. "Because they were so alive," he said and burst into tears.

He sat on the rough bench, face buried in his hands, and wept. All hope of pleasing his father was gone. He had had his chance, and he had failed.

Beside him his father crouched suddenly. "Here comes a single. Looks like a pintail. Let's try again."

Jeremy did not lower his hands. "It's no use, Dad; I can't."

"Hurry," his father said roughly. "You'll miss him altogether. Here!"

Cold metal touched Jeremy. He looked up, unbelieving. His father had taken the camera out of its case, was offering it to him. "Quick, here he comes. He won't hang around all day!"

In swept the single, a big pintail drake driving low across the water, skidding right into the decoys. Jeremy's father clapped his hands together, a sound like a pistol shot. The splendid bird soared up; the pressure of his wings sent him twelve feet. One instant he was there, not thirty yards away, feet **retracted**, head raised, wings flapping, white breast gleaming. The next he was gone, whistling like a feathered bullet downward.

Jeremy lowered his camera. "I got him!" His face was radiant. "I *got* him!"

"Did you?" His father's hand touched his shoulder briefly. "That's good. There'll be others along soon; you can get all sorts of shots." He hesitated, looking at his son, and Jeremy saw that there was no disappointment in his eyes, only pride and sympathy and love. "It's okay, son. I'll always love shooting. But that doesn't mean you have to. Sometimes it takes just as much courage not to do a thing as to do it. Think you could teach me how to work that gadget?"

"Teach you?" Jeremy felt as if his heart would burst with happiness. "Dad, there's nothing to it. It's easy, really it is. Look here, let me show you . . . "

"The sluggard will not plow by reason of the cold; therefore shall he beg in harvest, and have nothing." – Proverbs 20:4

The Plowing

Hamlin Garland

For the first few days after we arrived on the prairie, my brother and I had little to do other than to keep the cattle from straying, and we used our leisure in becoming acquainted with the region round about.

It burned deep into our memories, this wide, sunny, windy country. The sky so big and the horizon line so low and so far away made this new world of the plain more majestic than the world we had known before. The grasses and many of the flowers were also new to us. On the uplands the grass was short and dry and the plants stiff and woody, but in the swales[1] the wild oat shook its quivers of barbed and twisted arrows, and the crow's foot, tall and sere,[2] bowed softly under the feet of the wind. Everywhere, in the lowlands as well as on the ridges, the bleaching white antlers of bygone grass eaters lay scattered, testifying to "the herds of deer and buffalo" that once had fed there. We were just a few years too late to see them.

To the south, the sections were nearly all settled upon, for in that direction lay the county town. To the north and on into Minnesota rolled unplowed sod, the feeding ground of the cattle, the home of foxes and wolves; and to the west, we loved to think the bison might still be seen.

The cabin on this rented farm was a mere shanty, a shell of pine boards, which needed **reinforcing** to make it habitable. One day my father said, "Well, Hamlin, I guess you'll have to run the plow team this fall. I must help Neighbor Button wall up the house; I can't afford to hire another man."

This seemed a fine commission for a lad of ten, and I drove my horses into the field that first morning with a manly pride that added an inch to

---

1 swales: low-lying wetlands
2 sere: dry

my **stature**. I took my initial "round," which stretched from one side of the quarter section[3] to the other, in a confident mood. I was grown-up!

But alas! My sense of **elation** did not last long. To guide a team for a few minutes as an experiment was one thing—to plow all day like a hired hand was another. It was not a chore; it was a job. It meant dragging the heavy implement around the corners, and it meant also many shipwrecks, for the thick, wet stubble matted with wild buckwheat often rolled up between the coulter and the standard and threw the share completely out of the ground, making it necessary for me to halt the team and jerk the heavy plow backward for a new start.

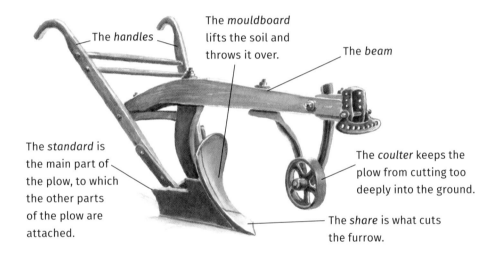

The *handles*

The *mouldboard* lifts the soil and throws it over.

The *beam*

The *standard* is the main part of the plow, to which the other parts of the plow are attached.

The *coulter* keeps the plow from cutting too deeply into the ground.

The *share* is what cuts the furrow.

Although strong and active, I was rather short, even for a ten-year-old, and to reach the plow handles, I was obliged to lift my hands above my shoulders; and so with the guiding lines crossed over my back and my worn straw hat bobbing just above the cross brace, I must have made a comical figure. At any rate, nothing like it had been seen in the neighborhood, and the people on the road to town, looking across the field, laughed and called to me. Neighbor Button said to my father in my hearing, "That chap's too young to run a plow," a judgment which pleased and flattered me greatly.

---

3 quarter section: a tract of land a half mile square, one hundred sixty acres

My sister Harriet cheered me by running out occasionally to meet me as I turned the nearest corner, and sometimes Frank consented to go all the way around, chatting breathlessly as he trotted along behind. At other

Hamlin Garland (1860-1940) is known for his stories of prairie farmers in the Midwest. He tried to realistically portray the toil and heartache these farmers faced.

times he was prevailed upon to bring me a cookie and a glass of milk, a deed which helped to shorten the forenoon.

The flies were savage, especially in the middle of the day; and the horses, tortured by their lances, drove badly, twisting and turning in their despairing rage. Their tails were continually getting over the lines, and in stopping to kick their tormentors from their bellies, they often got astride the traces, and in other ways made trouble for me. Only in the early morning or when the sun sank low at night were they able to move quietly along their ways.

The soil was the kind my father had been seeking—a smooth, dark, sandy loam, which made it possible for a lad to do the work of a man. Often the share would go the entire round without striking a root or a pebble as big as a walnut, the steel running steadily with a crisp, crunching, ripping sound that I rather liked to hear. In truth, the work would have been quite tolerable had it not been so long drawn out. Ten hours of it even on a fine day made about twice too many for a boy.

Meanwhile, I cheered myself in every imaginable way. I whistled. I sang. I studied the clouds. I gnawed the beautiful red skin from the seed vessels that hung upon the wild rose bushes, and I counted the prairie chickens as they began to come together in winter flocks running through the stubble in search of food. I stopped now and again to examine the lizards unhoused by the share, tormenting them to make them sweat their milky drops (they were curiously **repulsive** to me). I measured the little granaries of wheat which the mice and gophers had deposited deep under the ground, storehouses which the plow had exposed. My eyes dwelt enviously upon the sailing hawk and on the passing ducks. The occasional shadowy figure of a prairie wolf made me wish for Uncle David and his rifle.

On certain days nothing could cheer me. When the bitter wind blew from the north and the sky was filled with wild geese racing southward with swiftly hurrying clouds, winter seemed about to spring upon me. The horses' tails streamed in the wind. Flurries of snow covered me with clinging flakes, and the mud gummed my boots and trouser legs, clogging my steps. At such times I suffered from cold and loneliness—all sense of being a man evaporated. I was just a little boy, longing for the leisure of boyhood.

Day after day, through the month of October and deep into November, I followed that team, turning over two acres of stubble each day. I would not believe this without proof, but it is true! At last it grew so cold that in the early morning everything was white with frost, and I was obliged to put one hand in my pocket to keep it warm while holding the plow with the other; but I didn't mind this too much, for it hinted at the close of autumn. I've no doubt that facing the wind in this way was excellent discipline, but I didn't think it necessary then.

Father did not intend to be severe. As he had always been an early riser and a busy toiler, it seemed perfectly natural and good discipline that his son should also plow and husk corn at ten years of age. He often told of beginning life as a "bound boy"[4] at nine, and these stories helped me to perform my own tasks without whining.

Finally the day came when the ground rang like iron under the feet of the horses, and a bitter wind, raw and gusty, swept out of the northwest, bearing gray veils of sleet. Winter had come! Work in the furrow had ended. The plow was brought in, cleaned, and greased to prevent its rusting while the horses munched their hay in well-earned holiday.

---

4 bound boy: a boy required to work for someone for a set length of time, usually in exchange for passage on a ship from Europe

My Prairies

I love my prairies, they are mine
    From **zenith** to horizon line,
Clipping a world of sky and sod
    Like the bended arm and wrist of God.

I love their grasses. The skies
    Are larger, and my restless eyes
Fasten on more of earth and air
    Than seashore furnishes anywhere.

I love the hazel thickets; and the breeze,
    The never resting prairie winds. The trees
That stand like spear points high
    Against the dark blue sky

Are wonderful to me. I love the gold
    Of newly shaven stubble, rolled
A royal carpet toward the sun, fit to be
    The pathway of a deity.

I love the life of pasture lands; the songs of birds
    Are not more thrilling to me than the herd's
Mad bellowing or the shadow stride
    Of mounted herdsmen at my side.

I love my prairies, they are mine
    From high sun to horizon line.
The mountains and the cold gray sea
    Are not for me, are not for me.

– Hamlin Garland

Buffalo Dusk

The buffaloes are gone.
And those who saw the buffaloes are gone.
   Those who saw the buffaloes by the thousands
   and how they pawed the prairie sod into dust
   with their hoofs, and their great heads down
   pawing on in a great **pageant** of dusk,
Those who saw the buffaloes are gone.
And the buffaloes are gone.

– Carl Sandburg

Carl Sandburg (1878-1976) was an American poet, historian, and biographer. During his early life, he traveled as a hobo, served in the army, and worked as a newspaper writer. He wrote many poems, but his best-known work is his six-volume biography of Abraham Lincoln. He received two Pulitzer Prizes—for the biography of Lincoln in 1940, and for his poetry in 1951.

"For every kind of beasts... is tamed, and hath been tamed of mankind."

– James 3:7

Woof

Charles G. D. Roberts

The **gaunt** black mother lifted her head from nuzzling happily at the velvet fur of her little cub. The cub was only twenty-four hours old and absorbed every emotion of her savage heart. But her ear had caught the sound of heavy footsteps coming up the mountain. They were confident, fearless footsteps, taking no care whatever to disguise themselves, so she knew at once that they were the steps of the only creature that dares to go noisily through the great silences. Her heart pounded with anxious suspicion. She gave the cub a reassuring lick, deftly set it aside with her great paws, and thrust her head forth cautiously from the door of the den.

She saw a man—a woodsman in brownish-gray homespun and heavy boots. He carried a gun over his shoulder as he slouched along the faintly marked trail which led close past her doorway. Her own great tracks on the trail had been hidden that morning by a soft fall of late spring snow. The man, absorbed in picking his way by this unfamiliar route over the mountain, had no suspicion that he was in danger of trespassing. But the bear, with that tiny black form at the bottom of the den filling her thoughts, could not imagine that the man was approaching for any other purpose than to rob her of her treasure. She ran back to the little one, nosed it gently into a corner, and anxiously pawed some dry leaves half over it. Then, her eyes aflame with rage and fear, she scurried to the entrance and crouched there motionless to await the coming of the enemy.

The man swung up the hill noisily, grunting now and again as his foothold slipped on the slushy, moss-covered stones. He fetched a huge breath of satisfaction as he gained a little strip of level ledge, perhaps a dozen feet in length. A scrubby spruce bush grew at the other end of the ledge.

28

Behind the bush the man spotted what looked like the entrance to a little cave. Interested at once, he strode forward to examine it. At the first stride a towering black form, jaws agape[1] and claws outstretched, crashed past the fir and hurled itself toward him.

A man brought up in the backwoods learns to think quickly, or rather, to think and act in the same instant. Even as the great beast sprang, the man's gun leaped to its place and he fired. His charge was nothing more than heavy duck shot, intended for some low-flying flock of migrant geese. But at this close range, some seven or eight feet only, it tore through its target with a stopping force that halted the animal's charge in midair. She fell in her tracks, a heap of huddled fur and grinning teeth.

"That was a close call!" remarked the man.

Entering the half darkness of the cave, he quickly discovered the cub in its hiding place. Young as it was, when he picked it up, it whimpered with terror and struck out with its baby paws, recognizing the smell of an enemy. The man grinned at this display of spirit.

"Ye're chock-full o' ginger!" said he. And then, being of an understanding heart and an experienced turn of mind, he laid the cub down and returned to the body of the mother. With his knife he cut off several big handfuls of the shaggy fur and stuffed it into his pockets. Then he rubbed his hands, his sleeves, and the front of his coat on the warm body.

"There, now," said he, returning to the cave and once more picking up the little one. "I've made ye an orphan, to be sure, but I'm goin' to soothe yer feelin's all I kin. Ye must make believe as how I'm yer mammy till I kin find ye a better one."

Pillowed in the crook of his **captor's** arm, and with his nose snuggled into a bunch of his mother's fur, the cub ceased to wonder at a problem too hard for him and dozed off into an uneasy sleep. And Jabe Smith, pleased with his new pet, went gently that he might not disturb the animal's sleep.

Now it chanced that at Jabe Smith's farm, on the other side of the mountain, there had just been a humble tragedy. Jabe Smith's dog Jinny, a longhaired brown retriever, had been bereaved of her newborn puppies. Six of them she had borne, but five of them had straightway died.

---

1 agape: wide open

For two days, in her box in the corner of the dusky stable, Jinny had wistfully poured out her tenderness upon the one remaining puppy. Then, when she had run into the house for a moment to snatch a bite of breakfast, one of Jabe's big red oxen had strolled into the stable and blundered a great splay hoof into the box. That happened in the morning; and all day the mother had moped, whimpering and whining, about the stable, casting long anxious glances at the box in the corner. She was quite unwilling to either approach the box again or to forsake it.

When her master returned and came and looked in at the stable door, the brown mother saw the small furry shape in the crook of his arm. Her heart yearned after it at once. She fawned upon the man coaxingly, lifted herself with her forepaws upon his coat, and reached up till she could lick the sleeping cub. Somewhat puzzled, Jabe went and looked into the box. Then he understood.

"If you want the cub, Jinny, he's yers all right. And it saves me a heap o' bother."

Driven by hunger and reassured by the handful of fur that the woodsman left with him, the cub promptly accepted his adoption. Jinny was a good mother. She loved the cub with a certain **excess** and gave herself up to it utterly, and the cub repaid her devotion by imitating her in all ways possible. The bear is by nature a very silent animal. Jinny's noisy barking seemed to stir the cub's curiosity and admiration; but his attempts to imitate it resulted in nothing more than an occasional grunting *woof*. This throaty syllable came to be accepted as his name, and he speedily learned to respond to it.

In the course of no long time, Jabe Smith realized that Woof was growing up thinking himself to be a dog. The others in the household accepted this idea too. The cats scratched him when he was little, and with equal confidence they scratched him when he was big. Mrs. Smith, as long as she was in good humor, allowed him the freedom of the house, spoiled him with kitchen tidbits, and laughed when his bulk got in the way of her mopping or sweeping. But when she was in an ill mood, she regarded him no more than if he were an overgrown black poodle. At the heels of the more nimble Jinny, he would be chased out the kitchen door, with Mrs. Jabe's angry broom thwacking at the spot where his tail wasn't.

And so, with nothing to mar his content but the occasional fury of Mrs. Jabe's broom, Woof led the sheltered life and was glad to be a dog.

In his third year with Jabe, Woof felt the call of the wild and took to the woods for a time. But when the frosts came and the ground was crispy with new fallen leaves, Woof headed straight back for home. Now, in his absence, a fire had destroyed Jabe's farmhouse, and the Smiths had left for parts unknown. Greatly puzzled, Woof set off again on his wanderings. After about three weeks, forlorn and desperate with hunger, Woof found himself in a part of the forest where he had never been before. But someone else had been there; before him was a broad trail, just such as Jabe Smith and his woodsled used to make. Here were the prints of horses' hooves. Woof's heart bounded hopefully. He hurried along down the trail. Then a faint delectable savor, drawn across the sharp, still air, met his nostrils. Pork and beans—oh, to be sure! He paused for a second to sniff the fragrance again and then lurched onwards at a rolling gallop. He rounded a turn of the trail, and there before him stood a logging camp.

To Woof, a human habitation stood for friendliness and food and shelter. He approached, therefore, without hesitation.

There was no sign of life about the place, except for the smoke rising liberally from the stovepipe chimney. The door was shut, but Woof knew that doors frequently opened if one scratched at them and whined persuasively. He tried it, then stopped to listen for an answer. The answer came—a heavy, comfortable snore from within the cabin. It was mid-morning, and the camp cook, having got his work done up, was sleeping in his bunk while the dinner boiled.

Woof scratched and whined again. Then, growing impatient, he reared himself on his haunches in order to scratch with both paws at once. He happened to scratch on the latch. It lifted, the door swung open suddenly, and he half fell across the threshold. He had not intended so abrupt an entrance, and he paused, peering timidly but hopefully into the homely gloom.

The snoring had stopped suddenly.

Sir Charles George Douglas Roberts (1860-1943) was a native of New Brunswick who wrote many poems about its land and wildlife. His animal stories made him famous throughout the world.

At the rear of the cabin, Woof made out a large, round, startled face, fringed with scanty red whiskers and a mop of red hair, staring at him from over the edge of an upper bunk. Woof had hoped to find Jabe Smith there. But this was a stranger, so he held back his impulse to rush up and wallow delightedly over the bunk. Instead, he came only halfway over the threshold.

To a cool observer of even the most limited intelligence, it would have been clear that he intended to be friendly. But the cook of Conroy's Camp was wakened out of a sound nap, and he was not a cool observer—in fact, he was frightened! A gun was leaning against the wall below the bunk. A large hairy hand stole forth, reached down, and clutched the gun.

Woof wagged his haunches more coaxingly than ever and took another hopeful step forward. Up went the gun. There was a blue-white spurt, and the report clashed deafeningly within the narrow cabin walls.

The cook was a poor shot anytime, and at this moment he was at a special disadvantage. The bullet went close over the top of Woof's head and sang waspishly across the clearing. Woof turned and looked over his shoulder to see what the man had fired at. If anything was hit, he wanted to go and fetch it for the man, as Jabe and Jinny had taught him to do. But he could see no result of the shot. He whined again and ventured all the way into the cabin.

The cook felt desperately for another bullet. There was none to be found. He remembered that they were all in the chest by the door. He crouched back in the bunk, making himself as small as possible. He hoped that a certain hunk of bacon on the bench by the stove might distract the terrible stranger's attention and give him a chance to make a bolt for the door.

But Woof had forgotten neither Jinny's good example nor the discipline of Mrs. Jabe's broom. Far be it from him to help himself without leave. But he was very hungry. Something must be done to win the favor of the strangely unresponsive round face. Looking about him anxiously, he spied a pair of greasy cowhide larrigans[2] lying on the floor near the door. He picked one up in his mouth. Remembering the example of his

---

2 larrigans: high-topped leather moccasins

retriever foster-mother, he carried it over and laid it down, as a humble offering, beside the bunk.

Now the cook, though he had been undeniably frightened, was by no means a fool. This touching gift of one of his own larrigans opened his eyes and his heart. Such a bear, he was assured, could harbor no evil intentions. He sat up in his bunk.

"Hullo!" said he. "What ye doin' here, sonny? What d'ye want o' me, anyhow?"

The huge black beast wagged his hindquarters frantically and wallowed on the floor in his fawning delight at the sound of a human voice.

"Seems to think he's a kind of dawg," muttered the cook. And then the light of certain remembered rumors broke upon his memory.

"Well," said he, "ef 'tain't that there tame b'ar Jabe Smith, over to East Fork, used to have afore he was burnt out!"

Climbing confidently from the bunk, he proceeded to pour a generous portion of molasses over the contents of the scrap pail, because he knew that bears have a sweet tooth.

When the choppers and drivers came trooping in for dinner, they were somewhat taken aback to find a huge bear sleeping beside the stove. The dangerous-looking slumberer seemed to be in the way (none of the men cared to sit too close to him), and to their amazement, the cook smacked the mighty hindquarters with the flat of his hand and bundled him unceremoniously into a corner. " 'Peers to think he's some kind of a dawg," explained the cook, "so I let him come along in for company. He'll fetch yer larrigans an' socks an' things fer ye. An' it makes the camp a sight homier, havin' somethin' like a cat or a dawg about."

"Right you are!" agreed the boss. "But what was that noise we heard, along about an hour back? Did you shoot anything?"

"Oh, that was jest a little misunderstandin' afore him an' me got acquainted," explained the cook, with a trace of embarrassment. "We made up all right."

"Ask, and it shall be given you; seek, and ye shall find; knock, and it shall be opened unto you." – Matthew 7:7

Seek-No-Further

Part 1

Mabel Leigh Hunt

Evan McNeill crouched in the tall grass. He was playing a game of his own—spotting landmarks on this Illinois prairie, where the lone McNeill homestead stood. He peeped above the nodding grass heads. A half mile to the east stood the treeless homeplace, its buildings squat under the vast sky. There were the plodding oxen and his father guiding the plow that turned up fresh furrows to make the broad encircling firebreak. Beyond grazed the forty head of McNeill cattle.

He looked beyond the homestead and the cattle to Gopherville, a small settlement in the timber along Silver Creek. It was five miles away, but in the clear, dry air, Evan could see the curl of smoke and the shape of roofs and chimneys lifted against the trees. His gaze veered to the north, where, farther still, another grove thrust its wedge into the prairie. In the middle distance the heads and shoulders of three deer moved through the flowery meadow. Going back in a half circle, past home and Gopherville and around to the south, there was nothing but the tossing grass.

Evan turned toward the west. "Hey, there 'tis." Yes, there it was—the tree. Alone it stood, king of the prairie. Above the airy billows of the grass and nine miles distant, it seemed airy too, yet with a strength and majesty that had long stirred Evan's imagination.

If only he had a pony of his own! But he was not even allowed to ride his father's Hunter, and eighteen miles of pushing there and back through the thick grass on his own two feet would be hard going. Evan sighed.

"Where've you been, Evan McNeill?" complained six-year-old Janie, when he returned to the cabin. "I called and called you."

"Nowhere p'ticular," answered Evan. His mother turned and smiled at him. Suddenly he wanted to talk to her about the tree. He jerked his thumb over his shoulder. "How do you s'pose that tree ever grew there, all by itself?"

His mother placed her hand on his shoulder. They stood together, looking off across the shimmering miles to the west. "I've often wondered myself," she answered. "Your father's been close to it. He says it's an oak. Maybe an Indian dropped an acorn there long ago. Indeed, it's wonderful!"

"But how do you suppose it ever missed getting blown down when it was a sapling or burned up in a prairie fire?" Evan persisted.

"I couldn't tell you, boy. Maybe it was spared to give you and me something to dream about." Evan's mother had often seen him gazing into the distance. Now, after a moment's silence, her hand tightened on his shoulder. "Evan McNeill, you and I are going to visit that tree," she announced.

Evan looked up at her quickly. "When?" he asked.

"Maybe tomorrow. Long enough we've been aching to go. Let's ask Father."

"How shall we get there?" Evan couldn't quite believe it.

"We'll ride Hunter," answered Mother. "I'll fix it up with your father."

She waited until the end of the noonday meal. "Evan and I have got a hankering," she began gravely. "It's a tree-hankering, and there's only one cure for it. Tomorrow we would like to ride to see the lone oak, Father. Grandma will take care of you and Janie. Won't you, Ma?"

"I'd hate to think I couldn't look after them for a day," Grandma said. "You and Evan go, Ellie. It'll do you good."

"Hunter's full of spirit," cautioned Father. "He shies at a rabbit. Out there on the prairie, he's likely to throw. And you can see a passel o' trees at Silver Creek and not go half so far."

"I know," answered Mother meekly. "The trees are lovely at Silver Creek. But they grew up through the marsh without any trouble and with plenty of company. The lone oak away off yonder—it's a rare brave thing, pushing up by itself, so strong, meaning through all its years of growing and reaching to be the best of its kind. Evan and I, we'd like to go over and touch it, and look at it, and think about it.

"As for Hunter," Mother went on, with sudden spirit, "I can ride him almost as well as you can, Robert."

What a mother for a boy to have! Evan was up very early the next day. It was hard to wait until the morning chores were done and a lunch packed. "If the buttermilk clabbers in the heat, it won't harm us, and 'twill quench our thirst," laughed Mother. She was as happy as a girl again.

"Don't get reckless and ride on to St. Louis," teased Father. "It's about seventy miles due west of the oak."

Across the prairie rode Evan and Mother. The June grasses brushed against Hunter's flanks, against Evan's bare feet, and the flowing skirt of Mother's dress. Spot, one of the dogs, followed, flushing quail and prairie chickens and pheasants. Rabbits and field mice scurried here and there. Gophers and badgers ducked into their burrows. Dipping and curving, the field sparrows and meadowlarks made sweet music. The soft southwest wind ruffled the grass into waves, now rose, now green. Once the travelers came upon a patch of wild strawberries. "On our way back, we'll fill our lunch basket," promised Mother. "I'll make a pie."

"Um-m-m!" murmured Evan, his mouth watering.

But whatever new thing might claim their attention, the two never lost sight of their goal. The leafy top of the oak grew broader as they pushed steadily westward. At last Mother pulled on Hunter's reins. They had reached the tree.

The oak was more superb than Evan had guessed it would be. For how many, many years had it drawn through root and trunk the boundless fertility of prairie loam? Now it towered over them, a hundred feet high. Evan's heartbeat was quick as he slipped off the horse. With happy excitement he and Mother stretched arms wide to pass the tethering rope about the massive trunk, tying it securely so that Hunter might not stray. Their hands lingered on the thick rough ridges of bark. Evan saw tears in his mother's eyes as she looked up at the noble branches.

They spread their lunch under that cool-shadowing canopy, eating slowly, with scarcely a word spoken, but smiling at one another in deep content. And when they had thrown the scraps to Spot, Mother leaned back against the oak's trunk and told of the trees of her childhood. Evan realized then how hungry she had long been for their companionship. "The ones I liked best were the apple trees in

Mabel Leigh Hunt (1892-1971) was born in Indiana, where she worked as a librarian. After ten years, she quit her job and began to write children's stories full-time.

my father's orchard in New York state," said Mother. "In the spring—oh, the fragrance and beauty of their blossoms! There's something about an apple—well, I think it's a fruit that belongs especially to girls and boys. You, my poor Evan, can only guess what an orchard or an orchard apple is like.

"I remember that one tree bore apples which we called *Seek-no-furthers*. When they were ripe, some would fall on the house roof where it sloped at the back. *Thump, roll, tumble*—such a merry sound! I can hear it yet."

"Seek-no-further?" echoed Evan, his brow puckered. "Oh, of course," he said at last. "The apples were so good you didn't need to seek further for better ones."

"That's right," said Mother, and she sighed. "Oh, to taste one again!"

When they started homeward, Evan said, "D'you know, Mother, I think this oak might be called *Seek-no-further* too, because there couldn't be another tree so fine, surely. Besides, Mother, now that I know just how it looks, I shan't be so—so hankering to—to *seek* it."

It was easier to share the tiny sweet strawberries with the family that evening than the memories of the day and the tree. And when the milking was done, the stock penned for the night, and the dogs turned out to warn the wolves against preying on his pigs and chickens, Father began speaking slowly. He spoke as if he had been thinking deeply all day. He had something he wanted to say to Mother and Evan. "The forest is itself. The orchard is itself," he said. "And the prairie is itself. I'll take the prairie. I like it just as it is. A man feels like a king in the wide space, under the open sky. Land like ours is the highest, most level, the most fertile, although few have the courage to settle on it. In time they will come away from the trees that grow by the watercourses and breed the ague."[1]

---

1 ague (ā' gyü): fever

"Ellie," said Grandma, her eyes **impish**, "Robert's sticking up for the prairie because his conscience pricks him. After you left this morning, I told him he should plant some trees for Ellie McNeill that had such a hankering for 'em."

Father looked a little sheepish as he laughed and said, "I'll sow you a grove of locust tree seeds, Ellie. They'll grow into tall trees in no time. The prairie soil beats everything for richness."

"I like it on the prairie too, Robert," said Mother gently. "It will still be prairie, but lovelier, when we have the locust grove."

But his stock, his grain, and his hunting kept Robert McNeill very busy. He seemed to forget about locust seeds. And Mother was no woman to nag a man. The prairie grasses deepened to red and to yellow, and finally, to the brilliant gold of autumn. Then in the crystal air the lone oak seemed to draw nearer. Evan could almost distinguish its **ruddy** color. After Indian summer it was blotted out in the long-falling veils of rain that beat down the grass and filled up old buffalo wallows and the dry **sloughs**. Swirling curtains of snow hid it completely, but on certain clear winter days Evan could see it, a delicate penciling of bare boughs against the sky.

"And seek not ye what ye shall eat, or what ye shall drink, neither be ye of doubtful mind. But rather seek ye the kingdom of God; and all these things shall be added unto you." – Luke 12:29, 31

Seek-No-Further

Part 2

Mabel Leigh Hunt

When spring brought the prairie to life again with a green-like young wheat, Mother was ailing. Evan and Janie had to help Grandma with the household chores. One day Evan needed to walk the five miles to Gopherville to mail an important letter.

" 'Tain't bad going," he confided to Grandma, "but coming back it's about twice as long."

Grandma gave him a sharp look. "Never mind about that, Evan," she said. "When folks speak to you over there, hold up your head and answer **cordial** as a McNeill should. You'll enjoy yourself more if you aren't so bashful."

Evan flushed. He left without answering. He did have a craving to linger and talk to people, if only he could think of something to say. At the same time he longed to be back on the prairie, where he felt so free and easy. *Guess I'll* ***meander*** *along the creek on the way home. Maybe there'll be some violets I can pick for Mother. Wish I had something nice to take her—something she wants real bad.*

But when he came out of the general store and post office, Evan saw a crowd of children dancing alongside a lean, rangy[1] old fellow, hanging to his hands and his shabby coattails. His gray hair straggled to his shoulders. On his head was a pasteboard hat, the brim cut to form a broad front peak. His clothes were odd. Nothing matched. While Evan stared

---

1 rangy: tall and skinny

in curiosity, the man seated himself on a grassy bank, and the children grouped eagerly about him.

A boy came out of the store. He flung a look at Evan. "That's Johnny Appleseed," he said, answering the question in Evan's eyes. "Come on if you want to hear one of his good stories."

Evan hesitated, stumbled forward, catching up with the strange boy. "Appleseed—Johnny Appleseed," he stammered, "why is he called that?"

"Why, apple seeds and a place to plant 'em—that's his business," came the ready answer. "But not for money. One look at 'im will tell you that!"

Evan caught his breath. "You mean he doesn't want any money for his apple seeds?"

"Oh, if you've got it easy in your pocket, maybe. But he'd just as lief have an old coat or a shirt or a bit of cornmeal. Or, for that matter, nothing at all."

"Is he going to live in Gopherville?" asked Evan. He had never heard of Johnny Appleseed.

"Naw, 'course not. He says he's bound for St. Louis and the Mississippi."

Evan hung bashfully on the fringe of Johnny's audience. But his mind darted all around the planter's story, although it was a thrilling account of an Ohio hunter's adventure with a bear. *Apple seeds for nothing!* He *must* find out about them. When the story was finished and Johnny had gently shaken himself free of the children, Evan followed that long loping stride, fighting against his shyness.

"Mister Appleseed! J-Johnny Appleseed!" he called. "What kind of apples are them you plant? What's the name of 'em?"

Johnny turned around and looked into the eyes as dark and burning as his own. "Why, lad," he answered, "they're all kinds. *Rambos* and *Seek-no-furthers* and *Fall Wines* and *Golden Pippins* and—well, it doesn't make much difference. An apple is the sweetest and best of all God's fruits, whatever its name."

"It would make a difference to my mother," declared Evan earnestly, "because she's got a craving for the *Seek-no-furthers* she remembers from a long time back. And I'm asking, sir," stammered Evan, very red, "if you would stop and talk to my mother about apples on your way to St. Louis. We live off on yonder prairie. And—maybe—you do have some apple seeds left, don't you?"

"Of course I do," Johnny assured Evan heartily. "God willing, and Johnny Appleseed to do His will, there shall be orchards along the Mississippi. For your mother too, boy."

"When will you come?" asked Evan.

"I'm ready now," Johnny answered. "If you'll wait until I get my horse and my seed bags, we'll go together."

Evan never forgot that journey homeward. "I picked up this gray mare," Johnny explained, "so worn out with travel she was left by the wayside by some westward-going folks to fend for herself. I named her Gillyflower, for the apple. Pretty name, ain't it?" Johnny patted the mare affectionately. "I've fattened her up since I've had her."

Evan almost laughed, for he could have counted Gillyflower's ribs. "Are we going to ride?" he asked hopefully.

"No, lad," answered Johnny. "We're as able to walk as she is, and better. We'll burden her only with my few belongings." Johnny's bushel-bags of seeds were strapped to the mare's back, also his hoe. From the strap hung his kettle and cooking pan. *Tinkle, clink*—with Gillyflower's every step, they made a harsh, humorous music. Johnny talked. His voice had the wilderness in it, but gentle, so that Evan completely forgot his shyness. When they reached the cabin, he introduced his companion with rare pride.

"Welcome, Johnny Appleseed," said Father. "I've heard of you."

"Mother," Evan whispered, "he's got all kinds of apple seeds."

"I'll plant you an orchard, ma'am," Johnny spoke up. "There ought to be some Seek-no-further trees among them to give you extra pleasure."

"I'll let you have a plot of ground close to the house," promised Father.

"He was saving it for a locust grove," explained Grandma, and she stole a sly look at Father. "Gave Ellie hope of it 'most a year ago."

"We'll have both," Father said. "There's plenty of room for both."

"I declare!" sighed Mother. "Apple *and* locust trees!"

Evan was proud when Father said, "Thanks to you, son, for bringing Johnny Appleseed to us."

"Evan spoke up in Gopherville like a McNeill should," chuckled Grandma. "But I guess it was because he wanted to bring Ellie something nice."

Evan helped prepare the soil and sow the seeds. He listened carefully to Johnny's instructions: how to water the young seedlings through the blazing summer, how to protect them with wrappings of dried grass and cornstalks from winter frosts and the nibbling of rabbits. Father hauled fencing from Gopherville. Mother grew well and strong again. Grandma said it was because of the tonic of mullein leaves and milk which Johnny brewed for her. Deep in his mind, Evan thought it was the promise of apple bloom.

Johnny lent a hard hand to the chores. He made a cradle for Janie's doll. He told her about other little girls he had known—Nancy Metzger and Megan McIlvain, Rosella Rice of the lovely Mohican Valley, Eliza Rudisill of Fort Wayne. His eyes shone as he told Janie of his nieces, the Brooms, who, when they were little, could kite up the peg ladder that led to the loft of their cabin home like squirrels. The McNeill family listened spellbound to his stories of settlers and Indians. Through all his talk ran, like a silver thread, the flow of the western watercourses, and Johnny following creek and river to sow his apple seeds in some waiting plot. At bedtime he read from his tattered Bible. He slept on the floor, his weathered cheek resting on his palm.

From the master of the house to the scrubbiest dog, everyone loved him. When he said he must go, Janie shed tears.

"Johnny, how you have blessed our house and fields!" cried Grandma.

And Father, his hand on Johnny's shoulder, advised him, "Man, it's amazing to think how many nurseries you've planted in the West. Isn't it time to take your ease? Don't go. Stay here with us. You're getting old."

"Must be nearing the last of my sixties," Johnny answered, smiling. "But I'm still able, and my work not done. Besides, for an enduring time I've been cur'us to see where all the little cricks and runs and rivers of Ohio and Indiana and Illinois are bound for. Well, I know they're bound for the Mississippi, and so am I."

Evan and Mother rode across the prairie with Johnny as far as the lone oak. Evan felt no sadness. Indeed, it seemed to him he had never been happier.

He chattered and he whistled. He stood on his head. He turned cartwheels all around the oak.

"The boy is full of youth and the thought of an orchard full of apples," offered Johnny.

"Seek-no-furthers," Evan reminded him.

"Remember, lad," Johnny said, "*Seek-no-further* is a mighty fine name for an apple or for an oak. But *seek further* would be a better name for a boy."

Evan was thoughtful as he and his mother watched the old apple missionary and the nag Gillyflower plodding westward.

"There's no real sorrow in saying good-bye to Johnny," said Mother quietly, "for we know that wherever he goes, he will leave such promise as he left with us. He may not be great, but a man whose trace shall last as long in beauty and bounty as Johnny's, a man who plants for the future good of mankind in the way he can plant best, has greatness in him."

"I guess that's what he meant," answered Evan, "when he said I should be a *seek-further* one. Same as he has always been." One hand resting on the great trunk of the oak, Evan called across the prairie, "Good-bye, Johnny Appleseed."

Johnny turned, waving a last farewell.

"And out of the ground made the Lord *God to grow every tree that is pleasant to the sight, and good for food; the tree of life also in the midst of the garden, and the tree of knowledge of good and evil." – Genesis 2:9*

Trees

Bliss Carman (1861-1929), a Canadian poet, was born in New Brunswick and moved to New York City where he edited various journals. Many of his poems praise the beauty of nature.

In the Garden of Eden, planted by God,
There were goodly trees in the springing sod—
Trees of beauty and height and grace,
To stand in splendor before His face:

Apple and hickory, ash and pear,
Oak and beech, and the tulip rare,
The trembling aspen, the noble pine,
The sweeping elm by the river line;

Trees for the birds to build and sing,
And the lilac tree for a joy in spring;
Trees to turn at the frosty call
And carpet the ground for their Lord's footfall;

Trees for fruitage and fire and shade,
Trees for the cunning builder's trade;
Wood for the bow, the spear, and the flail,
The keel and the mast of the daring sail—
He made them of every grain and **girth**
For the use of man in the Garden of Earth.

Then lest the soul should not lift her eyes
From the gift to the Giver of Paradise,
On the crown of a hill, for all to see,
God planted a scarlet maple tree.

– Bliss Carman

Shade

The kindliest thing God ever made,
His hand of very healing laid
Upon a fevered world, is shade.

His glorious company of trees
Throw out their mantles, and on these
The dust-stained wanderer finds ease.

Green temples, closed against the beat
Of noontime's blinding glare and heat,
Open to any pilgrim's feet.

The white road blisters in the sun;
Now, half the weary journey done,
Enter and rest, O weary one!

And feel the dew of dawn still wet
Beneath your feet, and so forget
The burning highway's ache and fret.

This is God's hospitality,
And one who rests beneath a tree
Has cause to thank Him gratefully.

– Theodosia Garrison

45

"Let your conversation be without covetousness; and be content with such things as ye have." – Hebrews 13:5

The Chickens and the Mush

William E. Barton

Now Keturah considered the High Cost of Living, and she said, Let us buy an Incubator and keep Hens. So she sold her Waste Paper to the Rag Man, and she bought an incubator, and put Eggs therein. In thrice seven days the Eggs Hatched, and there came forth Little Chickens. And Keturah fed them.

And it came to pass one day that I went into the yard and beheld Keturah feeding the Chickens. And that whereon she fed them was Mush.

And she took the Mush from a Bowl with a Spoon, and she dropped a great Spoonful on the Ground. And all the Little Chickens ran every one of them after the Mush.

And she walked on a little farther and dropped another Spoonful. And all the little chickens forsook the first Spoonful and ran after the second. Yea, they trod every one of them upon the Mush which they had been eating that they might Hasten after the other Mush.

And she went on a little farther and dropped a third Spoonful. And all the little chickens forsook the second Spoonful and ran after the third. And the Mush of the first Spoonful and the Mush of the second Spoonful they despised.

And some of the chickens got none of any of the three Spoonfuls. But if part of them had gone to each Spoonful, they might all

William E. Barton (1861-1930) was the pastor of a Congregationalist church in Illinois. He was a famous preacher and wrote a book about Abraham Lincoln, but his best-known and best-loved writings were the parables that appeared each week in *The Christian Century*. He wrote them under the name *Safed the Sage*, and "The Chickens and the Mush" is one of them.

have had Mush. Nevertheless, did they all follow Keturah all around the Lot, and every chicken was Among Those Present when the last Spoonful was dropped.

And I **meditated** much thereon. And I said, Keturah, Men are like Chickens.

And Keturah said, What about Women?

And I said, No matter how good is the food they already have, yet do they forsake it and run where the last Fad droppeth. And what they **obtain** after all their running is but Mush.

And I spake again, and I said, Keturah, Men are like young chickens.

And Keturah said, So are Women.

Path of the Pioneer

Pioneering in Canada

Jack Miner

On April 22, 1878, we loaded our family into one wagon and all our belongings into another—the latter being by far the smaller load—and we were "hoff for Kanada," as Father would say it. As Father shook hands, I believe for the last time, with one of his tried and true friends, Mr. Calvin Pease, Calvin asked, "John, do you think you can make a living for your big family over in Canada?"

Turning his rugged face toward him in a manner of stern attention, Father replied in clear ringing tones: "Calvin, we are going to make more than a living. We are going to make a life."

At that time I was just a few days past thirteen years of age, and I doubt there was ever a teenage boy who experienced a more delightful change than this short migratory trip brought to me. In about twenty-four or thirty hours from the time we left Cuyahoga County, Ohio, we were liberated in the woods of Essex County, in the extreme sunny side of Canada.

Among the outstanding occurrences of that April, still fresh in my memory, is the way my sister Mary cut my hair. Mother had not taken the time to give me my "annual" haircut, and the day before we left Ohio, Mary said to me, "Jack, you are not going to Canada looking like that."

So Mother made me sit up and take notice, while sister cut my hair. Starting with Mother's old, dull scissors, she began chewing it off. She kept getting each side the shorter, until she ran out of hair, and I came to Canada by the name of "Sawhair." It was months before my name got back to just plain Jack.

I was not much concerned with human neighbors at that time, being much too interested in the immense variety of so-called "wild" creatures that were keeping the woods echoing with song and good cheer. While there were very few robins, mourning doves, and bobolinks, as were most plentiful in Ohio, I hardly missed them because of the countless variety of other birds. I have seen twenty-five full-plumed scarlet tanagers in sight at once; and there were warblers, flycatchers, thrushes, catbirds, and woodpeckers of all species, including the pileated woodpecker. In fact, I doubt if there is another country in North America where a greater variety of cheerful song and insectivorous[1] birds could be found.

As soon as the stars closed their eyes in the morning and the whippoor-will voices began to die out, the sweet call of the bobwhite could be heard in the distance, and the thud and boom of the drumming partridge seemed to come from all directions. As the rays of the sun drove the darkness away, the woods would grow more musical still, until it seemed that every creature on earth was shouting for joy. The throat of each singer appeared to be focused on that little ten-acre cavity we had chopped out of the virgin[2] forest.

That entertainment never ceased; there was only a change in the program. For shortly after the sun had missed the treetops in the west and bid the scattering clouds to the east a red-faced goodnight, the faint voice of the whip-poor-will would start again and get louder and louder, until every other sound was either hushed or drowned out.

However, there was one bird that we did not know. It was an extra big crow. Our name for them was "the big crows," until one day I said to a friend, "Isaiah, look at those big crows." Isaiah rolled his eyes at me and said, "Crows! Crows! Them's not crows, you Yankee. Them's ravens!"

When I told my mother, she said, "Why certainly, they are ravens. We should have known what they were." Then she added, smiling, "Well, I guess we will get along all right, for Elijah's ravens have found out where we are."

The weather was dry and warm, which permitted us to clear and burn off a small piece of land and plant our corn. But June was hot and wet, and this country being extremely level, there was over six inches of

---

1 insectivorous (in' sek' ti' və rəs): insect-eating
2 virgin: unchanged by human activity; never cut

stagnant water all through the vast forest. It was almost impossible for a human being to live in the woods because of the swarms of hungry flies and savage, bloodthirsty mosquitoes.

Soon our baby sister Florence took sick, and she continued to grow worse in spite of Mother's doctoring. Brother Ted volunteered to walk to Kingsville to try to get a doctor. It was a good long two miles and more from our home to Dr. King's office, but brother was back in an hour and a quarter, stating that Dr. King had said he would come right out. Our whole family anxiously watched, waited, and sighed for the coming of the doctor. Finally the next morning came, and Mother said Florence was a little better.

About nine o'clock someone saw a horse and buggy coming down the newly cutout road, and behold, it was the doctor. How can I paint the picture of that homesick, sad-hearted, barefoot family's anxious faces as we stood in a circle, fairly holding our breath, awaiting Dr. King's **verdict?**

Finally, he gave a long sigh and, turning to Father, said, "Mr. Miner, your child has malaria[3] fever. You will have to move out of this wet place or your children will all die."

Every face quivered with emotion. We clung to each other and cried.

"You could move out near the lake for the summer," the doctor spoke up, "and come back here in the fall."

"Doctor," Father answered, "Hi have no money to build another 'ouse. Hi don't know what to do."

While the doctor closed up his medicine case, Father stood there in deep study. Then he pulled his shirt sleeves a little higher. Turning his rugged face toward the doctor, he said in his clear-toned accent, "Doctor, hif Hi could locate a houtlet, Hi would soon 'ead this fever hoff."

In less than five minutes, Father was going down the clay road, looking for an outlet. Fortunately, we had brought with us two spades and a shovel from Ohio. By eleven o'clock we were ditching. Father took the top spading and I the bottom, and brother Ted did the shoveling. Ted and I were both barefoot.

In less than a week, we had a small ditch winding among the stumps.

---

3 malaria: a sickness causing chills and fever, transmitted by mosquitoes

To see the water running away and to hear Father's words of encouragement and cheer caused us to forget the thousands of mosquito bites. The ditch was completed, the water ran off, and all nature seemed to back us up; for the heavy rains ceased, the woods dried up, and dear little sister got well. Yes, thank God, she got well!

But Father, whom we all loved to hear sing, and who sang so much for us, hadn't uttered a note for a month. What had happened that he should be so silent and melancholy? Little sister was getting stronger every day, and we were all happy, except Father. Then the morning of June 30th I was awakened at daylight, hearing Father sing—

> Come Thou fount of every blessing,
> Tune my heart to sing Thy praise.

As soon as we children were up and downstairs, Father called us into the only bedroom and—can you imagine our surprise and delight? For, behold, we had another little baby sister! As the news spread over the house, every occupant crowded into Mother's bedroom to see the baby. As I stood looking, I noticed Mother's lips quiver with emotion. With tears trickling from her eyes, she turned her face to the wall.

I know now what those tears meant. They were tears of gratefulness. Her family was well; her baby was born. Then, with Mother and Father both so cheerful again, we were happy beyond expression.

Our log house was one hundred feet from the road, and the path that wound its way among the stumps to it was bordered on each side with Mother's choice flowers. The people came to "see the flowers those Yankees have got." The stumps in our five-acre cornfield were covered with the rank growth of corn. Indeed, I have never seen a more vigorous growth of vegetation in a glass hothouse than we had that summer.

September was soon upon us, and we were harvesting our crop. The ground was heaved up with potatoes—potatoes as clean and bright as silver and as large as goose eggs. We just took the fork or hoe and raked them out by the cartload. Hundreds of cabbages as large as peck measures. Tomatoes? Where we planted them around the black charred stumps, some of those low stumps were covered with tomatoes.

But this was not accomplished by sitting on a stump, wishing and wondering. Father was a big broad-shouldered man; and when he said, "Get in gear, boys," we didn't run downtown to find the interpretation of what he said, but got into gear immediately, if not a little sooner. For we knew if we didn't, he would soon put us in gear, and high gear at that. Father was kind but firm.

That October we found the woods fairly alive with game, small game especially. We shot black squirrels and partridge by the hundreds within a half mile of our house. We got a few wild turkeys and some choice venison too.

In December we killed the nine young pigs, and Father said they would average over one hundred pounds each. Mother and my sisters made over one hundred pounds of pork sausage, seasoned with our homegrown savory. Father took some of the choicest corn to town and had it ground fine for our cornmeal flour, which we usually made into mush and fried. Our table was loaded with fried mush and a platter full of those homemade and home-seasoned sausages, and another platter of squirrel, partridge, or venison steak, combined with those quickly grown, **mellow** potatoes and other vegetables. I tell you, one and all, I do wish every person in North America could have at least one meal like that!

By then we had enough to eat and to spare. Yet that was not our crowning blessing.

We were practically cut off from the world. Now and then a spell of homesickness for our Ohio friends would come upon us. But the great blessing in that little log house was the love and harmony that reigned there. Actually, if one of us got a toothache, the whole family would cry! The house was crude and small, but I say from experience: the smaller the house, the bigger the home.

Yes, the blessings of that winter will always remain fresh in my memory.

John Thomas (Jack) Miner (1865-1944) was born to a poor family and had to work hard as a boy. He loved nature and studied birds extensively. In 1904, he established a now-famous bird sanctuary on his farm in Ontario, to which thousands of ducks and geese come each spring and fall. Miner, sometimes called "Wild Goose Jack," learned about their migratory habits by banding and releasing them.

My father was one of the most beautiful singers I have ever heard, and after supper he would sit in his chair before the fire and sing for us. Our clearing and the bordering woods were clothed in their pure white winter robe. The frost sparkled on the few small windows of our home. With a big pile of wood in the corners and a roaring fire broadcasting warmth and cheer all over the house, night after night that lovable man would sit in his big chair with the baby in his arms and another child on his knee. And we older ones would coax him to sing.

I can almost hear him now, with his deep mellow voice, seasoned with just enough accent to make it fragrant. I remember that winter he often sang this song:

> *When the poor harmless hare*
> *She is chased to the woods*
> *And her footsteps are dinted in snow,*
> *And you sit by your fireside*
> *With your loved ones by your side*
> *That's the time to remember the poor.*

Mother would whack him on the shoulder and say, "John, you are singing *remember the poor,* and there isn't a dollar in the 'ouse."

She was right. There was not a dollar on the premises. But Father was right too. For we were rich and did not know it. We were warm. We had abundance to eat. And we were rich in health and harmony and love.

"When the poor and needy seek water, and there is none, and their tongue faileth for thirst, I the Lᴏʀᴅ will hear them, I the God of Israel will not forsake them." – Isaiah 41:17

Desert Miracle

Agnes Ranney

Heat already lay in a shimmering haze over the high desert that August morning, although it was not yet ten o'clock. The clump of ancient cottonwoods between the house and barn stood motionless, no hint of a breeze stirring their dusty leaves.

Janet washed the breakfast dishes in a scant two inches of water in the smallest dishpan, then carefully carried the water outside and poured it around the few bright marigolds and zinnias struggling to grow in the dry sandy soil near the back door.

She looked up as her brother Roger came in from the direction of Thirsty Creek. "How's the water, Roger? Is there still enough for the cattle?"

Roger pushed the damp dark hair back from his forehead. "A dribble," he said. "Gets lower every day though."

"Well, come in out of the sun," said Janet. Roger followed her into the kitchen, where bright curtains hung at the windows and their little brother Freddy sat building a block house on the clean wood floor. Roger filled a glass from the pail of water on the drainboard, paused, poured half of it back, and drank the rest.

It had been six months now since Janet and her family had come to live on the ranch in the high desert country of southeastern Oregon. They had come to Oregon because the doctor had told Daddy that an outdoor life was necessary if he were to live to raise his family. It seemed **providential** that they had been able to find this ranch, on sale for the back taxes, at a price they were able to pay. It had been a homestead long ago.

But no one could make a living farming that dry land, and the people had given up trying and gone away.

But you could make a living raising cattle on land you couldn't farm. So Daddy had patched up the old weather-beaten house, and they had bought a milk cow and a few chickens. Then they had put all the money they could spare into a few good cattle, hoping to add to their herd year by year.

"How much longer can the water last, Roger?" It was a question they'd been asking for the past month. Cattle could keep alive on surprisingly scrubby land—if they had water. Most years, the neighbors told them, Thirsty Creek kept running through the summer, giving water for livestock and even keeping a little pasture green along its banks. But last winter had been mild—little snow had fallen in the mountains. Thirsty Creek had shrunk to brook size. Soon it would be only a string of stagnant pools. Then they, too, would dry up.

"Don't know how much longer we'll have water," Roger said soberly. "I'd say not over a few days."

Freddy looked up from his building with solemn brown eyes. "Why don't we dig a well? Then we'd have water like the Careys, and Mother and Daddy wouldn't have to go after it every day or two."

"That's what we'd planned to do, until we found out how much it cost," Roger told him. "Some folks have gone four or five hundred feet deep and still haven't got water. It's not always as bad as that—but we can't afford to take a chance."

"Well, then, maybe Daddy can bring an extra barrel for the cows next time he goes after water."

"Water for twenty whitefaces?" Roger snorted. "Don't be silly, Freddy!"

"He's trying to help," Janet said. "We just couldn't haul enough water for the cattle in the station wagon, Freddy. It's all Daddy can do to get it for us to use at the house and for the chickens. I just hope the Careys' well doesn't go dry or something. I'm glad he and Mother started early this morning before it got so hot."

"If you're so hot, why don't you come to my dugout?" Freddy asked.

"It's another scorcher, all right," Roger said, ignoring Freddy. Janet's eyes followed his gaze across the desert to the faint, distant purple line of pine and juniper-clad mountains.

"It's a wonder any water at all gets across that desert!" Janet said. "Isn't there something we can do to get water for the stock?"

"Yes—work a miracle," Roger said shortly. "Make it rain—or find a few thousand dollars so we can have a well drilled. I tell you, Janet, we might as well give up."

"Give up?" Janet said. "And what then?"

"Dad talked to me about it," Roger said. "We'd have to move the cattle out to where there's water. There is on some of the ranches nearer the mountains."

"But we'd have to pay for the pasture," Janet said.

"Sure—we'd have to go back to the city, and he'd have to go to work there."

"But we can't let him do that!" Janet cried. "He's so much better now than he was when we came here—he can't go back!"

Roger shrugged. "Don't know how we can help it. Hope they don't try to come home until late this afternoon. It's too hot to drive now."

"It's cooler in my dugout," Freddy said patiently.

"Dugout? What's he talking about, Janet?" Roger asked.

"Oh, you know, that old root cellar dug into the bank of the wash. He plays there sometimes. It might be cooler there at that."

"That's what I'm trying to tell you," Freddy said. "Only nobody listens to me."

"I'm sorry, Freddy. We're just worried about the water," Janet said, rumpling the fair hair that was a contrast to the dark eyes. "Come on, let's go down to your dugout."

The sun beat down fiercely as they crossed the yard to the dry wash behind the barn. Water ran in a stream here in the spring when the snow was melting, but it was a dry gully the rest of the year. Someone—probably the people who had homesteaded the place—had dug a sort of cave into the bank and shored it up with rough planks.

Freddy plopped down on the sand in front of the dugout and took up the game he'd left the day before, with his toy cars traveling over roads marked out in the sand. Roger and Janet went into the dugout, grateful to be out of the sun.

"It is cooler in here," Roger said. "I'd almost forgotten this place. What do you reckon they used it for?"

58

"Storing potatoes and stuff, I s'pose," Janet said. "Look, there are even some old rough shelves. I expect they kept things here so they'd be cool in summer and not freeze in the winter."

Roger sat down on the ground near the opening, but Janet looked for something a little cleaner to sit on than the dusty ground. She poked about along the crude shelves. A battered basket lay on its side, and a broken box showed the marks of gnawing rats.

"Nothing here fit to sit on," Janet said, pushing the box aside. Then, suddenly, she forgot what she had been looking for.

"Roger!" she cried. "Look! A chest!"

"Say, it is! Looks like a treasure chest!" Roger said at her side. "Here—let's get it out into the light." Sandy dust filled the air as Roger pulled the chest off the shelf and carried it toward the mouth of the dugout.

Janet's heart beat fast. It did look like a treasure chest, made of metal, with a strong-looking lock. Janet's hands trembled as she pushed at the lock. It did not move under her fingers.

"Rusted shut. Locked too," Roger said, his voice shaking a little with excitement. "Maybe I can pry it off."

Freddy came to stand beside them, as excited as the others. Roger pried at the lock with his knife.

"What if it really is a treasure!" Janet breathed. "You said we needed a miracle, Roger—maybe this is it!"

The knife wouldn't work. Roger finally had to go to the house for a screwdriver. After working for ten minutes at the screws that held the lock, Roger pried it loose.

"Open it, Janet!" he said. Holding her breath, Janet raised the lid. Roger groaned.

"Some treasure chest!" he said in disgust.

"Well, it's not full of gold pieces," Janet admitted.

"There's a dolly," Freddy said, "and some beads—and a book."

"It must have belonged to a little girl," Janet said, lifting the doll from the chest. She was clad in a long full dress of blue calico. Her china head had painted hair and features, and her cheeks were still rosy after all the years she must have lain there.

"Isn't she darling?" Janet said. "And here are some blue beads, and look—

a sampler like Grandma made when she was a little girl—with the needle and thread still in it!" She unfolded the piece of yellowed linen and smoothed it so that she could see the cross-stitched letters. At the bottom she read:

ELIZA B. — AGE 12 YEARS — 1893

"Long time ago," Roger commented. "Must have belonged to the folks who homesteaded the place." His interest in the chest had fallen off since they found it contained nothing of **apparent** value. But Janet looked over the contents eagerly. What kind of girl was Eliza B? And why had she left her treasure box poked away here in the old dugout? What had become of her?

I suppose we'll never know, Janet thought. But she changed her mind when she picked up the book Freddy had seen.

"Why, it's a diary!" She didn't look for anything to sit down on now, but dropped down near the opening of the dugout and opened the little leather-covered book. The ink was faded, the paper yellow and brittle, but Janet was soon absorbed. Now and then she read a few lines to Roger and Freddy.

March 3, 1893. My birthday! Mama made me a new blue calico frock and a little one for Sarah. Papa planted the southwest field. I picked buttercups along Thirsty Creek.

So the doll's name was Sarah. Janet read on. The story of the early settlers was complete in Eliza's diary. It started with high hope—new fields plowed and planted, gardens put in, new livestock bought. But then hot, dry weather came, and the tone changed.

May 20. Dreadfully hot today. Mama doesn't like it when it's so hot. I think she is getting lonesome too. We don't often see anyone since the Dolan's moved away.

June 17. Thirsty Creek is getting low. The Wilson's well has gone dry. Mr. Wilson brought four barrels on his wagon to fill at our well. Papa says we should be thankful for the well, but Mama says that's all we can be thankful for.

"I'm hungry," Freddy said.

Janet went on reading, having to skip a faded word here and there, but following the story of that struggling family of long ago.

July 12. The spring wheat is drying up. Papa says the ground is too sandy—it doesn't hold water like the land back home. Mama gets lonesomer every day.

"I'm hungry," Freddy said again. "When will we have lunch, Janet?"

"Janet's a bookworm," Roger teased. "She'd rather have a book than a chest full of gold."

"It's fun reading about Eliza B," Janet said. "But come on—we'll have some sandwiches and milk. Aren't you glad we have a refrigerator to keep things cold? Eliza's family didn't."

The house was so hot they were glad to get back to the dugout as soon as they'd finished lunch. Janet picked up Eliza's story where she'd left off—a story of drought and discouragement. The team had been sold—it wasn't clear why. She read on.

August 14. Mama says she just doesn't see how she can stand it here any longer. But I like it, even if you do roast in the day and freeze at night. This country sort of grows on a person.

"I know just how she felt," Janet said. "The stars are so bright and close at night—as if you could almost touch them. Daddy says we're almost a mile high—that's why the air is so clear. And the desert is always changing. Don't you love it, Roger?"

"Sure," Roger said. "If we could just make a go of this cattle-raising, I'd like it fine. I guess it was even more lonesome when Eliza B. lived here."

"Oh, this is the end," Janet said, disappointed, as she turned a page. The last half of the book was blank. "Here's the last thing she wrote:

September 21. We're going away. Papa's just given up. I think if Mama liked it, we'd stay, but she can't stand the lonesomeness. Papa says we'll leave everything we can't carry, soon's we can get a ride out. He's sold the cows and covered the well under the cottonwoods, and we've packed our clothes.

"That's all," Janet said sadly. "They must have gone right away right after that. I wonder why Eliza would leave her doll and diary and her little chest?"

Roger shrugged. "Maybe they left in a hurry," he said. "Maybe she forgot 'em. Anyway, she'd be an old lady by now." They did some more speculating on what had happened to Eliza and her family. Then Janet told stories to Freddy, who had grown tired of his cars and was beginning to worry about when his parents were coming home.

"They won't be back yet, Freddy," Roger said, "but as soon as it cools off some, you can help me get Molly."

"I'd better feed the chickens," Janet said. "Then I'll try to think of something cool for dinner. Mother and Daddy will be tired and hungry when they get home."

The hens stood panting with their wings spread in an effort to keep cool. The sun had slipped down toward the horizon, and there was a faint stirring of air in the leaves of the cottonwoods. Janet's eyes searched the distant hills hopefully, but the sky was cloudless. She breathed a prayer for the miracle Roger had said they needed. Faith and work—they had used lots of both when they had moved to the ranch on the desert. Now it looked as if they could do nothing to get water for the cattle. But God had guided them this far—Janet could not believe He meant them to give up now.

"I'll do all I can to help and trust God for the rest," she whispered softly.

She turned on the fan in the living room to drive out the accumulated hot air. She was at the sink squeezing lemons for lemonade when her gaze drifted out to the clump of cottonwoods. A phrase from Eliza B.'s diary struck her—

She went flying out the back door, leaving the lemons strewn across the counter. When Roger and Freddy came up from the creek, walking slowly behind old Molly, they came upon Janet frantically raking away at the sandy ground beneath the cottonwoods.

" 'S'matter? You lose something?" Roger called. "Or did you lose your head?"

"Roger! Remember what it said in the diary? Remember? Eliza's father covered up the well under the cottonwoods! They had a well!"

Roger stared at her. Then he looked around at the sandy ground with its **sparse** growth of wild grass and scattered clumps of sagebrush. "Why, you don't even know for sure the girl lived here, Janet. And it's certain there's no sign of a well."

"But she said under the cottonwoods."

"There are clumps of cottonwoods all over this country, silly."

"I guess there are," Janet admitted. She was ready to cry. Freddy, tired from his walk, lay on the ground, letting the sand sift through his fingers.

"The creek's about dry," Roger said. "Hardly a trickle of running water left. We'll have to move the cattle in a couple of days, sure."

"Look, Janet," Freddy broke in. "Why does the sand go down that little hole?"

"Down the hole?" Janet repeated absentmindedly.

"See, it just runs into that tiny hole and disappears."

Janet looked down at him.

"Freddy!" she cried. "You found the well!"

Janet and Roger were both on their knees then, scratching away at the sandy earth. A few inches below the surface, they came upon an old barn door. The sand from Freddy's hand had sifted through a crack in the door.

"Get back, Freddy!" Janet said, when part of the door lay bare. She and Roger, struggling for a grip on the half-rotten boards, gave a heave, raised the door on edge, and flopped it backward in the sand. A big round hole yawned in the ground at their feet.

"The well!" Janet said. The sand, disturbed, slipped in little trickles around the edges of the hole.

"Not too close; that ground is awfully loose," Roger said. "And the well may be dry."

"Oh, no!" Janet said. "Here—let's see." She hunted for a good-sized rock, then, standing back, held it at arm's length above the well.

"Now!" The three held their breath as the rock fell down—down—down—

The station wagon coming in the lane made a good deal of noise. But not as much noise as the shouts of Janet and Roger and Freddy as they went to meet their parents. And not as much, Janet thought, as the beautiful sound that rock had made at the bottom of the well—Eliza B.'s well, the well Janet would always think of as a miracle.

For that sound was the splash of a rock falling into deep, deep water!

"But I say unto you, Love your enemies, bless them that curse you, do good to them that hate you, and pray for them which despitefully use you, and persecute you." – Matthew 5:44

Bless Them That Curse You

Mary Zook

Mahtako, son of Nauhaugus, chief of the Mashpees, strode along the path leading to the lake, enjoying the cool autumn twilight. As he rounded a curve in the winding trail, he saw a white man limping ahead of him. He recognized Simon Wenders, whose ill-kept property lay near the Mashpee village.

Wenders had never given the Mashpees any reason to love him, and Mahtako knew how easily a meeting with this man could lead to trouble. He decided to circle around him. Just as he was about to slip from the path into the forest, Wenders suddenly looked over his shoulder and called out. Mahtako hesitated, and then unwillingly advanced.

"Ho, Brother Mahtako! It is well we have met. A silver shilling will be yours for doing me a small favor."

Mahtako stood motionless, questions whirling in his mind. Even in times of peace, Wenders was not known to call an Indian *brother*, nor did he offer silver shillings for such favors as he might **wheedle** or browbeat from a Mashpee.

"I promised to deliver this keg of powder to the traders in the village just beyond your tribe," Wenders said. "But it grows late, and I cannot reach the village before dark—not with this sprained ankle. Would you take the keg, Mahtako, and keep it with you in your tent tonight? Tomorrow—no need for haste—deliver it to the traders. Here is your silver shilling, and I daresay it's easy earned."

Mahtako hesitated. Truly it was a good wage. But again suspicion arose, warning caution.

"The white men forbid the Mashpees to have powder in their wigwams," he said. For in that time of distrust between the races, with the warlike Wampanoag terrorizing the villages, the English had made laws to prevent even peaceful tribes from possessing any weapons of warfare.

Wenders spat. "Bah! That is a foolish law! Everyone knows the Mashpees are true friends of the English. 'Tis only overnight. No one need ever know. And," he added slyly, "silver shillings are not often so easy to get."

Still Mahtako hesitated. He did not feel bound by Englishmen's laws: laws which his people had no hand in making, and which he regarded as unjust. But Wenders had misused him more than once, and the memory rankled. Moreover, he distrusted the man's manner.

Then Mahtako thought of Richard Bourne, the man who had spent many years sharing the story of Jesus Christ among Mahtako's people. His Christlike life endeared him to the Mashpees, and they accepted his teachings. Now Mahtako remembered what Bourne had said only a few days ago.

"Trying times are upon us. The English have sinned against the Indian, and Indians against the English—even now the battle rages. You can expect little but suspicion and mistreatment, but you must bear yourselves meekly, as followers of Him who suffered for us. Show yourselves in every way to be friends, that none may have reason to complain of you in these perilous times. Remember the words of our Lord: 'Bless them that curse you. If you are smitten on one cheek, turn the other also.' "

Mahtako pondered, as Wenders shifted impatiently beside him. Why should he do a white man a favor? And of all white men, Simon Wenders? But Christ's love goes the second mile.

Mahtako made up his mind. "Mahtako will take the powder. But keep your shilling."

He took the keg, and in a moment had disappeared down the trail. Wenders stared after him in surprise; then he looked blankly at the shilling in his palm.

"Have I, indeed, been a fool?" the man exploded. "But no, even if the Mashpees are plotting, 'tis little they can do tonight; and after that—" He sped down the path, his limp mysteriously fled.

When Mahtako left Wenders, he did not immediately turn home. His fish traps in the lake needed to be checked, and he did not want to make a second trip. *I will tend the fish traps since there is no hurry to deliver the powder before morning,* he thought. *I am glad to show this kindness. Perhaps, someday, if we prove ourselves friendly, the English will trust my people.*

Much later, a string of fish in one hand and the powder keg on his shoulder, Mahtako followed the trail back from the lake through the forest shadows.

Suddenly he stopped. A light glimmered in the woods ahead—a fire where no clearing or village lay. Had a careless hunter left a spark in the dry leaves? Every Mashpee knew the danger of forest fires. An unattended blaze could spread through the dry underbrush in minutes. Mahtako moved forward.

As he neared the fire, he hesitated, hearing voices—English voices. He paused, and then, full of curiosity, crept nearer. What would Englishmen be doing here at night?

The voices grew louder—angry voices. " 'Twill be the end of the redskins in these parts. And 'twill go hard if we don't get the Mashpee's village and land and possessions for ourselves." The speaker laughed harshly.

Mahtako slipped forward along the shadow of a boulder overlooking a small forest hollow. There he could see the men who sprawled around the small fire. They were armed, and the scattered whiskey bottles showed how they had spent the evening. The whiskey had apparently killed all reason and caution; they raised their voices recklessly.

"Aye, 'tis a cunning plan," another agreed. "Before morning dawns, Wenders, Jones, and me will fire Woods' barn and drop a coat that everyone knows is a Mashpee's garment. About the same time the rest of you will fire shots into the Mattons' house. Woods and Matton already fear and hate the Mashpees."

Mahtako was amazed. *English destroying the property of other English? What can this mean? Surely, these men have no fear of God!*

Then he heard Wenders speaking. "After the shots are fired and the barn's ablaze, we'll run from the wood as rescuers.

"Already beneath the door of the village sheriff lies a note warning that Chief Nauhaugus has a goodly store of powder in his wigwam!"

Another laughed loudly, pouring himself a drink from the jug before him. "And a goodly store of powder they shall find too, thanks to Wenders!"

"Yes, it's a clever plan," applauded another. "When the powder is found, fate will be against the **scoundrels**. They'll be proven lawbreakers. After the battle we'll be the first to the field to claim the spoil."

"Will there indeed be a battle?" fearfully inquired a younger man.

Wenders laughed again and, with an oath, declared, "With the men of the village in such a temper, and the Mashpees being Indians, though more cowardly than most, there will indeed be a battle. But never fear," he added confidently. "With little but fish spears with which to fight, they can do no more than give excuse for their own slaying. And as for the truth, which may well be told after the battle, it's very little weight the word of any Indian will hold."

In the shadow of the boulder, Mahtako's eyes flashed fire. So this accounted for Wenders' sudden friendliness! But what could he do? The fiendish plot would likely work just as the men had planned.

Distrust of Indians ran throughout the settlement. Woods and Matton, honest men both, had openly declared their distrust of the Mashpees—a thing which would make the pretended attack upon them more **credible**.

Mahtako thought of his father, who had always befriended the English. Weapons or no weapons, were the Mashpees to be called cowards?

Weapons! Suddenly Mahtako realized what he held on his shoulder. Simon Wenders had given him the very means of revenge! There was the fire, and these hateful men crowded around it in the cool of the night. A twist of the plug from the powder keg, a toss of the keg into the flames! Mahtako would be protected by the boulder. But they would die a death far more terrible than they had plotted for the peaceful, praying Mashpees.

Slowly the keg rose above Mahtako's head. But something stayed his hand—the words of Jesus, which Mahtako had heard Richard Bourne read in the rude chapel he had built with his own hands: *Do not **render** evil for evil. Bless them who curse you. Do good to them who despitefully use you.*

Like the night that closed about him, long ages of **vengeance** lay behind Mahtako. But the words and life of Jesus promised a way better than the ancient law of revenge. Silently as he had come, Mahtako slipped away from the boulder.

Behind him, the white men plotted on, never dreaming how closely the death shadow had hovered above them.

Long past midnight, a rapid knock brought Richard Bourne to the door of his cabin. The faint glow of the candle in the aged pastor's hand flickered across Mahtako's anxious face. Richard Bourne looked from the troubled eyes of his visitor to the keg on his shoulder. "Tell me," he said.

Mahtako related his story, bit by bit, until the minister understood the intention of the wicked plot.

"Come," said the pastor. "Sit here and calm yourself."

"Do you believe me, my friend?" Mahtako asked. "Here, see the keg! And I did not kill them."

Richard Bourne sighed. "Yes, my brother, I believe you. I know the wickedness of these men. Too often I have heard of their evil deeds. The day will come when God will punish the land because of such men as these."

"Almost I regret that I spared the lives of those murderers," Mahtako said fiercely. "But for the love of my Saviour, those men were dead men now."

Bourne shook his head. "It is well for you and for your people that you held your hand, Mahtako. God grant you grace never to take revenge. Had you killed these men, their bodies would have witnessed against your people as an unprovoked attack. Open warfare would certainly have followed—and the fault would lay with you."

Mahtako drew in his breath sharply. He had not thought of that. "Can we save my people?" he demanded.

"Yes," said Richard Bourne. "I will send trustworthy men to guard the clearings where the attacks will take place—men who will witness against the plotters you overheard. We will prevent the mischief they plan."

He laid his hand on the young Indian's shoulder. "You and I, Mahtako, have cause tonight to thank the God of peace that you have followed His way of peace."

Our Heroes

Here's a hand to the boy who has courage
To do what he knows to be right;
When he falls in the way of temptation,
He has a hard battle to fight.
Who strives against self and his comrades,
Will find a most powerful foe.
All honor to him if he conquers:
A cheer for the boy who says, "No!"

There's many a battle fought daily
The world knows nothing about;
There's many a brave little soldier
Whose strength puts a **legion** to **rout.**
And he who fights sin single-handed
Is more of a hero, I say,
Than he who leads soldiers to battle
And conquers by arms in the fray.

Be steadfast, my boy, when you're tempted,
And do what you know to be right.
Stand firm by the colors of manhood,
And you will o'ercome in the fight.
"The right," be your battle cry ever
In **waging** the warfare of life,
And God, who knows who are the heroes,
Will give you the strength for the strife.

– Phoebe Cary

Phoebe Cary (1824-1871) and her sister Alice published four volumes of religious poems and hymns. Her best-known poem is probably "One Sweetly Solemn Thought."

"God ... hath made of one blood all nations of men for to dwell on all the face of the earth, and hath determined the times before appointed, and the bounds of their habitation." – Acts 17:26

Standing Bear's Vision

Author Unknown

Standing Bear was in jail. He had been there for two years. Although he had not committed any crime nor broken any law, he might remain in jail forever because the United States government said that Standing Bear was not a person.

Standing Bear was the chief of the Poncas, a tribe of North American native peoples; and in those days, every Indian in the United States was under the authority of the United States Secretary of the Interior. If the Secretary happened to be a tyrant, Indians suffered. At first the Secretary of the Interior had made treaties with the Poncas. But in 1858, a new Secretary forced the Poncas to sell most of their land to the government, assuring them that the remaining acres would always belong to the Poncas people. Eight years later, the government demanded another third of their land. Before long the government took the rest of the Poncas' land, saying they wanted to give it to the Sioux.

In 1877 the U.S. Army raided the Poncas' village along the Niobrara River in Nebraska. At bayonet point the soldiers forced men, women, and children to walk eight hundred miles south to "Indian Territory," poor land in what is now Oklahoma. Once the Poncas had been driven away, the Secretary began to sell their homes and land to settlers moving west.

Standing Bear and his people arrived in the new territory without food. For many months they were without basic necessities. More than one-third of them died, including Standing Bear's young son. The chief refused to bury his son in a strange land. He gathered together thirty brave men and set out with his son's body for their ancient burial grounds in Nebraska. For many, many generations Poncas chiefs had been buried there, and Standing Bear intended to bury his son among them.

Word reached Secretary Schurz: Standing Bear has returned to Nebraska. The order went out: capture the Poncas runaways, arrest them, and put them into prison. U.S. Army General George Crook arrested Standing Bear and his men and took them down to Omaha, along with the wagon containing the bones of Standing Bear's son.

That is how Standing Bear ended up in jail for two years with no charges made against him, for he had not broken any law. The United States did not recognize Native Americans as persons, so Standing Bear could be held in jail forever without even being charged with a crime—he was not a person.

At last a newspaper reporter named Thomas Henry Tibbles asked Standing Bear for an interview. Tibbles was moved by Standing Bear's story, and he arranged for the Poncas chief to tell his story to a group of people gathered in an Omaha church house. When Standing Bear told his story to Nebraska's leading citizens, they became angry about the mistreatment of the Poncas. One man who was there—a lawyer—decided to do something about it, if he could. In the meantime, Standing Bear and his men remained in the Omaha jail.

The lawyer devised a plan. He called for a trial in the United States court in Omaha. That trial was one of the most important ever carried out in the West. In fact, you could almost say that the outcome of that trial was as important as the outcome of any trial ever tried in this country; because based upon its decision, 100,000 Native Americans were first recognized as persons.

The courtroom was packed with Omaha's leading citizens. Many ministers were there; they had been greatly troubled by Standing Bear's arrest. Every lawyer in Nebraska, and many from large eastern cities, squeezed into the room. Businessmen came. General Crook and his staff were there; and, of course, the Poncas were there.

On one side of the courtroom stood the army officers in the uniform of the United States Army. On the other side was Standing Bear, in his official robes as chief of the Poncas, and with him, his leading men.

The **attorneys** for the Poncas had carefully prepared their arguments, and for two days Attorney Poppleton stated the case for Standing Bear and his men. On the third day, another attorney, Mr. Webster, spoke for six hours. All through the trial, the courtroom was full.

As the third day of the trial moved toward its close, the tension in the courtroom increased. Mr. Webster detailed each of the wrongs inflicted on the Poncas, and the people in the courtroom grew more and more indignant. The judge, Mr. Dundy, made no attempt to **suppress** the people's excitement. At last, a lawyer for the government made a short speech. The court listened in complete silence.

It was already late in the afternoon. But before the trial ended, Mr. Dundy announced that Chief Standing Bear would be allowed to make a speech in his own behalf. The audience became restless. Few people in the courtroom had ever heard a Native American speak publicly. Most wondered if this mild-looking man, with the lines of suffering and sorrow already drawn on his 52-year-old face, dressed in the robes of a Poncas chief, could make a speech at all. A good interpreter was present—one who understood the language of the native chief.

Standing Bear rose. He faced the audience. He held out his right hand and stood motionless and silent. The silence stretched on and on. It became almost unbearable.

Finally, turning to the judge, Standing Bear said, "That hand is not the color of your hand. But if I prick it, the blood will flow, and I shall feel pain. God made me, and I am a man. I never committed a crime. If I had, I would not stand here to make a defense; I would suffer the punishment and make no complaint."

Then Standing Bear looked past the judge, gazing out of the window, as if at something far in the distance.

"I seem to be standing on a high bank of a great river, with my wife and my little girl at my side. I cannot cross the river, and **impassable** cliffs arise behind me. I hear the noise of great waters. I look and see a flood coming. The waters rise to our feet, and then to our knees. My little girl stretches her hands toward me and says, 'Save me.'

"I stand where no member of my tribe has ever stood before. I have no tradition now to guide me. The chiefs who came before me knew nothing of the circumstances that surround me. I can only hear my little girl cry, 'Save me.'

"In despair, I look to the cliffs behind me, and I seem to see a dim trail that may lead to a way of life. But no Poncas ever passed over that trail. It looks impassable. But I must make the attempt.

"I take my child by the hand, and my wife follows after me. Our hands and feet are torn; our trail is marked by our blood. At last I see a rift in the rocks! Just a little beyond there are green prairies! Yes, the swift-running water of the Niobrara runs down through the green hills. Beside it are the graves of my fathers. Beside it we will pitch our tepee and build our fires. I see the light of liberty, just ahead."

The chief became silent again. All was quiet.

Standing Bear turned to the judge.

"But in the center of the path there stands a man. Behind him I see soldiers in number like the leaves of the trees. If that man allows me, I may pass on to life and liberty. If he refuses, I must go back and sink beneath the flood.

"You are that man."

Standing Bear sat down. Tears ran down over Judge Dundy's face. General Crook leaned forward and covered his face with his hands. Some of the women in the room were sobbing.

All at once, the audience rose to its feet, and a shout went up as was never heard in a Nebraska courtroom. No one heard Judge Dundy say, "Court is dismissed." Everyone in the room rushed to reach Standing Bear, to receive him back into Nebraska.

A few days later, Judge Dundy gave his important decision. He ruled that an Indian is a person, entitled to the full protection of the law. Standing Bear and his men must be released—their imprisonment was illegal. The judge also said that the Poncas could not be forced from their homelands in violation of the many treaties that the U.S. government had made with them.

With his old wagon and the body of his dead son, Standing Bear returned to the hunting grounds of his fathers; and there he buried his son's body in the tradition of his tribe. In 1881, the Poncas were at last allowed to return to their homes along the Niobrara, where Standing Bear died in 1908.

Stopping by Woods on a Snowy Evening

Whose woods these are, I think I know.
His house is in the village though;
He will not see me stopping here
To watch his woods fill up with snow.

My little horse must think it queer
To stop without a farmhouse near
Between the woods and frozen lake
The darkest evening of the year.

He gives his harness bells a shake
To ask if there is some mistake.
The only other sound's the sweep
Of easy wind and downy flake.

The woods are lovely, dark and deep.
But I have promises to keep,
And miles to go before I sleep,
And miles to go before I sleep.

– *Robert Frost*

Robert Frost (1874-1963) was born in San Francisco but spent most of his life in New England where he was a farmer, editor, and schoolteacher. Much of his poetry was inspired by the people and landscape of New England. "Stopping by Woods" is probably his most famous poem.

"But when thou makest a feast, call the poor, the maimed, the lame, the blind." – Luke 14:13

Even Uncle Henry

Miriam Sieber Lind

Everyone who ate at our house that day still says it was the best Thanksgiving dinner they ever had. Even Uncle Henry!

It all started the year before when we were eating at Uncle George's. We always eat Thanksgiving dinner together. One year they come to our house, then it's Uncle Jim's turn, then Aunt Sadie's, Uncle Henry's, Uncle George's, and then around to us again. We all ate together— wherever it was, the twenty of us around the big table, grown-ups and children mixed.

It was that chicken gizzard I was eating. Did you ever try to cut a slippery gizzard with a spoon? I did, because Mary Ann, or whoever was supposed to see that everyone got knives and forks and spoons, didn't give me a fork. So I thought I wouldn't say anything about it but just use my spoon instead. It went all right until it came to cutting the gizzard. Then all of a sudden there was a brown flip high into the air and that wonderful gizzard, the gizzard I'd reached way under the pile to find, disappeared beneath the table.

"There goes my gizzard!" I wailed, and, tight as our table room was, I promptly dived under the white tablecloth to recapture the truant gizzard. I felt and I fished, and finally I found it, right at the tip of Aunt May's plump foot. Up I came with it and popped it into my mouth just as Aunt Marie let out a little scream.

"Child! From the floor!"

It was too late. I don't usually eat things that fall on the floor, but a gizzard—!

"Ooh! She put it in her mouth!" echoed Aunt May's Lois and Suzy in horror.

"Hey, Dave," laughed Uncle Jim, "are you starving Jeannie at home that she has to eat the crumbs off the floor?"

Daddy smiled at me and at Uncle Jim, and then looked serious. "No, but I guess there are plenty of little girls that are hungry enough to do that for less than a little piece of gizzard."

"Oh, isn't it the truth," sighed Aunt Laura. She and Uncle Henry both shook their heads in sympathy. "It just makes a person feel wicked to eat at this table when so many little ones are hungry!" She sighed again and took a great bite from the mountain of mashed potatoes on her plate.

"Yeah," said Uncle Henry, who was our favorite because he was so lively and funny. Now his voice was sad, but his eyes looked eagerly over the feast in front of him. "But what can a person do? We might as well enjoy it while we've got it!"

"You know," Aunt Sadie, who was a widow, put in rather timidly, "I was just thinking to myself before Jeannie let fly the gizzard, I wonder if the Lord would feel welcome here at this table?"

Everything was so quiet you could hear Uncle Henry's teeth click softly over the choice forkful of turkey breast that he had just hauled up to his mouth.

"I fink vat'd be nice!" piped up my little cousin Jamie. "I'd let Jesus sit by me!"

"No-sirr, by me!" shouted his older brother Johnny.

"By me!"

"By me!" All the children were laughing and shouting at once.

"I know what," I said. "We'd have a children's table all to ourselves, in the front room, and Jesus'd tell us stories. An' the big people could have the dinner all to themselves!"

Aunt Sadie went on: "Yes, I suppose that's what would happen. I imagine Jesus would be more comfortable talking with the children or eating a bowl of rice with some poor heathen."

Everything was quiet again. All the grown-ups had strange looks on their faces. But pretty soon Uncle Henry said something funny, and everyone laughed and started eating once more.

Then, after the mince and pumpkin pies had gone the rounds, and Uncle Henry had **declined** a third piece, they let us children go. I was going out the door as I heard Uncle Henry say to Uncle Jim, "No sir, Jim,

76

for a man to be as chock-full of food as I am at this moment is a sin. But these wonderful womenfolks just cook too much and too good!"

That night I said to Daddy, "Daddy, Uncle Henry is so funny. He said he ate so much it was a sin. Then why did he eat so much?"

Daddy didn't pay any attention to my question. "Mother," he said firmly, "next year it's our turn. And it's going to be a different Thanksgiving than any of us ever had. And no one's staying home from services at church to baste the turkey or cook potatoes. Sadie's not so dumb."

"But, Dad, we always have turkey dinner at Thanksgiving. Isn't that what Thanksgiving's for, to eat? That's what Uncle Henry always says!" My brother Joe looked at Dad in disbelief. But Dad didn't pay any more attention to Joe than he had to me.

"See, Mother!" he said. "See what they think Thanksgiving means!"

Well, the year rolled around, and finally Thanksgiving Day came again. We felt as if we had all been wound up like an alarm clock, it was so exciting. Joe and I were just waiting for Daddy and Mother to give us the signal, so we could let go with the secret. Not a soul but us four knew the plans. How we had planned for this day! But the day came quietly, and that morning everything was in order at our house. We didn't have to hurry to get ready for church. We arrived early! When we came home again, Joe and I rushed into the house ahead of everyone so we could see their faces as they came in.

Uncle Henry came in first. He gave his usual welcome laugh. "Ah, ah-h-h! Smells like—" "Like Thanksgiving" was what he always said, but this time he didn't finish the sentence, because, to tell the truth, there wasn't much smell! One by one the clan came in, and as they came, we almost burst with laughter to see the silly looks on their faces.

"Could I help you in the kitchen, Anna?" Aunt May asked, with a worried little glance at Mother, who wasn't hurrying around the way Thanksgiving mothers usually do.

"Oh, no, May. I have everything in hand."

"Do let me set the table!" offered Aunt Marie.

"No, Jeannie will do all that's necessary." I put twenty spoons around on the table, and Joe got twenty chairs. We had to use rockers and stools and all sorts of odd chairs, but there were twenty.

"Dinner's ready. Call the children down, Jeannie," smiled Daddy.

I wish you could have seen the expression of dismay on everyone's face.

"Dinner?" Jamie blurted out.

"Dinner?" was the question in every pair of eyes.

But somehow, we finally got them around the empty table. Empty except for the white tablecloth and the shining silver spoons. Then Daddy stood up at the end of the table.

"Let us pray," he said.

Each one obeyed him, with strange looks in their eyes as they bowed their heads.

"Our Father in Heaven and Giver of all good gifts," Daddy began, and went on to thank God for all His blessings. "And, O Father," he concluded, "when we gathered last year, Sadie set us all thinking about true thankfulness. And none of us were real sure that You would have been pleased to be our guest. Now this year we want You to step in and sit down with us and feel at home. Amen."

Then Daddy slipped out into the kitchen, and he and Mother started serving the Thanksgiving feast.

When Daddy set a bowl full of steaming rice cooked in chicken broth before Uncle Henry, Uncle Henry sort of gulped and said, "Well now." Aunt Mary's eyes flew open. Uncle George laughed a little. Jamie cried, "Rice!" and all of us children giggled. Aunt Sadie smiled at Daddy, laid her hand on his, and said, "You're very brave, you and Anna, and Jeannie and Joe. I think the Lord is here, in a way He's never been with us before."

Everyone seemed to like the rice. The table was soon busy with talk, but it was quiet talk.

"Uncle Henry's done with his rice, Mother!" Joe cried. "May Jeannie and I bring in the dessert?" Uncle Henry was always the last one through eating, and every year we joked about waiting on him for the dessert.

"All right, if you like," Mother smiled. Joe and I giggled and ran to the kitchen. Together we carried the big trayful of "dessert," and Daddy and Mother helped us put it in the middle of the table. Then while the questions started flitting across the faces again, Mother explained.

"You know"—she looked at Uncle Henry, Uncle George, Uncle Jim,

Aunt Sadie, and Daddy—"that your sister Elizabeth never can spend Thanksgiving with us. But she did send a letter this year. I'll pass it around the table so you can read it."

"Why not let Uncle Henry read it to all of us?" Uncle Jim suggested. And so that was the way we did it. Uncle Henry read the long letter that told all the latest news from the little mission up in the hills where Aunt Elizabeth worked.

"Dave," she wrote, "I wonder if you could get a Sunday school class interested in furnishing some dollar Bibles to distribute here. We have so many calls for them—right now we could use a hundred at least—and if you could interest them in **contributing** even a fraction of that number, it would be wonderful!"

When Uncle Henry was finished with the letter, Daddy went on to explain the dessert. "We thought we should give it a try among our own brothers and sisters first. Anna made a list of what she would have spent if we had made our usual Thanksgiving meal, and with the money we saved by serving rice, we were able to buy these—not half as many as they need—but a starter at least." He pointed to the twenty Bibles piled on the tray. Everyone clapped and shouted, and Uncle Henry started singing, "Praise God from whom all blessings flow"—just like that, without any warning. All of us joined in.

"How about **supervising** the packing, Henry?"

"Yes, sir!" Uncle Henry beamed. "Come on, all you children! Get the string, Joe; binder twine'll do. Jeannie, you and Suzy find a big strong box out in the garage." All of us children ran this way and that at Uncle Henry's orders. Aunt Marie helped with the cards. Into each Bible went a card with the name of one of the clan. "From Jeannie Miller," I wrote. "From Joseph," wrote Joe.

"Silly, how will they know which Joseph?" Mary Ann asked.

"Doesn't matter, silly," retorted Joe.

Aunt Marie helped Jamie and Sarah and Danny write their names. Soon the Bibles were all packed, and it was time for everyone to go home. Uncle Henrys were the last to leave. "The best Thanksgiving we've ever had!" cried Uncle Henry. "I feel better here—" he put his hand over his belt buckle, "and here!" he shifted his hand up over his heart. Then he pulled out his checkbook and went over to the desk.

"Do you have a pen, Dave?"

"Sure, Henry." Daddy took one out of his desk drawer. Uncle Henry wrote fast.

"Here." He handed the check to Daddy. "Get the rest of those Bibles. And tell Elizabeth they all come from the clan—and thanks again, Dave and Anna, for the grand Thanksgiving!"

"Give us this day our daily bread." – Matthew 6:11

The Day I Made Bread

Sem Sutter

I have always thought homemade bread was very special. The **tantalizing** aroma that filled the whole house while it baked ranked among my favorite smells. And eating fresh bread, so warm that the butter melted and honey filtered down through the holes, seemed better than almost any dessert.

But baking bread was supposed to be difficult—my mother was a good cook, but she never did it. Our friend Edna would sometimes bake bread and rolls when she came to visit us, but she was a professional cook and could prepare almost any food. Baking bread just did not seem like something that a thirteen-year-old, especially a boy, could do.

It wasn't that I was a total stranger to the kitchen, you understand. My mother sometimes let me make things like cake mixes and Jell-O. But when I tried out my own ideas, the results could be **disastrous**. Once I thought I could make cornmeal mush a nice shade of brown by putting equal parts of red and green food coloring in it. But it turned out greenish gray, and my sister refused to eat it.

But I finally got a free hand in the kitchen the week my mother and my sisters went to Grandpa and Grandma's, leaving my father and me to "bach it."[1] I decided this was my golden opportunity to try baking bread. If I told no one beforehand, then no one needed to know if my experiment was a miserable failure.

After my father had left for work one morning, I spread out the cookbooks and studied the recipes. I decided that the whole wheat bread in the Betty Crocker cookbook sounded good—besides, it had pictures showing what to do, step by step.

I reread the recipe several times, knowing that I could still back out.

---

1 bach it: to live as bachelors

Then I took a deep breath and plunged in, landing squarely on my first problem—the yeast. I was supposed to dissolve it in two cups of "warm, not hot water—about the temperature of a baby's bottle." How did I know how warm a baby's bottle was? I remembered seeing people testing formula on the undersides of their wrists, so that's where I tested the water, until it seemed "warm, not hot." I hoped it was right and hadn't killed the yeast.

The next steps went smoothly—adding oil, honey, salt, and half the flour, and beating with the electric mixer. I stirred in the second half of the flour with a wooden spoon because the dough was getting too stiff for the mixer.

Then another problem developed—kneading. I figured this could be fun, but I was also afraid I might not do it right. I studied the pictures carefully, then sprinkled flour on the counter, dumped the dough on it, and began pushing, poking, folding over, and flattening again. The stuff immediately stuck to my fingers! Betty Crocker said if this happened to keep sprinkling more flour on, a little at a time. This seemed to help, but then I noticed gray smudges on the dough and suddenly realized that I had forgotten to wash my hands. Oh, well, I decided, baking would **sterilize** the dirt. Ten minutes of kneading dough seemed awfully long, but as time went on it became easier to manage and more elastic, and it was fun to push and feel it pushing back.

Having no idea how much the dough might expand, I put it in the big green dishpan to rise, covering it with a towel. I couldn't resist checking its progress every few minutes and could soon tell that it was indeed rising. Fortunately, Betty Crocker told me that it should take an hour and a half to double in size, because I had a hard time judging when it looked that big.

The next step was punching down the dough, which I did by landing a fist smack in the middle of it. It was fun to hear it "poof" and then watch it sinking slowly down like a revival tent being taken down. With the help of Betty Crocker's diagrams, I managed to shape the dough into two loaves and put them in pans. They looked small and slightly lopsided, and I was discouraged, remembering they had to rise a second time before baking. I wished this project weren't taking so long to complete.

At last the dough was even with the tops of the pans and ready for the oven. I was glad that our oven door had a window so that I could watch the bread baking. Soon the mouth-watering smell filled the air, increasing my impatience for the bread to be done. There was certainly no danger of its burning because of baking too long!

As soon as the bread was out of the oven, I had to taste it. It was so hot that I nearly burned my fingers slicing it. I smothered the crust piece with butter and honey and took a bite—it tasted even better than I had expected. I sat down and basked in my success, slicing and downing piece after piece until I noticed that nearly half a loaf was gone and my stomach was feeling heavy.

When my father returned from work, the rich smell of bread still hung in the air. Before he could ask questions, I offered him a sample. When he proclaimed it the best he had ever eaten and reached to cut another slice, I glowed with pride and a feeling of accomplishment. I was glad I had tried doing something that thirteen-year-old boys "don't do."

The Sense of Smell

The sense of smell is wonderful,
A marvel of design:
Mere vapors move with powerful force
The channels of the mind.

Uncanny[1] smells spark memories—
A passing bus's fumes
Recall a childhood walk along
A Paris street in June.

Repulsive odors knot the gut
And make us gasp for air:
The sulfury stink of paper mills,
The musky stench of bear.

Imagination wakes at spicy scents,
Dreams of exotic brigs[2]
That reek of lavender and nard,[3]
Sharp sandalwood and figs.

Consider smells that make you feel—
Aromas strong and sweet—
Hot blacktop steaming in the rain,
Mown grass or smoky peat.

But chicken sizzling on the grill,
Hot loaves, fresh-baked just right,
And spicy cider are the best:
Smells that stir your appetite!

– Tim Kennedy

---

1 uncanny: eerie, mysterious
2 brig: a two-masted, square-rigged ship; shortened form of *brigantine*
3 nard: spikenard, a fragrant ointment

"There hath no temptation taken you but such as is common to man: but God is faithful, who will not suffer you to be tempted above that ye are able; but will with the temptation also make a way to escape, that ye may be able to bear it." – 1 Corinthians 10:13

The Boy Judge

from Arabian Nights

In the days of the Caliph[1] Harun al-Rashid, there lived in Baghdad a merchant whose name was Ali Cogia. He had been very successful in business and at length decided to go on a pilgrimage to Mecca.[2] He therefore disposed of his shop and merchandise, rented out his house, and made ready to join the next caravan to the city of Mecca.

Now Ali Cogia had a thousand pieces of gold over and above the sum he had set aside for his pilgrimage; and not knowing what else to do with them, he put them into a jar and then filled the jar with olives. The next day he carried the jar to a merchant named Hassan, who was his friend.

"Brother," he said, "you know that I am about to start to Mecca. Here is a jar of olives, which I beg you to take care of till my return."

Hassan answered, "Certainly, my friend. Here is the key to my warehouse. Carry the jar thither yourself and place it where you choose. As you leave it, so shall you find it."

Ali Cogia therefore set his jar on a shelf in his friend's warehouse and soon afterward started to Mecca. He made the pilgrimage in safety; and then, desiring to see still more of the world, he journeyed to many other famous cities, and then proceeded to India. Thus seven years passed before he set his face homeward.

Meanwhile the jar of olives stood in its place in the warehouse of the merchant Hassan, who had almost forgotten his friend Ali Cogia. But one evening, about the time Ali Cogia was returning to Baghdad, Hassan was eating supper with his wife when she happened to speak of olives.

---

1 caliph: title of the successors of Muhammad as the leader of the Islam religion
2 Mecca: the city of Muhammad's birth and the holy city of the Islam religion; devout Muslims are to take a pilgrimage to Mecca at least once in their lifetime if possible

"You know I am so fond of them," she said, "and now I have not tasted one for more than a year!"

"Well, well," said Hassan. "That reminds me of something. When Ali Cogia went to Mecca, he left a jar of olives in my charge. Seven years have passed, and nobody has heard from him. He is no doubt dead and will never return to claim his olives. Give me a dish and I will go and fetch some. I think we might as well eat them."

"But, Hassan, will that be honest?" said his wife. "A trust should be guarded, whether for a long time or a short. We have left the olives alone these seven years, and can't we do without them still? Think no more about them!"

Hassan would not listen to the words of his wife. He found for himself a lamp and a dish and started out. Again his wife warned him: "Remember, Hassan, that I have no share in what you are about to do."

Hassan laughed and went straightway to his warehouse. When he opened the jar, he found that the olives were spoiled. Hoping that some good ones might remain toward the bottom, he emptied the jar upon the floor, and to his great surprise, a number of gold pieces fell out.

Arabian Nights and Harun al-Rashid

The *Arabian Nights*, from which "The Boy Judge" is taken, is a collection of Oriental stories. Most probably the stories were passed down for years and were written down at different times.

The tales are set in a "frame story," which tells of a king who married and killed a new wife every day. When Scheherazade marries the king, she begins an interesting story, but cleverly stops, promising to finish it the next day. The next day she did the same thing—and so on for many nights, until the king decides not to kill her.

This frame story gives *Arabian Nights* its other name, *The Thousand and One Nights*, the number of tales Scheherazade supposedly told the king.

While "The Boy Judge" is likely a folktale, the caliph Harun al-Rashid was a real man. He was an important ruler of the Muslim empire during the late 700s, when it was at the height of its power. He appears in several of the stories from *Arabian Nights*.

Now Hassan was not uncommonly honest. He put the money in a bag, which he carefully hid away, returned the rotted olives to the jar, and quitted the warehouse.

"O wife," he said, "you were right about those olives; they are all spoiled. So I put the cover on the jar again, so that if Ali Cogia ever returns again, he will never notice that it has been touched."

"You did wisely," answered the wife, "but you would have done better still had you never meddled with the olives."

Hassan lay awake all night, planning what he would do with the gold. In the morning he went out very early and bought a quantity of fresh, sound olives of that year's growth. Returning to his warehouse, he threw away the old olives and filled the jar with the fresh. Then he covered it as it had been before and set it in its place.

Not long after this Ali Cogia arrived at home, much to the surprise of his friends. The next day he went to see his friend Hassan, and the two spent a pleasant hour together. Then, at length, Ali Cogia said, "Brother, you remember the jar of olives which I left with you. I will now trouble you for it again."

"Yes, certainly," said Hassan. "I had really forgotten about it. But it stands just where you placed it. As you left it, so you find it."

Ali Cogia thanked him and carried the jar to the inn where he was staying. He shut the door of his room, took a large dish, and poured the olives into it. What was his astonishment when he found no gold, but only olives! "Is it possible that the man whom I trusted has robbed me?" he cried.

He hastened back to the merchant's house. "O Hassan," he said, "there were a thousand pieces of gold in that jar when I left it with you; but when I emptied it just now, there was nothing but olives."

"Indeed!" answered Hassan. "What do I know about any gold? You said that the jar contained olives. And as you left it, so you found it."

Then Ali Cogia besought him to confess that he had taken the money; but he angrily denied having so much as touched the jar and was finally about to drive his old friend from his door.

Some of the neighbors, hearing loud words between the two men, came forward and tried to **pacify** them. "Refer the matter to the cadi," they said.

So to the cadi they went.

"This man, Hassan, has stolen a thousand pieces of gold which I entrusted to him," said Ali Cogia, and he told the whole story of the jar.

"Have you any witnesses?" asked the cadi.

Ali Cogia answered that he had not taken the precaution to have any, because he had firmly trusted in his friend's honesty.

Then the cadi bade Hassan state his side of the case. The merchant thereupon declared that he had neither taken the gold nor so much as opened the jar; and he offered to take an oath to that effect. The cadi accepted the oath and dismissed Hassan as innocent.

Ali Cogia was not at all satisfied with the cadi's decision. He drew up a request to the caliph, Harun al-Rashid, and **contrived** to have it presented to him. The caliph read the request carefully, pondered upon it, and then commanded that both Ali Cogia and Hassan should appear before him the following morning.

That same evening the caliph, with his friend Jaffar, went out in disguise for a stroll through the city. As he was walking down a back street, he heard a clamor of children's voices in a vacant yard and, looking in, saw several small boys at play.

"See, Jaffar," he said. "You and I often played together in that way when we were boys. Let us wait here by the wall and watch those little fellows awhile."

So they sat down on a stone bench and looked at the boys playing in the moonlight.

Presently one of the lads said, "Let's play cadi's court, boys."

"Yes! Yes!" cried the others. "That will be great fun. Who will be the cadi?"

"I will," answered the boy who had proposed the game. "I am the cadi. Now bring before me Ali Cogia and the merchant who stole the gold pieces from him."

At hearing this, the caliph whispered to Jaffar, "Now we're going to have some rare sport. Perhaps I will learn a lesson in judgment," and he smiled and stroked his beard.

The boy cadi took his seat with great pomp and dignity. Then his chief officer led forward two other boys whom he presented as Ali Cogia and Hassan.

The boy cadi spoke and said, "O Ali Cogia! Wherefore comest thou before me? What is thy complaint?"

The boy Ali Cogia bent low and told the story of the jar and the olives and the gold. After this the boy cadi demanded of the boy Hassan why he had not returned the jar of olives as he had found it. The boy Hassan declared that he had really done so; no one had so much as opened the jar, and he was ready to take an oath that such was true.

Here Harun, the caliph, jogged the elbow of Jaffar and whispered, "Now see what will happen!"

"Not so fast, Hassan!" said the boy cadi. "Before you take any oath, I wish to see and taste some of those olives. Hast thou brought the jar with thee, Ali Cogia?"

The boy Ali Cogia answered that he had not. The boy cadi therefore bade him run and fetch it, which he did without delay.

Not to omit any formality, the boy cadi then said, "Hassan, dost thou admit that this is the same jar that was left with thee?"

"Yes," said the boy Hassan, "I do."

"Open it then, Ali Cogia."

The boy Ali Cogia obeyed.

Then said the boy cadi, looking into the jar, "The jar is indeed quite full of olives, and it appears that none have been taken out. I will taste some of them. Ah! They are fine but rather fresh to have been in this jar seven years. Go! Bring hither some olive merchants. We must have their opinion."

Soon two boys came forward who said they were olive merchants.

"Tell me, O olive merchants," said the boy cadi, "how long can olives that are put up in this manner be kept fresh and fit to eat?"

The first boy merchant answered, "O Cadi! It is impossible to preserve them longer than the third year. They lose their flavor and color and are fit for nothing."

"Taste these olives," said the boy cadi.

The boy merchants pretended to taste. "O Cadi! These olives are fresh and of the present year!"

"You are mistaken," said the boy cadi. "This man Hassan tells me that they have been in this same jar for seven years."

The boy merchants looked at each other **derisively**. "It is impossible," they said. "The olives would have shrunken very much, but the jar as you see is quite full. Every olive merchant in Baghdad will tell you, O Cadi, that these olives were grown this year."

The boy Hassan tried now to say something, but the boy cadi bade him hold his tongue.

"Hassan, the case is plain. There is no getting around it. Thou art a thief, and thou shalt be hanged."

At hearing this judgment, all the boys shouted their pleasure, and the Caliph Harun al-Rashid joined in their **acclamations**.

"What do you think of the boy cadi, Jaffar?" he said.

"I am surprised at his wisdom," answered Jaffar.

"Well, he shall judge the case of the real Ali Cogia," said the caliph. "Bring him to me tomorrow. Bring also the real cadi who acquitted Hassan; he shall learn wisdom from the child. Have also present a couple of olive merchants and bid Ali Cogia bring his jar of olives."

On the morrow Jaffar conducted the young lad to Harun al-Rashid. The child was frightened and trembled.

"Fear not," said the caliph. "I saw and heard thee last night when thou wert playing the cadi. I approve thy judgment."

Then the boy's fear departed, and Ali Cogia and Hassan were brought forward. The caliph called them by name, and each bowed low and pressed his forehead upon the ground before the throne.

"Now," said the caliph, "you may each plead his cause, and this child will hear and give judgment. If it needs **amendment**, I will see to it."

So Ali Cogia told his story and made his accusation; and Hassan answered it as before and offered to take an oath.

"Not so fast," said the boy. "The jar of olives must be examined before any oath is required of you."

Then to Hassan's great surprise, the jar was carried in and placed at the feet of the caliph. Ali Cogia opened it.

"Hassan, is this the jar?" asked the boy judge.

"It is," answered Hassan.

The caliph tasted an olive and found it good and fresh. The two olive merchants were called and bidden to examine the olives.

"How old do you pronounce them to be?" asked the boy judge.

"They are of this year's growth," they answered.

"Nay!" said the boy judge. "This man, Hassan, declares that they are the same olives left in his charge by Ali Cogia seven years ago."

The merchants shrugged their shoulders and said that such was utterly impossible. Never could olives be preserved fresh for that time.

And now Hassan, pale and trembling, was called to stand before the judgment. He was so confused that he could not say a word in his own defense. The boy judge, after a moment's silence, looked up into the caliph's face and blushed.

"O Prince," said he, "this is no child's play but a matter of life and death. I can give judgment only in make-believe sport; it is for you to give judgment in earnest."

Then the caliph ascended the throne and solemnly pronounced judgment against the thieving merchant. And Hassan, overcome with shame, confessed his fault and told where he had hidden the thousand pieces of gold. Thereupon they were restored to Ali Cogia; and the caliph embraced the young boy and sent him home with a hundred pieces of gold to his mother.

"Judge not according to the appearance, but judge righteous judgment."

– John 7:24

The Judge's Sentence

Archibald Rutledge

Only after a desperate struggle had state policeman Julian Broderick mastered the fugitive. Broderick could not remember ever having so relentless and prolonged a chase or so sudden and fierce an encounter. The incident happened too on a peculiarly lonely stretch of beach between a remote pine forest and the **desolate** sea marshes of rural Charleston County, South Carolina. Broderick knew that had the struggle ended differently, many a day would have passed before his friends learned of his fate—if they had ever learned of it.

After the **posse** had abandoned the pursuit, Broderick had dogged his man through swamps and across rivers, until at last he had come upon him just as the fellow was about to cross a deep tidal estuary.[1] In the clash that followed, the law had triumphed; and as soon as Broderick had handcuffed his man, the two began the march to Sellers, the nearest settlement.

The prisoner was Jason Jones, a powerful man, whose reputation in the community at Rosemary up to the time when he robbed Ashton, the storekeeper, had been good. Jones had robbed the store on Friday and fled that very night. It was now the following Tuesday; and in all that time, the silent man who now marched before Broderick had eaten hardly a mouthful.

Compared to Broderick, Jason Jones was a giant; and the policeman felt that he should have had a small chance against so formidable an opponent if the man had not been exhausted by the pitiless pursuit. Broderick was sorry for the fellow, and he intended when they reached Sellers to see that the man was decently cared for.

---

1 estuary (es' chə wer' ē): an arm of the sea at the mouth of a river

The two men arrived in the seacoast village at sunset, but a strange sort of darkness had already set in. A sharp misty rain, driven by an insistent east wind, had been falling for an hour. The huddled houses of the small settlement were well-lighted. It was an evening to be indoors.

Broderick, weary physically and mentally, at last brought his captive to the post office. Sellers was the kind of village that has only one officer of the law, who is police officer, storekeeper, and postmaster. Broderick was an old friend of this man.

"Jim," he said, "I've got a man here with me. Guess I'll have to ask you to let me keep him here tonight."

"Right, Julian," the other answered, gazing with interest on the powerful form of Jason Jones. "Tell me what you need."

"I must take this man on the truck to Charleston first thing in the morning. We've had nothing to eat, Jim, for a good while."

The postmaster busied himself behind the counter and soon set out cheese, crackers, canned salmon, and some ancient gingerbread cookies.

"Jason," said his captor, not without kindness, "I'll take the cuffs off now so you can eat your supper."

The prisoner muttered thanks.

The postmaster, who had been about to close up shop when the two men arrived, slouched into his overcoat. "Stormy wind coming up," he remarked. "If it doesn't get too bad, I'll have my wife send you up a pot of hot coffee." In a lower voice he added, "Come to the door." There he whispered, "Julian, do you want any help with this fellow tonight? I can come back if you think you might need me."

"No, I think I can manage him," Broderick replied. "No reason for you to come back."

The postmaster opened the door, and the wind slammed it violently back against the wall. The two smoky lamps in the room flared **convulsively**.

"Regular storm," Broderick commented, closing the door behind the postmaster and shutting out the rain and the night.

Then he turned back to the room. "Jason," he said, raising his voice to make himself heard above the wind, "there's a couch over there, where you can get some sleep. I'll put the cuffs back on you, that being according to orders and regulations."

Jason made no protest. He seemed to be sensible of the kindness that Broderick had shown him. When the handcuffs had been adjusted, he went to the rude couch and lay down. There was something resigned about his manner, as if he had realized that there was no use running from the law.

Jason soon slept, though the night was no night for sleeping. In a chair tilted against the counter sat Julian Broderick, trying to read a week-old paper by the dim lamplight. Outside, the wind had slowly increased until now it was almost a cyclone. The policeman was sure he heard a great tree blow down. The wood frame post office began to creak and groan.

"No chance for Jim to send that coffee now," he said to himself. As the hours wore on toward midnight, the violence of the gale increased. Jim Laws' store was especially exposed to the force of the blast. The storm was coming off the sea, and there was nothing in the village between the stormy sea and the post office.

About an hour before midnight Julian, now alarmed, went to the window. In the darkness a storm-lashed tide raged before a seventy-mile gale. Salty seawater was already creeping under the building. Julian realized that this was a hurricane out of the West Indies. At any moment the rising tide might sweep the rickety post office from its foundations. Water began to puddle on the floor, and salt spume came driving through the cracks in the wall.

There was no chance that the postmaster would get back, for he and his neighbors would be fully occupied in getting their families inland to safety. Julian and Jason would have to shift for themselves. Julian tossed three mail sacks and some boxes of store goods up on the counter and turned to his prisoner.

With Jason, exhaustion had had its way; he was sleeping heavily, his large form cramped on the small couch. Julian would have been glad for the prisoner to rest, but the time had come to waken him. Suddenly there was a grinding crash. Rain poured heavily through the roof. A live oak tree had fallen on the building.

"When live oaks go," Broderick muttered, "it's time for us to leave!" He laid his hand on Jason's shoulder.

Even after the fall of the tree through the roof, the prisoner slept. Julian shook him. "Jason, sit up and listen to me."

He waited until he was sure that his prisoner had full possession of his senses.

"Jason, we are caught in a storm—you understand? You and I have to leave this place. Now, I want to give you the best chance I can, so I am going to take the cuffs off. Stay with me as long as you can, Jason. If things get so bad that you have to save yourself from drowning, look out for yourself. But when the storm is over, you come back to me. Is that fair?"

"Yes, sir, more than fair." Both men spoke calmly, in high contrast to the howling gale.

Just then came a heavy thud against the windward side of the building and a smashing, splintering blow. A heavy pine post, drifting from the sawmill nearby, had been driven like a ram through the side of the building. The waves drove it farther in and twisted it. Seawater rushed in through the gaping hole. The two men stood for a moment. Julian was afraid that Jason might not be willing to risk the storm. He turned to call to Jason and at the same time stepped downward into the wild tide.

"Take my hand, Jason; let's try to get through this together."

Even while he was speaking, he was thrown violently against the building, and the hand that reached out for Jason's clutched empty air. With a groan, Julian sank into the seething black waters. A heavy timber, companion to the one that had rammed the building, had driven against his leg. His thigh was broken; he could neither swim nor stand; he would surely drown.

Into the wailing darkness came the sound of Jason's voice. His bulk loomed monstrous in the doorway. "Where are you?" he shouted.

With his fingers trailing idly against the side of the building, his breath almost gone from another savage thrust of the cruel timber, Julian called back faintly, "I'm done for, Jason. Save yourself. Keep the wind at your back, and you'll reach the woods. Save yourself."

Unconsciousness surged down upon him, and the doomed man in the water was hardly aware of the giant form towering above him.

It was noon the following day; and though the wind was still high, the clouds were breaking up. What had been the village of Sellers was now a desolation. Three miles inland, in a stout cabin in the pine lands, lay Julian on a pallet in the corner. The first thing the aching eyes of the state policeman caught as he opened them was his prisoner, seated near the fireplace.

"You've come back, Jason," Julian said. "You are a man of your word."

"I never went, sir," Jason responded simply.

Then the owner of the cabin told what Jason had done. In the end he said with some show of feeling, "He carried you just like a woman would carry a baby, and he would not rest till we had you as comfortable as you could be made. He must be a mighty faithful man of yours."

"He is," said Julian Broderick.

Two weeks later Jason Jones, accused of robbing the Ashton store in Rosemary, was on trial in Charleston. Judge Napier had heard the evidence; and in his charge to the jury, he had suggested that if the twelve men came to a verdict of guilty, he would see that the punishment met the offense. He **intimated** that the robbing of country stores was a practice that, so far as he could help it, would have to cease in Charleston County.

Then he turned to the prisoner. "Jason Jones, the law gives you the right to make any statement you may wish to make; do you wish to say anything for yourself?"

"Please, sir," Jason replied, "make my fine as light as you can. I'm mighty sorry I broke in the store. My wife is dead, and I got seven children. I broke in the store 'cause they were hungry."

At that moment there was a stir at the rear of the courtroom. Julian Broderick, lying on a cot, was carried in. The doctors at the hospital had not yet permitted him even to use crutches. From his bed of pain he told, with evident effort, the story of the storm. Through it all the listeners were spellbound. Judge Napier cleared his throat suspiciously.

"Gentlemen of the jury," he said at the conclusion of the policeman's story, "retire for your verdict. Find according to the evidence."

In a few minutes the men returned with the verdict—guilty.

"Jason Jones, stand up and hear your sentence," said Judge Napier. "We find you guilty of robbing the Ashton store. But we also find you guilty of saving your captor's life at the risk of your own and of staying by him as you had promised to do. The amount of damage you did to the store was about five dollars, which I, in an unofficial **capacity**, will pay. The charges against you are cleared by your conduct in the storm.

"Return home now and work hard for those seven children. Mr. Broderick here and certain other gentlemen in the room have thrown together and now hand you this little gift of a hundred dollars. Jason, I am convinced that you are a brave and good man. Be brave and good always. You may go. You are free."

Living for Others

"For all the law is fulfilled in one word, even in this; Thou shalt love thy neighbour as thyself." – Galatians 5:14

The King's Questions

Leo Tolstoy

"What is the most important time in a man's life?" the king wondered one day as he walked alone through his gardens. "And who are really the right people to be with? And if I only knew the thing that was most important to do of all things and could do it—then I would always be successful."

The king was always thinking thoughts like these, but these three questions puzzled him most of all. So the king made an announcement throughout his kingdom that he would give a large reward to anyone who could answer these three questions: What is the most important time? Who are the most **essential** of all people? And what is the most important thing to do?

Well, many learned men came to the king from every corner of the kingdom—and they answered his questions with many different answers, trying to win the reward.

In answer to his first question, one professor said that to know the most important time, you must make a timetable for all the days, months, and years and follow it strictly. "Then," he told the king, "you can do everything at the right moment." But another said it was impossible to know before it came which moment was the most important! "Give close attention to what is going on around you, and do whatever needs to be done as soon as you can." Still another said that one man could never figure out for himself the most important time in his life and so he must hire a council of wise men to advise him.

The king's second question was also given many answers. Not one answer agreed with the others. Some of the learned men said the most essential people were the king's counselors, others said the priests were more important, and still others told the king to rely most upon his soldiers.

100

To the third question the answers were likewise varied. "The most important occupation," one man said, "is science." "No," said another, "the really essential thing to do is to prepare for war against your most fearful enemy."

The king had already considered most of these answers, and he agreed with none of them! So he did not give the reward to anyone. However, he was not satisfied either, and when he heard that there was a **hermit** in his kingdom famous for his wisdom, the king set out to ask his counsel.

The hermit lived in the woods, which he never left. He received only common people into his home, because none of the wealthy or mighty people in the land wanted anything to do with his simple, old home. For this reason, the king put on very plain garments. He sent his bodyguards away before he reached the hermit's shack, dismounted from his horse, and walked the rest of the way alone.

The king found the hermit digging in his garden in front of his hut. The hermit looked up, greeted the visitor, and went on with his digging. He was frail and thin, and each time he dug his shovel into the ground and turned the soil, he gasped for breath.

The king watched for only a moment before he said, "I have come, wise man of the woods, to ask you to give me the answers to three questions."

Since the hermit said nothing, the king at last posed the questions to him: "What hour should we always remember and not let slip away? Which people are the most important—the ones with whom we should associate? What is the essential thing we should do—do first above all others?"

The hermit heard the king but made no answer. He went on digging.

"You're tired," the king said. "Give me the spade—I'll dig for a while."

The king took the shovel and began to dig. After a while he stopped and asked the hermit his questions again. Again, the hermit did not answer him. He just reached out his hand for the shovel: "You rest now, and I'll work."

But the king wouldn't give up the spade. He went on digging. An hour passed, and then another, and the sun began to set behind the trees. Finally the king stuck the shovel into the ground and said, "I came to you, wise man, to find the answers to my questions. If you can't answer them, I'll be on my way home."

"Wait. Listen. Someone is running up!" the hermit said. "Let's see who it is."

The king turned and saw a man running toward them. The man's hands were clasped over his stomach, and the blood flowed from beneath them. He fell at the king's feet and lay motionless, rolling his eyes and moaning faintly.

The king and the hermit opened his shirt. He had a large wound in his stomach. The king bathed the wound as well as he could and bandaged it. The blood did not cease flowing, and several times the king had to remove the bandages soaked with warm blood, rebathe and rebandage the wound.

When at last the blood stopped flowing, the wounded man came to and asked for water. The king brought him fresh water and raised it to the wounded man's lips.

"Only wet your mouth with a little, for now," the king advised.

The sun had set by this time and it was turning cold, so the king and hermit carried the man into the hermit's shack and laid him on the only bed. The man shut his eyes and fell right to sleep. The king was so tired from traveling, spading, and tending to the stranger's injuries that he curled up on the floor by the door and fell into a sound sleep. He slept through the whole summer night, and when he awoke in the morning, he couldn't remember where he was at first. A strange man lay across the small room, staring at him with glistening eyes.

"Forgive me," the man said suddenly, in a faint voice when he saw that the king was awake and looking at him.

"I have nothing to forgive you for. I don't even know you," the king said.

"You don't know me. But I know you. I am your enemy!" the other man said. "I was going to kill you last night, because months ago you imprisoned my brother and seized our family farm. I knew you had come alone to see the wise man, and I had decided I would follow you and kill you when you went back home through the forest. I waited all day, but you didn't come; so I came out of hiding, thinking I would follow you and find you here. I stumbled onto your bodyguards, who recognized me. They attacked me and wounded me before I could escape. I would have bled to death if you had not dressed my wound.

"I wanted to kill you, and instead you have saved my life," the man went on. "Now, I have been lying here thinking—if I live, and if you will allow me, I will serve you as your most faithful servant. I will insist that my sons do the same! Please forgive me!"

The king was glad to make peace with this enemy so easily. He not only forgave him but also promised to return the farm and to have his own servants and the royal physician come to care for him.

He left the wounded man there and went to find the hermit. *Perhaps,* he thought, *I should ask him my questions once more before I leave.* He found the old man on his knees, sowing seed in the beds they had dug the day before.

"I must leave. But I'll ask once more—will you please answer my questions, if you can?"

"But they've already been answered," the old man said, squatting on his thin legs and looking up at the king.

"How?" the king asked.

"Don't you see?" the hermit responded. "If you had not had compassion on me yesterday and dug these beds for me—if you had gone back home alone—that man would have attacked you and perhaps would have killed you. So the most important time was when you dug these beds for me, and I was the right person for you to be with—don't you see? The most important thing for you to do was to show me kindness!

"Later, when that man ran up, the most important time was when you cared for his wounds, for if you hadn't bandaged him up, he would have died without making his peace with you. He was the most essential man to you at that time, and what you did for him was the most important thing to be done.

"This is always true," the hermit said,

Leo Tolstoy (1828-1910) was born near Moscow, the capital of Russia. He studied for a time at a Moscow university and joined the army. Later he came to believe that war was wrong; he also sold his possessions and committed himself to a life of poverty. Many of his writings express his views opposing violence and involvement with the world.

"that the most important time is now. Now is the only time when we have any power over ourselves. The most important person to be with is the person you are with at the moment. You can never be sure that you will ever be with anyone else! And the person you are with is the only person you can help right now. As for the most important thing to do—well, that's obvious enough. The most important thing to do is to show kindness to the man you're with, because that is why God has left us in the world."

"But the stranger that dwelleth with you shall be unto you as one born among you, and thou shalt love him as thyself; for ye were strangers in the land of Egypt: I am the LORD your God." – Leviticus 19:34

The Family

Savannah Lee

Many stars lighted the white winter night. Tonight they hung low, especially the one in the southwest that always appears first. I trudged over the field, the squeaking of my rubber boots the only sound in the night. Everything was muted by a covering of snow and the grayish starlight: the farm buildings in the distance, the still woods, even the humps of stone along the fence. Sal's place was down this hilly field, across the road in a grove of trees.

That's where I was headed, all because of Mom. Every year it happened. About a week before Christmas she would corner Jim, Eva, or me. "You know," she would say sweetly, "I think it would be nice to have Sal Smithinson come for Christmas Eve again this year. Would you please walk down and give him a personal invitation?"

This year she cornered me—out in the shop. Tonight I had raised my head from the sawdust and given her a patient look.

"What's the use, Mom?"

"He always comes, Miles!"

"I know he always comes—and goes away again, with nothing in between!"

Mom's eyes had shadowed a little, but she kept smiling and looking at me. I **relented**. After all, how could I say no to an angel?

Of course, it was the Christlike thing to do for a retired bachelor— invite him to share your family's Christmas Eve. To Mom, this must be a family time: no supper invitation, no skating, or youth get-together could interfere.

I jumped a snow-filled ditch and jogged down toward Sal's house. I could see it now—the boxy, clapboard structure that looked more like a chicken coop than a house. Pale yellow light filtered through the one front window, and I could hear the twang of music as I mounted the sagging porch and knocked on the storm door. He might actually be expecting me, I thought, grinning. I stamped my tingling feet on the wooden floor.

The inside door squeaked open, and Sal's bearded face peered through the glass. He saw me and unbolted the storm door.

Holding it half open, he greeted me with a yellow-toothed smile. "How're ya, lad? Yer out on this cold night?"

"Oh, it's good exercise," I said, smiling. "Uh, Mom was wondering if you would come for our Christmas Eve supper again this year? Next Friday evening."

Sal stood there and looked at me. "Yeah," he said after some moments, "I supposed she was. But this year," he paused, his dark eyes holding mine, "this year, I'm askin' you to come 'ere. Not yer whole family, jist you."

I stared back until I collected my thoughts. "Well, Sal," I hesitated, "that might be fine, but Mom's pretty determined, you know, about having the whole family together on Christmas Eve."

"I know." He smiled an odd smile and ran a massive hand over his heavy beard. "But I'm askin' anyway, laddie."

What could I say, standing there in the cold while this bearded giant waited **expectantly**? "I'll mention it to her," I promised.

"Fine. G'night." He pulled the storm door shut, and I slowly walked back to the road.

Well. This'll be a new one for Mom. What's she gonna do now? Maybe this'll cure her.

Sal had always come, at every invitation since we had moved here five years ago. He came scraping over the snow in his clumsy snowshoes and orange parka. He parked the shoes on the porch, hung the parka behind the door, and dropped into the chair at the foot of the table. He ate. All the food he tucked away in hearty bites! Especially stuffing. He always grunted when he ate the stuffing. He rarely looked at Mom or addressed her, other than a "Thanks, mem," as we left the table.

From there we trooped into the living room to sing carols and hear Dad read Luke 2. At this, Sal closed his eyes and locked his square-tipped fingers behind his head. Then Dad would pray, asking that more folks would come to know the Giver of peace and goodwill this season. Then Sal left, without asking Dad any of the questions I thought he should—soul questions, you know.

And this year he obviously won't, I thought as I again jumped the ditch. Then I grinned as I thought how Mom felt about Christmas Eve—how she would never consent to my going to Sal's and breaking up the family on Christmas Eve. Sal was harmless enough, just odd. It would've been a strange way to pass a Christmas Eve! No turkey, I suppose. Pork and beans out of a can, maybe? I had no idea what Sal cooked. I didn't know much about him at all; just bits I had heard from the area folks.

He's a social reject, I thought. It really was a shame that he wouldn't come over this year, and I knew Mom was going to feel especially bad about it.

Mom did feel bad, but not for the reason I expected her to. I found her in the warm parlor, mending a shirt. "Sal isn't coming, Mom," I said.

Her head jerked up, and she stared at me.

"He asked me, instead, to come over and spend the evening with him."

I stood there waiting for her protests, but she just sat still, with her needle poised in midair, until a faraway look softened her eyes. She sighed. "Well, Miles, we're going to miss you. But we'll have our big meal on Christmas Day this year instead."

"What?" I protested. "You aren't thinking I'll go, surely. Why, what about all your ideas about only family, and, and . . . "

Mom looked at me and smiled, and I could tell it was one of those moments she wished I was ten years younger, and she could hug me and rumple my hair.

"I think I'll have to compromise this time. That is, if you'll agree to go."

It took me a few days to agree, and then mostly because Mom was so sweet about it, actually wanting me to go yet letting me decide. I was also a little curious as to why this invitation changed her traditional way of thinking, and I figured I'd have to find that out myself.

I think the whole thing is a little strange, I thought, as I bundled up the next Friday evening.

Mom waved me out the door, looking after me a bit anxiously. *She should be concerned*, I murmured to myself. *After all, no one I know has ever been inside his dingy house. And whatever are we going to talk about?*

I had to have a talk myself with the Giver of peace as I trudged down the field and vaulted the fence. So I was in a settled frame of mind when I knocked on the storm door. There was a light again tonight, but no music.

Sal's steps were heavy as he came to the door, and his look startled me as he swung it open. His eyes darkened, and some sort of **spasm** twisted his features for a moment. He just stood there for the longest time, saying nothing.

"Ya came," he said finally.

I grinned, tapping my foot on the wooden floor. "Yup. Mom actually gave me the okay."

He sighed and rubbed a hand over his eyes. "Well, I guess ya can go home agin, 'n spend the evenin' with yer family."

My foot stilled. "But, Mr. Smithinson—"

"Go."

I stared into those dark eyes. Was this man sane? Or had he gone mad? "Mr. Smithinson," I tried again in a guarded tone.

"Laddie," Sal took a deep breath and held up his hand. "I was niver really in'trested in servin' ya a meal." He held my eyes. "For the past five Christmases, I came by yer house and heard ya folks all singin' and prayin' about the Baby who came at Christmas. Laddie, that family up there in Heaven was broke up fer men. I jist wanted to see whither ya actually believed it. I wanted to see whither ya'd break yer family apart fer me."

It was the longest speech I had heard from Sal. It left me wordless for a moment. We stood there—he the big, lonely, family-**estranged** bachelor, and I, the secure and well-loved teenager.

"Sal," I said finally, "about the family that was broken up for man, uh—" I stopped. I needed Dad to help me out. "Sal, you may as well come on home with me. Keep up the tradition, you know."

He came, and the two of us walked silently over the fields together. The stars were bright again tonight. Sal breathed heavily beside me as I looked upon the star in the southwest sky. It was then that God showed me what He must have shown Mom before. Earthly families and traditions were important, but there was a more important family still. One that could include all the Sal Smithinsons across the world.

The House by the Side of the Road

There are hermit souls that live withdrawn
    In the place of their self-content;
There are souls like stars, that dwell apart,
    In a fellowless firmament;
There are pioneer souls that blaze their paths
    Where highways never ran—
But let me live by the side of the road
    And be a friend to man.

Let me live in a house by the side of the road,
    Where the race of men go by—
The men who are good and the men who are bad,
    As good and as bad as I.
I would not sit in the scorner's seat,
    Or hurl the **cynic's** ban—
Let me live in a house by the side of the road
    And be a friend to man.

I see from my house by the side of the road,
    By the side of the highway of life,
The men who press with the **ardor** of hope,
    The men who are faint with the strife.
But I turn not away from their smiles nor their tears,
    Both parts of an infinite plan—
Let me live in a house by the side of the road
    And be a friend to man.

I know there are brook-gladdened meadows ahead
    And mountains of wearisome height;
That the road passes on through the long afternoon
    And stretches away to the night.
But still I rejoice when the travelers rejoice,
    And weep with the strangers that moan,
Nor live in my house by the side of the road
    Like a man who dwells alone.

Let me live in my house by the side of the road—
    It's here the race of men go by.
They are good, they are bad, they are weak, they are strong,
    Wise, foolish—so am I;
Then why should I sit in the scorner's seat,
    Or hurl the cynic's ban?
Let me live in my house by the side of the road
    And be a friend to man.

                                    – *Sam Walter Foss*

Sam Walter Foss (1858-1911) was an American editor and humorist. He wrote much light verse, but the serious piece "The House By the Side of the Road" is his most-remembered poem.

"Greater love hath no man than this, that a man lay down his life for his friends." – John 15:13

Journey by Night

Norah Burke

This story takes place in eastern India, near modern Calcutta, called in this story by its Bengali name, Kalikata. Several Hindi words appear in this story. Hindi is the most widely spoken language in India.

Sher Singh's little brother lay in the hut with a pain in his stomach that was getting worse. Sher Singh himself was only about twelve years old, brown and cheerful, a child of the jungle, and his brother was several years younger. There had been other children, of course, but they were dead, carried off by cholera and influenza and such, and by jungle accidents. Now there was only this Sher Singh and the little brother Kunwar.

"I will wring out rags in boiling water and lay them on his stomach," said their mother. She did not smile. She did not weep. She had lived through everything over and over again.

"What shall I do?" asked Sher Singh, who was feeling ill inside him because of this brother. "I will get sticks for the fire. And the dung. I will get the water. Let me tear up the rag."

He ran for these things.

They used fuel recklessly to get the water hot soon. They laid steaming cloths on the child's little belly. But after a while Sher Singh's mother said, "He must be carried in to the hospital at Kalikata."

Then Sher Singh knew that his brother was dying. When she said the word *hospital* he knew it, for all jungle people are well aware that the hospital is the last **resort** of the doomed. Something took him by the throat.

"I will run for my father," he cried.

"It may be days before you find him."

Sher Singh's father was known far and wide as Sher Singh Bahadur—
The Brave; a famous shikari,[1] with the title *Bahadur* added to his name
like a medal because of all he had done. He lived his life here in Laldwani
village, grazing his animals, cultivating his bit of land. But whenever
there was an expedition into the jungle in search of big game, either to
shoot or photograph them, they sent for this man, Bahadur the Brave.

He could find tigers where there were no tigers at all. He could look
at the dry grass and tell everything that had happened there. He could
listen to chital[2] calling and say, "A panther has just killed one of them,
and they can still see him with his kill." All down his skull and back
and shoulder went a scar where claws had opened his flesh to the bone
when he was pulling a comrade away from a **mauling** tiger. On his leg
was a place where a snake had bitten him and he had cut and burned the
wound. He had two fingers missing, and his face marked . . .
Sher Singh Bahadur.

Now he was away in the jungle with a photography expedition. All
the men of Laldwani village too, as beaters.

In this mud and grass hut, upon the floor of trodden earth, upon the
low string charpoy,[3] Kunwar lay crying, and sometimes coughing from
the smoke, but mostly glazed and silent.

Sher Singh, the son of his father, looked at his young brother, and he
saw death in his eyes.

"There are no men in the village," he said. "I will take him."

His mother must stay behind to mind the cattle and work the land
without which they would all starve; and he and she both understood
this without saying so.

But she was a hill woman. She knew about carrying loads. Her
own home was way up in the high mountains above these foothills
around Laldwani. She knew how to sling a load from a band around
the forehead down the back, so that the shoulders and strong muscles of
a thick neck could take fabulous weights up hill and down dale all day
without complaint.

---

1 shikari: Hindi for a big game hunter or guide
2 chital: a deer common in Asia. It has a brown coat with white spots.
3 charpoy: a low frame bed made by stringing ropes from one side of the frame to the other

She took one of her two saris[4] and she made a sling for Sher Singh to put around his forehead and down his back, and she lifted up the child Kunwar, who was doubled with pain, and put him into it.

Sher Singh could feel immediately the heat of the boy's body burning through the cotton cloth. He felt the weight too, and he wondered how he was going to manage.

"He is too big for you," said his mother. She spoke in a whisper of despair. "You will never get there."

Sher Singh said nothing. He set off.

It was evening. All the huts of Laldwani village lay in a strong orange glow. Around the village were spread their bits of cultivation and the maidan[5] where they grazed their cattle, and the hedges made of piled-up thorn branches, and the pound into which the forest guards locked any cattle they caught feeding in the government-reserved forest. Then there was a good deal of burnt grassland, which had been burned off to save the village in case of any forest fire. Beyond that, the jungle began.

Scrub at first, rough grassland dotted with thorn trees, then with willow trees, from which they got railroad ties for the railway at Kalikata. Kalikata was as far as the railway came. It was fifty miles away, but Sher Singh hoped that if he could get through the jungle and cross the two rivers that lay between him and his goal, he might get a lift in a cart or even a broken-down truck for the last part of his journey.

But not yet. Here, where the path was rutted with cart wheels, and his bare toes disappeared into silk-soft dust, he was alone on the track that wound into the forest, into night.

Not quite alone, though. Some unknown jungle sense made him hesitate between one step and the next, and a cobra that had been sunning itself on the path in the last of the daylight contracted and rose with a hiss, its hood spreading to show the spectacle mark on its back.

Sher Singh stood frozen. Then very slowly he backed away.

The cobra swayed, watching him, its tongue playing in and out like a leech. But this beautiful creature of metallic scales, with poison in its teeth, wanted only to get away, as the boy himself did. It subsided and slipped off into the matted grass.

---

4 sari: the traditional Indian woman's dress, a long wide band of cloth wrapped around the body
5 maidan: an open grassy area

Sher Singh drew a breath. The snake-feeling left his legs, and he was able to walk on.

Kunwar, twitching and groaning on his back, was already getting heavier. Oh, for a rest, to let aching muscles draw up from the painful stretching and strain. But it was too soon to rest yet, and presently he got his second wind.

Around him lay ancient forest in which the struggle of vegetation and the struggle of life continued as they had done since the beginning of the world. Dense bamboo growth sprang fast from its roots; impenetrable thorn thickets fought for air; trees and undergrowth and scrub and grass grew wild. And in this jungle lived the animals of the forest, the monkeys and **boisterous** peacocks, tiger and panther and bear and elephant. Since the deer were now so poached and **decimated**, the beasts of prey were obliged to kill domestic animals for food. Sometimes even man.

Night fell. The sky blushed purple. Black. It blazed with stars. Sher Singh had good eyes; he could still see, and presently the moon rose.

The sight of bear tracks in the dust—the square front paw and the long back one with the shaggy claws—made him glance round uneasily. He had once seen a man who had been mauled by a bear, all the face torn away. He quickened his step.

Presently, on a cliff above a riverbed, he knew he could go no farther without rest. Sweat was running off his shaking flesh.

He got his burden against a tree and pushed the band up off his forehead and over his straining hair, and he let Kunwar down as gently as he could.

"Oh!— O-h-h—," cried Kunwar at the jolt.

"What can I do for you?" sobbed Sher Singh, but the child was **delirious** and answered nonsense.

Suddenly all Sher Singh's muscles, shrinking back to their natural positions, thrilled with piercing pain. Where the band had pressed into his forehead, blood returned under the skin. He lay against the tree with his eyes shut, recovering.

It was then that he heard the jostle and squeal of elephants.

There is seldom need for elephants to travel silently in the jungle, and this herd was coming up the ravine, perhaps to new feeding grounds. Sher Singh was glad he was outside the ravine and above them.

Below him the broad riverbed shone like ivory in the moonlight. A spread of white pebbles, edged by thorn, lay on each side of the shallow chuckling water full of little trout. Sand, too, lay in long swaths and banks down the watercourse, and on this the elephants traveled, leaving behind them a jumble of tracks as if a forest had walked.

He could see the cows and the babies, and one great old tusker with the dark oily flow of the musk[6] discharge on his cheeks. In that condition he might chase and kill men.

Their ears flapped, their tails swung, their shadows were black on the white sand. They were so near he could smell elephant, hear the squeak of sand crushed under the feet, and the brush of rough hide, one against the other. He could see the toss and hustle of great heads and black backbones.

The tusker was playing his trunk to and fro to learn whatever the breeze could tell him; and suddenly he hesitated. The trunk came round toward the boys.

Sher Singh chilled with fright. With Kunwar to carry, he could neither climb nor run. If he shouted, it could not but bring catastrophe upon them. Prayer after prayer fled up like birds from his frightened spirit.

The tusker snorted, trumpeted, shook his head. Suddenly he hurried on

---

6 musk: a substance with a strong odor, which many animals have in their skin or special glands

angrily up the riverbed, and all the herd with him. They disappeared.

Sher Singh breathed one more prayer, of thanks this time, and made ready to move at once. He sat down with his back to Kunwar and got the band around his forehead again.

He could not rise. He tried again with all his might, but it was no use. All at once, in the distance, he heard an elephant trumpet, and the next moment he was on his feet, loaded. He scrambled down into the riverbed.

He had been here often by daylight, and he knew that at this time of year, before the snow melted in the hills, before the snow-water came flooding down like boiling green milk, he could easily ford it. The water was broad but shallow. You could hear how shallow it was as it raced along over the pebbles. A small trout rolled, and the moonlight flashed from it as from a looking glass.

He stepped into the river.

It was colder than usual; there was an icy edge to it, and in the middle it was deeper than it had been. He had to go slowly because of slime on the stones. He had to feel for footholds and be sure not to fall. The water was almost waist deep. Perhaps snow-water was already coming down.

Sher Singh was thankful there was a bridge at the second river, seeing it already as his spirit strove forward faster than his body. It was a flimsy thing, but it was at least a bridge. Rings of bamboo poles had been driven into the stony riverbed and tied round and filled with stones to make the piers of the bridge. Then more bamboo was laid from pillar to pillar and across, and laced with thick grass, and surfaced with river gravel.

As Sher Singh swashed up on to the shore, water twinkled in his footprints before sinking into the sand. Coming up out of the river went another set of prints—a tiger's, and there was glitter in them too. Even as he looked, it dried.

He plodded steadily on.

Every hour or so he had to rest, and each time it became more difficult to go on, although he had now mastered the knack of loading himself again. His body panted and sobbed, no matter what he himself wished to do.

But toward midnight he heard the second river ahead of him. He heard it from far away, and what he heard was the steady roar of a flood. When he came out on the shore, he saw it.

A big head of snow must have melted yesterday, and here it was. From bank to bank, the river foamed. He looked for the bridge. It was not there. Only a fierce crest of water to show where it lay, **submerged**. That, and a drowned goat held against it by the torrent. Branches rose like dying arms in the whirlpool and caught against the bridge and feathered the wild fall of water. Underneath, boulders moved. He could hear the river grinding its teeth.

Then on the flood appeared an entire tree, churning slowly over and over, gathering speed and crashing against the drowned bridge. In all the thunder came a loud tearing sound; the bridge moved like a monster, heeled over and broke, throwing up its bamboo ribs like a fan. A fresh gush of flood poured over it.

So, now, how to cross? There was not a chance to swim. Even alone he would be lost. But perhaps among the wreck of the bridge there was a way?

He set Kunwar down and brought him water from the river in his hands.

"My brother . . . " the little boy whispered, and he drank.

Sher Singh gathered grass, and he braided it into a rope. The blades were sharp; they cut his fingers. He tied the rope around his brother and himself so they would keep together. Then he entered the water just above the bridge. The river seized them and flattened them against the wreck. At first he could not move, but then he began to edge forward in the maelstrom,[7] holding on to this and that, feeling forward in the storm of water for things to hold, and finding the split ends of bamboo that were sharp enough to stab a man.

The roar deafened him; timber banged and bruised him. It was so cold he could hardly keep his hold. He could not get his breath in the spray. Water poured past and over him in one long icy cascade. He did not know if his brother lived or died, but he kept the child's head above water, and inch by inch he got along. He was deaf—blinded—frozen—drowned. It went on and on.

They slipped, they recovered, they clung and gasped in mortal struggle. Presently the river seemed to lose power. They were through.

---

7 maelstrom: a powerful whirlpool that sucks things into its center

After that, Sher Singh did not know what happened. He was wet and ice-cold. His nose hurt with the water inside it. He stumbled on. He was walking. Walking. His knees bent and trembled. They gave way. He was crawling. There was a road. There was a better road.

Far away, in another world, there came the yap of dogs heralding a village.

Suddenly, somehow—people. After that, the next thing he knew they were in a bullock cart, then a truck.

"Where have you come from, boy?"

"Laldwani."

"You carried him alone? Across the river in flood?"

They were at the hospital.

Sher Singh always felt shy in a house. He did not go in. But he had no money, so when morning came he went down to the rail yards to get work loading coal. He labored all day in the noise, and he earned a few pence with which to buy a little coarse flour and some mustard oil and chilies, and he could cook a meal between three stones. Up till now he had been laboring with all his strength and unable to feel the full force of anxiety, but now it came.

Presently the doctor called for him. He did not send an orderly;[8] he came out himself onto the porch, and he called out, "Sher Singh Bahadur, are you there?"

"My father is not here," replied the boy, going up to the porch. He was ashamed to shake so much, and of the marks of tears washing the coal dust away from his cheeks. "But I am Sher Singh."

"You are the boy who brought the child in from Laldwani?"

"Yes."

Then a smile broke all over the doctor's great gentle face so that he looked like a brown moon.

"Sher Singh Bahadur!" he said strongly. "Your brother will live. Come and see."

---

8 orderly: a special assistant who helps doctors and nurses in a hospital

"Woe to him that is alone when he falleth; for he hath not another to help him up." – Ecclesiastes 4:10

The Cloak

Part 1

Patricia St. John

The gray light was stealing into the city streets when Mustafa awoke, shivered, and pulled his ragged old cloak tightly around him. His face was covered by the hood, but he pushed it back just a little and peered around. He wanted to see what was happening, but he didn't want to let in the drafts.

The other boys lay around, sleeping uneasily. Their lodging was a café in an evil street, and the air was still thick with last night's stale tobacco smoke. Dirty glasses stood on the tables, and the boys were unwashed and homeless. Most of them lay huddled up as though conscious of the cold, and some muttered a little at the pale light.

Mustafa stared at them gloomily from under his hood. He had not been long in the city, and he hated the daily chilly awakening in this wretched place. It was not comfortable sleeping on the floor, but he was used to that, and at least in sleep you could forget that you were hungry and dirty and outcast. Sometimes in his dreams he drifted back to the time, not so long ago, when he had lain down at night beside his mother in their mountain home, and the folds of her dress had kept him warm. He must have been dreaming about her that morning, for while he was still only half-awake, he found himself thinking about her; she was a simple tribeswoman, but her love for him had been very strong. How often she had given him bread and gone hungry herself; perhaps that was partly why she had died so young. It was three years since he had seen the mountains near her home, and he wondered what they looked like now—probably all under snow, with the gales tearing down the ravines. It was warmer in the city, but the mountain air had been clean and **untainted**. He suddenly wrinkled his nose, got up with an expression of disgust, and made his way stiffly to the door. He had paid for his lodging the night before and had nothing to do but go.

The cold air of the street seemed to hit him, and he trotted along fast, his teeth chattering. It was only 6 a.m., but oh, how he wanted some breakfast! From the mosque nearby came the dawn prayer call, but Mustafa had never learned to pray. He had nowhere to go and nothing to do, and with his dream of the mountains fresh in his mind, the streets seemed unbearable.

He would go down to the beach; there, at least, he would find clean breezes and wide spaces, and there he could run and get warm. He pattered down a broader alley with shuttered shops on each side; at the bottom was a wharf and a stone jetty running out to the port where big ships rode at anchor, but away to the right stretched the long curved sands of the bay, bounded by scrubby hills. And over the waters of the bay and the lighthouse on the headland, the sky was aflame with sunrise. Even the sullen boy was struck by its beauty and stood wondering for a moment. It was so lonely. Just himself and the wheeling gulls and the little crisp waves tinted with gold.

Then his eyes, sharp with hunger, caught sight of something else. Far away, on the beach across the bay, a fishing boat was moored, and some men were coming down to the margin of the sea in a group. Mustafa knew what that meant—a net to be pulled in. He might get his breakfast yet! Slipping off his cloak, he girded himself with it and began running along the firm sands, the gulls rising up in front of him screaming, his bare feet leaving a track on the tide-washed stretches.

He arrived panting to find them all in rather a bad mood. They had been quarreling over the division of the price of the haul, and two boys had gone off in a rage, refusing to work. Mustafa had arrived in the nick of time.

"I'll pull with you," he panted, drawing himself up straight, "and help you carry it up to market."

His tone was a little too eager. The fisherman recognized that the boy was desperate for work and would probably take anything. He mentioned a very small sum; Mustafa's eyes flashed.

"It's too little," he protested angrily.

"All right, you can clear out," replied the fisherman, rolling up his sleeves. "There are other boys about."

There were too. Already they were scudding along the beach, and Mustafa had to decide quickly. He must either accept such meanness or go hungry. Scowling with rage, he flung his old cloak on the sands and took his place at the tarry rope. The other men fell into line, and at a word from the fisherman, they all hauled together.

The drawing in of a net is a beautiful sight. Men and boys strain backward, their brown limbs straining, their heels digging deep into the sand. Then, as one man, they all relax and clasp the rope farther down before the next great pull. They work in silence, to a perfect rhythm, adding their little strength to the might of the incoming tide, and the net, far out at sea, is borne to the shore. Then, with a last great heave and a sudden shout, the net is landed and a frenzied mass of silver fish writhes on the sand, sparkling in the sunshine, while the men run forward to examine and sort the catch. Much of it is no good and is thrown on one side on a bright heap of red starfish and orange jellyfish; but the sardines, the octopuses, the herrings, and the mackerels are piled into flat wooden boxes which drip at the joints, and the boys carry them on bowed shoulders to market, their clothes becoming soaked with fishy saltwater.

Mustafa lost no time in seizing a box of sardines, for other boys were eager for the job as well as himself, and he deemed it better to go as soon as possible. He set off at a steady trot, the cold water leaking down his neck; but he was happy, for he had not long now to wait for his breakfast, and he wanted his breakfast more than anything else on earth.

It was quite a climb to the market, and his shoulders ached and his fingers were numb. But the market was full these days, for it was the season when the Christians celebrated the birth of Christ. It was only eight o'clock in the morning, but already the streets were thronged with French, Spanish, and English shoppers with big baskets on their arms making their last bargains. For tomorrow was Christmas.

Mustafa dumped the fish before its owner and received his payment with a scowl. It should have been far more than that; the man was a cheat and a robber of the poor! Still, Mustafa was used to that, and the coin would buy him breakfast—four fried dough rings for a peseta[1] and a glass of coffee. He would feel better after that and would spend the morning in the market in hopes of carrying a Christmas basket for some overloaded housewife. The day began to look brighter, except that his damp garment clung to him, and there was very little warmth in the winter sunshine. Where was his old cloak?

He suddenly remembered. He'd left it on the beach. In his haste to get away, and warm with the exercise of pulling and carrying, he had forgotten all about it.

He forgot his hunger, for to lose his cloak was about the worst thing that could happen to him. Turning his back on the market, he scudded down the streets as fast as he could and reached the sea front. Now he was on the shore again, running, running. The tide had come in, and the river that flowed into the sea had filled up and was quite deep. He plunged in almost to his waist, but hardly noticed the cold, for the thought of his loss made him forget everything else. Eagerly he scanned the beach; yes, that was the place. There was the boat and the useless heap of jellyfish and the sand churned up by their feet. But the cloak had gone.

Yes, it had gone, and it was no use searching anymore. He was warm with running now, but he had to get back across the river, and soon he would be frozen. There was no hope of getting another cloak, and the cold weather was just beginning. He'd have to save up for a sack, and he'd better save up in good earnest too. He would start by going without his coffee and making do with two dough rings.

Bitterly angry, he wandered back toward the town. The sun was high now, and the sea a sheet of sparkling blue. The coast of Spain across the Straits was hidden by a silver haze. Why was the morning so beautiful, and men so wicked? He had been cheated of half his wages. His cloak had been stolen. He hated everybody.

The packet boat[2] from Gibraltar arrived at 11 a.m., and as it came round

---

1 peseta: a Spanish coin
2 packet boat: passenger boat that also carries mail and cargo

the headland, Mustafa hurried down the stone jetty that led to the port so as to get there in good time. This was usually the best hour of his day, the hour on which he depended for his dinner. The thing was to be there early, for there were many other hungry ragamuffins who also depended on the Gibraltar packet for their dinner, and there wasn't always enough work to go around.

With the scream of sirens and the rush of steam, and the thrashing of a backward revolving propeller, the ship drew in and cast anchor. Every boy was alert and on his toes then as the passengers streamed through the customs with heavy cases, or better still, as heavy cargo was piled on the wharf to be lifted onto trucks. As far as passengers were concerned, the game was to attach yourself to the greenest, most bewildered-looking tourist, preferably an American, as they had the most money, and offer to show him around the town or take him to a hotel for a fabulous price. The art was to appear so charming that the tourist would be unable to believe that anyone so considerate and anxious for his welfare could be capable of cheating him. But if this failed, there were usually cases to carry.

Mustafa was not much good at the tourist trade. He was too thin, and his dark eyes were too sad. Besides, years of mountain **solitude** had left him unsure of himself in crowds. Tourists had not come to be reminded of poverty and hunger. They had come to enjoy themselves, and they liked jolly, amusing, self-confident boys. Still, he did occasionally get a catch, and today he pranced up to a young lady slung about with binoculars and camera—obviously over for the day and most uncertain of herself. She was silly to come alone and should be easy prey.

"I show you all," he chanted, airing the three stock sentences of English that he knew, gamboling about a little in a desperate effort to be jolly and amusing. "I very good. Hundred pesetas."

The girl hesitated and might have fallen into the trap. But a man came to her rescue.

"Not a cent more than twenty, young lady," he remarked firmly, "and if I were you, I would get a proper guide. These boys are thieves and rascals."

The girl stalked off with an indignant look at Mustafa, who stood scowling. What did that man know about hunger? There he was, taking the girl off himself, probably to some expensive restaurant up on the boulevard to gorge and drink. However, it was no good wasting time brooding. He must look sharp or he'd get nothing. There was a tired-looking Spanish woman with a baby and a heavy suitcase, the type who could not afford a taxi; not very profitable, but there was nothing else left; he must get all he could out of her. He rushed forward and seized the case. She gave it up and he hurried along the wharf with it, casting angry, envious glances at a friend of his who had got hold of an expensive-looking young man in a brilliant tie and was making him laugh! Make 'em laugh, and they'd hand out anything. That boy would get a good dinner.

He hadn't gone five yards before a man came running down the wharf and kissed the tired woman and took the baby in his arms. Then he reached out for the suitcase and dropped two pesetas into Mustafa's outstretched hand without looking at him; and it was no use arguing or making a fuss, because it was all that was reasonably due to him, and anyhow, the husband and wife were far too interested in each other to take any notice of him.

The big chance of his day was over, and he'd earned two pesetas.

He loafed along the beach, sick of everything and watching the waves. It was midday. He had no heart left to rush straight back to the milling market. He would wait a little. The beach, if you walked on past the footballers, was the only quiet place in the town, and Mustafa some-times hungered for quietness. The city was a cruel place where every man lived for himself, and the strongest and the most cunning came out on top. He suddenly longed to turn his back on it all and go back to the rocks and rivers of his tribal village. But his father and mother were dead, and there was no place for him there—nor anywhere else, he thought, staring dully at the sea.

He reached the spot where they had hauled in the net that morning. The boat still lay on its side on the beach, and a dark-eyed boy with a shaved head was sitting cross-legged on the sand, mending a net. When he noticed Mustafa, he stared at him intently.

"Were you on the net this morning?" he asked.

"Yes," replied Mustafa, disinterestedly.

"So was I," said the boy. "I saw you. Did you lose your cloak?"

"Yes," answered Mustafa, suddenly eager. "Where is it?"

The boy threw a pebble in the air and caught it. He was silent for a moment.

"What will you give me, if I tell you?" he asked cautiously.

Mustafa felt desperate. "I have nothing to give you," he cried. "I haven't had any dinner yet, and the fisherman cheated me over my wages. Tell me where it is, and I'll pay you another day."

The fisher lad shook his head shrewdly. It was a land where no boy would trust another boy.

"One peseta," he bargained, "and I'll show you the house. The man who stole it has gone out with the boats and won't be home for a couple of days. There's only a woman there. You can just take it. I live next door, and I saw him carry it off."

He went quietly on with his work without looking up. There was no moving him. Mustafa flung the peseta down on the sand beside him, and the boy, gathering up the net, rose to his feet.

"Come on," he said, "follow me!"

They hurried up the beach and over the railway line and across the road to the salt meadows. There seawater was stored in hollows and ditches, and as it evaporated under the scorching summer sun, the deposit of salt was left behind. But in the winter the meadows were dry, and the only signs of life were a few ragged children playing around a cluster of black tarry huts, where fishermen and salt-makers lived.

Patricia St. John (1919-1992) was born in England and spent much of her childhood there. Her parents had been missionaries in Brazil, and her father occasionally left on mission trips to conduct Bible schools. During one of these trips, her mother took the children to Switzerland, where they lived for two years. *Treasures of the Snow* contains many of Patricia's memories of those years. She grew up to become a nurse and went to Morocco as a missionary. She lived there for many years and later wrote about her work with the children of Morocco in *Star of Light* and *Three Go Searching* and shorter stories such as "The Cloak." Later she worked for short periods of time in Rwanda, Lebanon, and Ethiopia. She wrote fifteen books and many short stories and poems.

"That's it," said the boy very quietly, giving a nod toward the smallest hut. "Good-bye, and may God help you!"

He disappeared into his own home, and Mustafa hesitated a moment. He felt rather frightened, but anger made him bold. Marching to the door, he knocked loudly and stuck out his chest in an effort to look manly.

There was silence for a moment. Then a weak voice said, "Come in."

It was a very bare room and rather dark. In one corner lay a pile of fishing tackle and a baby donkey, and in the other lay a girl on a straw mat, hugging a clay pot of ashes and moaning a little. A neighbor sat beside her, and at her feet tossed a restless little figure covered with Mustafa's cloak.

Ha! The boy had spoken the truth. This was the den of thieves, and now he had caught them! He would seize his cloak and threaten them with the police till they cried for mercy. Not that he intended to carry out his threat, for Mustafa's whole life was spent avoiding the police, and it would be a great mistake to have anything to do with them. Still, it would sound good.

"Where's the man who stole my cloak?" he shouted gruffly, trying to disguise the childish break in his voice. "You'd better hand it over quickly and pay me for having taken it, or the police will be here in half an hour. Do you hear me?"

The young woman turned her head wearily. She seemed to be thinking of something else. Mustafa realized that he had made very little impression and his loud, gruff voice sounded foolish and cheap. His boasting was quite lost on the tired mother and the sick child, for they had neither the heart nor the strength to resist him, had they wanted to. The neighbor, a worn old granny, just stared at him, for it was none of her business. Only the baby donkey seemed frightened and backed into its corner. Mustafa was sorry about that, for he had been brought up with a baby donkey.

"Take it," said the young woman, lifting her head and pointing to the little heap at her feet. "My husband has gone out with the boats. He won't be home till tomorrow night. I have no money in the house."

She turned her face to the wall and shut her eyes. There was nothing left to do but to take it. It was an **abject** victory. He dragged it defiantly off the child who cried out and shivered, as though awakened suddenly

126

from a restless dream. Even Mustafa could see that it was a very sick child. The old neighbor rose up slowly, every joint creaking, and carried the feverish mite to its mother's side and laid it under the cotton wrap that covered her. Perhaps her arms would keep it warm.

No one spoke. There was nothing to do but to go away. As he left the cottage, the cloak over his arm, a cold cloud blew across the sun and dark shadows brooded on the sea.

"I will not leave you comfortless: I will come to you." – John 14:18

The Cloak

Part 2

Patricia St. John

Back along the beach, Mustafa was feeling almost faint with hunger now and strangely miserable. Usually his feelings were perfectly simple. If he came out on top, he was happy; and if someone else came out on top, he was unhappy. And as he was a country boy, not very sharp or cunning, and no match for city urchins, he was usually unhappy. But today he had won, hands down, and he was wretched; he wondered why.

He bought a hunk of bread and two fried sardines and looked around for a social spot to eat it in. He did not want to be alone. He wanted noise and company, loud racy talk and perhaps a fight—anything to make him forget the quiet room, the tarry smell of fishing tackle, the white-faced woman and the sick child. He joined a group of bootblacks and café assistants lounging on the pavement by the bus stop, and sat down to enjoy his dinner as best he could.

The bootblacks were doing well, for everyone wanted to be smart for Christmas. They had been up in the market and were full of tall stories, for this feast was an interesting time of year—so much food in the shop windows and a certain amount of generosity in the hearts of buyers.

"What do these Christians do at this feast of theirs?" asked one lanky boy **contemptuously**.

"They eat turkey," replied a scruffy-looking man. "I used to work for one of them. And they give presents to their children. It was a wonder how much they ate! But they didn't offer me any. I was only the gardener's boy."

128

He spat contemptuously and lounged against the wall.

"And why do they keep this feast?" asked the lanky boy again. He seemed interested.

"They say it's the day their prophet Jesus was born," replied another lad. "They say He is the Son of God. Lies and **blasphemy**! May God preserve all faithful Muslims!"

"I know all about it," chipped in a third lad eagerly. "I've been in the Christian hospital. I had a fight with a chap, and he knifed me in the shoulder. I stayed at their hospital four days, and at night they came and preached their religion and taught us wicked words. This is what they tried to make us learn: 'God so loved the world that He gave His only begotten Son.' "

He mimicked the voice of the foreign speaker perfectly, and his performance was greeted with a roar of laughter.

"The good Muslims get under the bedclothes," went on the speaker, much encouraged, "but some listen and even repeat the words because they think they'll get better treatment. **Hypocrites**! However, I must say that the doctor was kind. He treated us all alike, whether we listened or not, and he made no favorites of the rich."

An older man, who had been chewing gum thoughtfully while he listened, suddenly broke in.

"Not all are hypocrites," he remarked. "Just now and again one is deceived and believes. There was that boy Hassan who worked at the port. He was in that hospital for two months with typhoid, and they bewitched him good and proper. He said he wasn't a Muslim any longer. He lost his job, and his family turned him out, but nothing would move him. And the strange thing was that he never shouted back at them or argued—just went quietly on; said he'd found the way of peace."

"And where is he now?" inquired the former gardener's boy.

"I don't know. He begged in the streets for a while, but no Muslim would help him. Anyhow, he's no longer of our company. Poor fool!"

The talk moved on to other subjects. The bootblacks returned to the market, but Mustafa and a few others lingered on, for a long-distance bus would be coming soon, and there might be work for one or two of them. The afternoon was drawing on. The ex-gardener put his hand in his pocket and gave a loud exclamation. His pocket had been picked.

Furiously he set on the nearest boy, who happened to be Mustafa. The lad struggled, but his cloak was dragged off his back, and he was cuffed into silence while they searched him. Finding him innocent, they pushed him aside and made off to find a policeman to round up the bootblacks.

What a fight and commotion there'd be! Mustafa, bruised and shaken, decided to get as far away as possible. He made for his one and only refuge, the seashore; and for the third time that day, he paced the shore, sick at heart.

For a long time he did not look up. What a miserable day it had been! All days weren't like that. Some days the sun shone; they laughed and joked and managed to make money, and then there was food and keep. But, come to think of it, they nearly always laughed because someone had been hurt or cheated or robbed. Today, on that deserted stretch of beach, Mustafa suddenly seemed to see things as they were and hated all the greed and **malice** and fear and quarreling and uncleanness that made up their daily lives. Tired and bruised, he flung himself down on the sand and stared at the sea.

He looked up. The soft colors of the sky were reflected in the water. A gull rose toward the last light on shining wings. Why had they spoiled the world like this? And was there any escape from such a rotten existence? He did not know. He had never really thought about it before.

Then he suddenly remembered fragments of the conversation by the bus stop. He remembered quite clearly because they used words so seldom heard. "God so loved that He gave . . . he said he had found a way of peace!"

Loving . . . giving . . . peace. Like three bright signposts in a wilderness, these words seemed scrawled across the rosy sky; words that, as yet, meant almost nothing to Mustafa and his gang. Hating, grabbing, fighting—that was their code; but it did not lead to any way of peace.

And yet Mustafa had known about these words in years past. His mother had loved him and given, given, given until she had nothing left at all. And Mustafa remembered that she had lain down at peace on the night she died. It was snowing, and she had wrapped him in the only warm covering in the house. It was the last she had to give.

What was peace? Early summer mornings on the mountains, sunset over the sea . . . *loving* . . . *giving.* But he had frightened a helpless woman and stripped the covering from a sick child. Suddenly, quite clearly, he knew where his own path of peace lay, and he turned his head to look at it. The stretches of water in the salt flats looked bloodred in the last light, and the boats rose up like black silhouettes against the sunset.

He got up like someone in a dream and crossed the railway line and the trenched meadows. The door of the fisherman's hut was not locked, for the neighbor was returning later and had left it on the latch. Mustafa opened it very softly without knocking and stepped inside.

A little lamp was burning and all was quiet, save for the labored breathing of the child—but Mustafa knew at once that something had happened. The young woman was propped up on a pillow looking down at the new baby she held beside her, and her tired face was utterly peaceful, for she, too, was loving and giving.

It must have been born soon after Mustafa left, for the room was clean and tidy, the baby washed, and the mother had slept and awakened again. The little donkey had drawn close and stood watching on long wobbly legs, and the sick child tossed and moaned under the cotton covering. Then the woman suddenly looked up and saw Mustafa standing shyly in the doorway.

She gave a cry of fear and would have beaten on the wall to call her neighbor, but Mustafa ran forward.

"Don't be afraid," he said. "I'm not going to hurt you. I came to lend you my cloak—just for tonight, because your child is ill. Tomorrow I must take it back, but I'll try to bring you a sack. Tonight, in any case, she shall keep warm."

He stooped and covered the little girl, and the woman looked at him very curiously. When he had come before, he had stuck out his chest and shouted and swaggered like a man; but now as he stood there, humble and deflated, she realized that he was only a young boy, fourteen at the most, a mere child, not yet quite hardened to wickedness.

"Sit down," she said in a weak voice. "The teapot is on the fire. Pour yourself out a glass."

He huddled over the dying charcoal and drank with relish a glass of hot sweet mint tea. It was days since he'd tasted any.

"Why did you bring it back?" asked the woman, still very puzzled.

"Hakada," replied Mustafa, which is a convenient way of saying, "What is, is; but I couldn't give any reason for it if I tried." As a matter of fact, he couldn't understand himself what had made him do such a thing.

"Where do you live?" went on the woman.

"Nowhere," answered the boy. "I've been here only three years. I came down from the tribes."

"Why, so did I," said the woman eagerly. "My husband brought me down when I married him seven years ago, and I've never been back since. What village do you come from?"

Mustafa named his village. It was only a few miles from hers on the eastern side of the same mountain. They had traveled the same paths to market, picked olives on the same slopes, and burned charcoal among the same rocks. She was too tired to talk much, but he poured out his homesick heart to this alien sister of his, for in three years she was the first person he had met who knew his village.

He talked of spring, with its swollen streams and foaming cherry and apricot blossoms—of summer, when they cut the harvests and slept on the threshing floors—of autumn, when they gathered figs and grapes and Indian corncobs and spread them out to dry on the baked cactus in front of the huts—of winter, when the villages were snowbound and the cattle slept indoors. He was back again in thought on his mountain, a happy child, running up the rocks after the goats, and coming home to his mother at night. He talked and talked, and she lay and listened, occasionally asking a few questions. But she was not as homesick as he was, for her children had been born in the hut on the salt flat, and that anchored her heart fast. Home to her was the baby in her arms and the child who lay tossing at her feet.

She gave a sudden, sharp cry, and the mother dragged herself painfully forward to quiet it. The child had awakened and wanted water. The mother held a glass to the child's lips, and she drank feverishly and wept with little gasping sobs to come into her arms. She laid the new baby on the floor and dragged the sick child toward her.

"What is the matter with it?" asked Mustafa.

"I don't know," answered the woman, rocking it wearily to and fro. "She has been ill three days. Each day I ask my husband to take her to the hospital; but he does not love her, because he wanted a boy, and he always says he hasn't time. I am too weak to go, so I suppose she will die, but if I could carry her to the doctor, she would live."

"How do you know?" asked Mustafa.

"I took her before," explained the woman simply. "She had fever as she has now and could neither suck nor draw breath. The doctor gave her the needle, and her fever went away. He would do it again, for he is a kind man, but who can carry her? We have no money to ask him to come here."

Mustafa thought for a moment. Then he said, "I will carry her. I know where the hospital is."

The woman looked at him as though weighing him up. She was an ignorant woman, who knew very little about sickness, and she was desperately afraid her child would die. She did not like sending it out by night in the cold, but she had unbounded faith in the needle and thought this was probably the only chance. As for Mustafa, the fact that he came from her district made her trust him as she would have trusted a kinsman.

The little girl, finding herself at last where she had longed to be all day, safe in her mother's arms, had fallen fast asleep and did not wake when Mustafa picked her up. They wrapped her in the cloak, and nodding good-bye, he set off across the flats at a quick pace. The moon was coming up over the sea, making a silver track across the waves, and Mustafa was glad for its light, for he had quite a long way to go. The child lay with her head on his shoulder, and the pressure of her burning little body kept him warm. He took the shortcut back along the beach; the tide was out and the stretches of sand were moon-washed and glistening. There was no one else about at all, just he and his little burden; once or twice she stirred and whimpered, but he soothed her and rocked her a little and whispered tender words learned long ago and almost forgotten. *If only she gets better,* he thought.

He had almost reached the pier now and must cut straight up through the town. The market would be grand tonight, a blaze of noise and color, but Mustafa had no wish to leave the beach. Here on the silver sands he felt peaceful, as though there was healing and forgiveness in the Christmas moonlight.

He did not know why he felt peaceful. He hardly noticed that he, Mustafa, was loving and giving.

"Glory to God in the highest, and on earth peace, good will toward men."
– Luke 2:14

The Cloak
Part 3

Patricia St. John

Oh, yes, the market on Christmas Eve was a merry sight, the stalls glittering with lighted Christmas trees and shop windows blazing. The place swarmed with prosperous children out for walks in their best clothes and seeing the sights with their parents—also with wretched beggars, some blind and deformed, hoping to profit from people's generous giving. Mustafa's friends were all there too, and on any other night Mustafa would have been among them enjoying the fun and out for what he could snatch. But tonight he had an errand, and he did not want to meet his friends. He chose the more deserted back streets and hurried on past the town center up the cobbled steps that led to the top of the cliff, where stood the hospital.

He had some **misgivings** about this doctor. From all accounts he might be celebrating with the rest. Mustafa was rather weak from insufficient food, and the hot baby in his arms seemed to grow heavier and heavier. He hoped he had not come for nothing.

He had reached the double gates that led to the hospital compound, and he hesitated, wondering which way to go. There seemed to be several big lighted buildings and a bewildering number of doors. Then, as he stood wondering, a man of his own race crossed the garden between the houses, and Mustafa, taking his courage in both hands, went up to him and asked timidly for the doctor.

"He's in the house," said the man, jerking his thumb over his shoulder, "but he's busy."

"But this little girl is very ill," faltered the boy. "I've brought her a long way."

The man glanced at her and heard the labored breathing. He shrugged his shoulders. "You'd better go and see," he said. "Knock at the door, and show him the child."

Mustafa crept on. The door of the house was shut, but light streamed from the windows, and there was the sound of music and laughter from within. The boy hesitated. No doubt they were celebrating. But no; as he listened, he realized that the sounds he heard were the laughter and shouting of little children. Perhaps, after all, a little child would be welcome here.

So he knocked and stood ready for flight should things turn out badly.

The doctor himself opened the door; he looked flushed, and his hair was standing on end. He had merely been playing musical chairs, and he carried his own fat, rosy son of three in his arms.

He stood blinking at Mustafa for a moment, his eyes unaccustomed to the darkness. He saw a boy with a hungry, dirty face and dull eyes, very thin and dressed in a cotton garment that had once been white; and in his arms he carried an unwholesome looking baby wrapped in a ragged cloak.

"It's ill," said Mustafa and held it out.

The doctor, who was a father, put his own son down in the passage. The little boy toddled off to rejoin the party in the room on the left. Then he stretched out his arms and took in its place the other baby—thin, dirty, and sick—and carried it into the warmth and light of his own home. Years later, when Mustafa had become a Christian, he often remembered that moment, for to him it **embodied** the whole meaning of Christmas. A father—a son—the dark night outside—and the needy outcast welcomed in.

The doctor fetched some things from his study and then sat down in the passage and listened to the child's chest with a strange tube. He took its temperature, which made it scream and reach out for Mustafa, to whom it had taken a liking. It was ill, but not as ill as the mother had feared—just a very bad cold and a touch of bronchitis. He would take it across to the hospital, and the nurse would give it the needle that Mustafa had tremblingly suggested, and then it could go home again. He told Mustafa to wait in the passage till he returned.

Mustafa sat quietly, listening to the noise within and wondering where all these children came from. Surely they could not all belong to the doctor! Never before had he heard little children laugh so much or sound so happy. Then someone came out, and he craned his neck to get a glimpse inside, and what he saw surprised him. For they were mostly children of his own race—little girls in dark plaits and little boys with shaved heads and baggy trousers, all eating cake. He had not known that the Christians shared their feast with Muslim children.

Quick steps outside and the doctor returned with a howling baby. Mustafa bowed and kissed his hand, and held out his arms for his little charge, who cast herself into them and relapsed into snuffles and hiccups. He must get back quickly.

But the doctor had not quite finished. He saw a great deal of poverty every day, but seldom had he seen anything as pinched and wretched-looking as this boy.

"Just a moment," he said. "She'll need another tomorrow. Where does she live?"

"Down on the salt flats on the road to the lighthouse," answered the boy. "She can't come again. Her father won't bring her. He's away today."

"And who are you?" asked the doctor. "Her brother? Why can't you bring her?"

"I'm not her brother," said Mustafa simply. "I'm nobody; just a street boy. Her father will not let me bring her once he comes back."

"And her mother?" inquired the doctor. "Why doesn't she come?"

"She had a new baby this afternoon," explained Mustafa. "She is still too weak."

"Very well," said the doctor. "I'll go myself. You must show me the house now. I have to visit a man outside the town, and it's not much farther to drive on to the salt fields. Come along!"

Mustafa beamed. He had never before traveled in a private car, and the prospect thrilled him. He was for starting at once, but once more the doctor detained him.

"And you," he said, "you look very cold. Haven't you a cloak?"

"This is my cloak," replied Mustafa. "It is around the little girl."

"And there is no blanket to wrap her in?"

"No; the baby born this afternoon was wrapped in the blanket. She has no other."

"Then I think you had better leave your cloak to keep her warm. I think I can find you something else."

He ran upstairs two steps at a time, and Mustafa waited, quite dazed. Whatever was going to happen next? Surely it couldn't mean that the doctor was going to give him clothes? But he did! Among the Christmas gifts for the hospital was a bale of old clothing. There was a warm coat and pullover just right for Mustafa and little wooly coats for the fisherman's children. He pulled them out and ran gaily downstairs.

"See," he said, holding them up. "These will keep you warm."

Mustafa stared, dumb and unbelieving. He did not understand this sort of thing. Perhaps the doctor was trying to sell them—but perhaps he wasn't.

"I have no money," he whispered uncertainly.

"That's all right," said the doctor. "It's a present. We give presents at our Feast."

He held the baby while Mustafa struggled into his new clothes. They were old and darned, but warm, and Mustafa felt like a prince in them. He had never had such garments before. Then, rather clumsily, they managed between them to dress the baby, who was screaming again.

"Now come along," said the doctor, but as he passed the room on the left, he popped his head in to say good-bye to the Sunday school party that was about to break up. He came out with a handful of nuts and sweets and cookies.

"There," he said, holding them out. "You shall share our party."

Mustafa wasn't sure whether life was real any longer or not. He found himself whizzing through the lighted streets, warm and cozy, and nibbling sugar cookies. There! They'd passed a bus, and there the policeman was waving his hand to beckon them through—down the bright boulevard in a stream of cars—getting up speed on the straight lighthouse road. It was heavenly.

They went straight to the fisherman's hut, and the doctor was glad he had taken the baby home because the scene was like Bethlehem. The hut was so poor that it might well have been a stable, with the little donkey asleep on a heap of straw, and the woman, young, tired, and a stranger, with the baby in her lap, **immortal** symbols of the love of God.

She was waiting anxiously for Mustafa's return but had not expected him so soon. She looked a little worried as the doctor entered, for she had no money in the house till her husband came home, and he would not be at all pleased if she ran up a bill in his absence. But she smiled when they laid the little girl down beside her, none the worse for her adventures.

"There," said the doctor, "she's had her needle, and she'll be all right. Keep her warm and give her plenty to drink, and I'll be in tomorrow. See, we have put on her a wooly coat, and here's one for her brother."

"But I have no money," said the woman nervously.

"That's all right," said the doctor. He was kneeling on the mud floor, peeping at the tiny crumpled newcomer blinking at him from between the folds of the blanket. He had forgotten that one usually charged a fee for a visit. No one paid anything at Bethlehem.

Mustafa followed the doctor out into the starlight. They crossed the flats by the light of his torch. It was getting near 9:00, and he wanted a lift back into town.

"Where do you sleep?" asked the doctor as the lamps of the city came into sight around a bend in the road.

The boy hesitated. He had not yet decided where he would sleep. The cafés all seemed pretty dreary after the strange experiences of that evening. He suddenly realized that he had to go back from this new world that he had entered for a few moments, where men loved and gave, and little children laughed and played. Tomorrow he would grab and steal and fight and swear again, and those three different hours would all seem like a dream.

"I don't know," he said at last, in rather a desolate voice. "Drop me in the market."

"I know somewhere where you can spend the night," said the doctor kindly. "There's a woman near the hospital who keeps a room for boys; no, there's nothing to pay—she does it because she's sorry for them. She'll let you have a blanket. We'll go along and ask her."

Mustafa had almost come to an end of wondering what would happen next. They stopped in front of a little house in a narrow street near a water pump. By the light of a lamp, women and girls were still filling their buckets, and they called out friendly greetings to the doctor, who seemed to be well-known.

He knocked at the door, and it was opened at once by a merry-looking woman with a baby in her arms. At the sound of the doctor's voice, the whole family ran to the door and urged him to come in and have supper with them. He entered, and they all sat down again around the bowl of steaming mush and the charcoal pot—father and mother, grown-up daughters, a baby, and five scruffy street urchins like himself. He knew them a little, for they all shared the same hunting grounds, and they all, like him, were mountain boys driven to the streets by hunger and homelessness. He had often wondered where they bedded down at night, but they had never betrayed their secret, for this was a Christian household, and they might get into trouble for going there.

The family itself was a tribal family. They had the brown skin, broad cheekbones, and strong muscles of the mountain-born. Their house was small, poorly furnished but clean, and the boys had a room to themselves on the roof. They were all pleased to see the doctor, and the family smiled welcomingly at Mustafa, but the boys stared suspiciously. They were a gang, and another member meant less room; also on nights when they failed to scrounge for themselves and Zohra took pity on them, it probably meant less supper.

"I've brought you a Christmas present," said the doctor, his hand on Mustafa's shoulder, "a new boy."

"Welcome to him," replied the women, and they moved up to make room for him at the pot. Mustafa shyly took his place, and one of them broke her piece of bread in two and handed him a scoop. It was the rough food of the very poor, but to Mustafa it tasted delicious.

"And now," said Zohra triumphantly as the doctor, who was glancing at his watch, rose to go, "you have come on Christmas Eve, and you must read to us."

She fetched a book from the shelf and put it in the doctor's hands, and he turned the pages and began to read. The boys already looked half asleep, warm, and satisfied, but the woman seemed to be hanging on his words, and Mustafa, too, listened as he'd never listened before. For the doctor read of a young woman great with child and an outcast baby lying in a manger, and Mustafa thought of the fisherman's cottage. Then he read about shepherds (Mustafa had been a shepherd himself once) and the angels' song.

"Unto you is born a Saviour ... Glory to God in the highest, and on earth peace, good will toward men."

Very simply he spoke on those three words: *a Saviour*, outcast that night, but waiting to be received into every humble, contrite heart. The Saviour that God gave because He loved.

On earth, peace. The peace of the heart that knows forgiveness of sin; the peace of a life committed to the Saviour, the peace of knowing that you need never again feel lonely or afraid.

Goodwill toward men. The love of God born in the heart that accepts the Saviour; the goodwill that makes Christians count all men their brothers, and open their hearts and homes, and help and serve and give—to see Christ wherever the least of His little ones is hungry or naked or sick.

Mustafa sat cross-legged on the floor, his eyes fixed on the doctor's face. He understood very little, but that little had explained a lot. He knew now why the little sick girl had been accepted and cared for, why he had been clothed and fed, why he had been welcomed in out of the dark and given refuge.

It was all most bewildering; he was beginning to feel drowsy. Zohra was telling the boys to take him upstairs and give him a blanket. The doctor had given him a pat on the head and gone off.

And outside the stars shone brightly for Christmas Eve, and all over the world men of every kindred and tribe and nation lifted up their hands to God. Christ was born, to preach the Gospel to the poor, to heal the brokenhearted, to preach deliverance to the captive, to set at liberty them that are bruised.

And one little bruised captive, half-seeking, dimly understanding, turned his face to the light of that coming. But in the dens and haunts of the city, hundreds more slept and woke as usual, neither knowing nor caring.

"Thou shalt love the Lord thy God with all thy heart, and with all thy soul, and with all thy strength, and with all thy mind; and thy neighbour as thyself." – Luke 10:27

The Hippie

adapted by Tim Kennedy

As I boarded the Los Angeles-bound bus that morning in Eugene, Oregon, I was glad I was not making the twenty-five-hour trip all the way to LA. It was July and, early in the day as it was, sweltering hot. It would be a long enough ride to Sacramento, where my sister and her family lived.

I chose a seat, sat down, and looked around. Across the aisle sat a tired, ill-looking girl of about twenty, holding a baby. I had never seen a more discouraged, despairing look than the look on that young mother's face. Her little daughter was obviously sick—too sick even to cry. She moaned and sobbed, while shafts of sun spilled over her sweaty little forehead.

The air in the packed bus was stifling. I sighed, hoping the boarding process would soon be over and we would be moving.

Finally the last passenger boarded—a ragged-looking young man. His shirt was holey and wrinkled, though clean, and he wore jeans so patched and ragged I could hardly see the original material. The seams on his canvas tennis shoes boasted several generous splits. His hair, while neatly combed, was very long. He swaggered down the aisle and sat in the seat in front of me, his head perched high.

Looks as though he just wished someone would challenge him, I thought, sizing up this character in front of me. *A member of the hippie species.* I began to speculate on the likely quality of the heart lying beneath those **rebellious** clothes. I knew the type: selfish, independent, bucking all authority and the ties of responsibility. I had just about perfectly figured out this scoundrel, when he startled me, leaning back into the narrow aisle to speak to the tired girl beside me.

"Miss, is there any way I can help you out? Would you let me hold your baby for you for a while, so you can get a bit of sleep? You look awful tired." His voice was warm, his face friendly.

"Oh!" The young woman hesitated, but she was clearly on the **verge** of exhaustion. She looked around, as though considering the safety of handing her baby over to a stranger. The bus, after all, was crowded, and he could go nowhere with the child.

He seemed to understand her thoughts. "Here, now," he said gently. "The baby will come to me. Aw, she's too sick even to object. I'll hold her carefully, miss."

Apparently, the girl didn't harbor the same prejudices about the man that I did. She handed her child to him, saying, "Thank you, sir. Thank you. I am so tired."

"Now you lie back and rest awhile. Have you traveled far?"

"From Seattle."

"On the bus? Where'd you sleep last night?"

"The Eugene bus station," she explained. "When I left Seattle, my baby just seemed to have a cold, but now she's getting worse. I'm going to my parents' home in Los Angeles."

She must have been worried about what the people around her were thinking—a young, single mother on her way back to her parents' home— because she said, "My—my husband—passed away, last—" That was all she could manage before her voice choked and she stopped, blinking back tears.

"I see," the hippie said, nodding. "You probably don't have enough money to stop and see a doctor for the baby?" He put the question **bluntly**, but somehow it did not seem impolite. He looked down at the baby whimpering in his arms and gently smoothed his fingers over the hot little forehead.

The poor girl blushed and lowered her head. Tears dropped freely into her lap. Finally she closed her eyes and leaned back to rest in her seat.

I felt rude for watching. I turned away from her, a mist coming over my own eyes as I revised my opinion of the rumpled young man in front of me. He was looking thoughtfully, tenderly, down at the baby, as though he had held more than one sick child.

The woman sitting behind the young mother had heard the conversation too. She leaned forward to speak to the hippie. "Let me take the baby. I'm ashamed I didn't offer to take her before," she told him.

She laid her hand on the tired mother's shoulder. "I saw how weary you looked," she said, "but I guess I just wasn't thinking." She turned back to the young man and held out her arms. "Poor thing! Look, she's asleep."

"So she is, but I'll surrender her to you, if you like," the man said cheerfully. I'm sure he sensed that the mother would feel more comfortable with her baby in the arms of an older woman.

The grateful mother thanked this second good Samaritan and closed her eyes again. After she fell asleep, the hippie stood in the aisle behind us. He produced a little cap from somewhere—his back pocket, I guess—and in a clear, not too loud voice spoke to the folks around him.

"Ladies and gentlemen," he said, every trace of the swagger gone from his posture, "here's an opportunity for us to do something good for a neighbor. This poor woman has come all the way by bus from Seattle and won't get off till LA. Her husband is dead; her baby is ill. She spent last night in the Eugene bus station. She doesn't have enough money for a doctor or to get off and sleep in a motel. She's worn out and discouraged. What shall we do about it?"

"Take up a collection!" a man in the back called out. He stood up, came forward, and dropped some money in the cap.

The effect was electrical. The cap went down one side of the bus and up the other, while voices buzzed back and forth about the offering. When it came to me, I saw dollars, fives, and tens in the cap. I dropped something in too. Finally, the hippie added some of his own—several bills rolled up together.

The girl slept through it all, but I wish you could have seen the look on her face when she woke and we gave her the money. She tried to speak, to thank us, but she couldn't. She just broke down completely and cried. But we didn't need any thanks.

I heard the man making plans with the middle-aged couple behind me. They were getting off the bus in Medford, just an hour away. They agreed to accompany the young mother to their family doctor, so she could get help for the child. Then they would see she got a room in a good motel by the bus station in Medford.

"I know it could take a little more than what we collected here," the young man said, "but I come back through Medford on Tuesday, and I promise I'll stop and make up any difference." He wrote down their phone number, but they said they wouldn't need the money. They'd be glad to help out.

I couldn't hear what the young mother said when he told her good-bye at Medford. I know I had a different **perception** of the "hippie" when he returned to his seat to finish his journey.

"Take heed that ye do not your alms before men, to be seen of them: otherwise ye have no reward of your Father which is in heaven." – Matthew 6:1

Betsy's Sewing Society

Dorothy Canfield Fisher

In the one-room schoolhouse in Hillsboro, Vermont, there was one child who never played with the girls nor ran and whooped with the boys—little six-year-old 'Lias, who shared the first grade with Molly.

At recess time 'Lias generally hung about the school door by himself, looking moodily down and knocking the toe of his ragged, muddy shoe against a stone.

The little girls were talking about him one day as they played. "My! Isn't that 'Lias Brewster the horridest-looking child!" said Eliza, who had the second grade all to herself.

"Mercy, yes! So ragged!" said Anastasia Monahan, called Stashie for short. She was a big girl, fourteen years old, who was in the seventh grade.

"He doesn't look as if he *ever* combed his hair!" said Betsy. "It looks just like a wisp of old hay."

"And sometimes," little Molly proudly added her bit to the talk of the older girls, "he forgets to put on any stockings and has his dreadful old shoes on over his dirty, bare feet."

"I guess he hasn't *got* any stockings half the time," said big Stashie scornfully. "I guess his stepfather drinks 'em up."

"How *can* he drink up stockings?" asked Molly, opening her round eyes very wide.

"Sh! You mustn't ask. Little girls shouldn't know about such things, should they, Betsy?"

"No, *indeed*," said Betsy, looking mysterious. As a matter of fact, she herself had no idea what Stashie meant, but she looked wise and said nothing.

Some of the boys squatted down nearby for a game of marbles.

"Well, anyhow," said Molly resentfully, "I don't care what his stepfather does to his stockings. I wish 'Lias would wear 'em to school."

"I wish he didn't have to sit so near me," Betsy complained. "He's *so* dirty."

"I don't want him near *me,* either!" cried all the girls at once.

Ralph glanced up at them, frowning, from where he knelt nearby with his middle finger crooked behind a marble—ready for a shot. He looked as he always did, very rough and half-threatening.

"Oh, you girls make me sick!" he said. He sent his marble straight to the mark, pocketed his opponent's marble, and stood up, scowling at the girls. "I guess if you had to live the way he does, you'd be dirty too! Half the time he don't get anything to eat before he comes to school, and if my mother didn't put up something for him in my box, he wouldn't get any lunch either. And then you go and jump on him!"

"Why doesn't his mother send his lunch?" Betsy challenged.

"He hasn't got any mother. She's dead," said Ralph, turning away with his hands in his pockets. He yelled to the boys, "Come on, fellows, beatcha to the bridge!" and was off, with the others racing at his heels.

"Well, I don't care; he *is* dirty and horrid!" said Stashie **emphatically**, looking over at the drooping, battered little figure, **listlessly** kicking at a stone.

But Betsy did not say anything more just then. Betsy, who lived with Uncle Henry and Aunt Abigail Putney, knew very well what it meant to be without a mother.

The teacher, who boarded around with each school family, was staying at the Putney farm just then; and that evening, as they all sat around the lamp, Betsy looked up from her game of checkers with Uncle Henry and asked, "How can anybody drink up stockings?"

"Mercy, child! What are you talking about?" asked Aunt Abigail.

Betsy repeated what Anastasia had said and was flattered by the startled attention given her by the grown-ups.

"Why, I didn't know that Bud Walker had taken to drinking again!" said Uncle Henry. "That's too bad!"

"Who takes care of that child anyhow now that poor Susie is dead?" Aunt Abigail asked of everybody.

"Is he living there *alone,* with just that good-for-nothing stepfather? How do they get enough to *eat?*" asked Betsy's Cousin Ann, looking troubled.

Apparently Betsy's question had brought something half-forgotten and altogether neglected into their minds. They talked for some time about 'Lias, the teacher confirming what Betsy had said.

"And we sitting right here with plenty to eat and never raising a hand!" cried Aunt Abigail.

"How you will let things slip out of your mind!" said Cousin Ann **remorsefully**.

It struck Betsy vividly that 'Lias was not at all the one they should blame for his **objectionable** appearance. She felt quite ashamed to go on with the other things she and the girls had said. She fell silent, pretending to be very much absorbed in her game of checkers.

"Do you know," said Aunt Abigail suddenly, "I wouldn't be a bit surprised if Elmore Pond mightn't adopt 'Lias, if he was gone at the right way."

"Who's Elmore Pond?" asked the schoolteacher.

"Why, you must have seen him—that big good-natured-looking man that comes through here twice a year, buying livestock. He lives over Digby way, but his wife was a Hillsboro girl, Matey Pelham—awfully nice girl she was too. They never had any children, and Matey told me once that she and her husband talk quite often about adopting a little boy. Mr. Pond has always wanted a little boy. He's such a nice man! 'Twould be a lovely home for a child."

"But goodness!" said the teacher. "Nobody would want to adopt such an awful-looking ragamuffin as that 'Lias. His stepfather is so mean when he's been drinking that it's got 'Lias so he hardly dares hold his head up."

The clock struck loudly. "Well, hear that!" said Cousin Ann. "Nine o'clock and the children not in bed! Molly's 'most asleep. Trot along, Betsy! Trot along, Molly. And, Betsy, be sure Molly's nightgown is buttoned up all the way."

Betsy went on thinking about 'Lias while she was getting ready for bed and answering absently little Molly's chatter. She was thinking about him even after they had gone to bed, had put the light out, and lay snuggled under the covers.

She was thinking about him when she woke up too, and as soon as she could get hold of Cousin Ann, she poured out her plan.

"Cousin Ann, couldn't we girls at school get together and sew—you'd have to help us—and make some nice, new clothes for little 'Lias Brewster, and fix him up so he'll look better, and maybe that Mr. Pond will like him and adopt him."

Cousin Ann listened attentively and nodded. "I think that would be a good idea," she said. "We were thinking last night we ought to do something for him. If you'll make some clothes, Mother'll knit him stockings and Father will get him some shoes. Mr. Pond makes his spring trip in late May, so we'll have plenty of time."

Betsy was full of importance that day at school and, at recess time, got the girls together on the rocks and told them all about the plan.

"Cousin Ann says she'll help us. We can meet at our house Saturday afternoons till we get them done. It'll be fun! Aunt Abigail telephoned down to the store, and Mr. Wilkins says he'll donate the cloth if we'll make it up."

Betsy spoke very grandly of "making it up," although she had hardly held a needle in her life, and when the Saturday meetings began, she was ashamed to see how much better Ellen and Eliza could sew than she. To keep her end up, she was driven to practicing her stitches around the lamp in the evenings.

Cousin Ann supervised the Saturday afternoon sewing and taught the girls whose legs were long enough how to use the sewing machine. First they made a little pair of trousers out of an old gray woolen skirt of Aunt Abigail's. This was for practice, before they cut into the piece of new blue serge from the storekeeper. Cousin Ann showed them how to pin the pattern on the goods, and they each cut out one piece. Those flat, odd-shaped pieces of cloth looked less like a pair of trousers to Betsy than anything she had ever seen.

Then one of the girls read aloud very slowly the mysterious-sounding directions from the wrapper of the pattern about how to put the pieces together. Cousin Ann helped here a little, particularly just as they were about to put the sections together wrong-side up.

Stashie, as the oldest, did the first basting, putting the notches together carefully, as they read the instructions aloud. And there, all of a sudden,

148

was a rough little pair of trousers, without any hem or waistband, of course, but just the two-legged, complicated shape they ought to be! It seemed like a miracle to Betsy.

Dorothy Canfield Fisher (1879-1958) was born in Kansas. She wrote many books and biographies for both adults and children. "Betsy's Sewing Society" is taken from her book *Understood Betsy*.

Then Cousin Ann helped them sew the seams on the machine, and they all worked at basting the facings and finishing. They each made one buttonhole—the first one Betsy had ever made, and when she got through, she was as tired as though she had run all the way to school and back. Tired, but very proud; although when Cousin Ann inspected that buttonhole, she covered her face with her handkerchief for a minute, as though she were going to sneeze, although she didn't sneeze at all.

It took two Saturdays to finish up the trial pair of trousers, and when they showed the result to Aunt Abigail, she was delighted. "Well, to think of that being my old skirt!" she said, putting on her spectacles to examine the work. She didn't laugh either when she saw the buttonholes, but got up hastily and went into the next room, where they soon heard her coughing.

Next they made a little shirt out of some new blue gingham that Cousin Ann had left over from a dress she was making. This thin material was much easier to manage than the gray flannel, and they had the little garment done in no time, even to the buttons and buttonholes. When it came to making the buttonholes, Cousin Ann sat right down with each of them and supervised each stitch. They were a great improvement over the first batch.

Finally, making a great ceremony of it, they began to work on the store material. They worked twice a week now, because May was slipping along fast, and Mr. Pond might be there any time. They knew pretty well how to go ahead by this time, and Cousin Ann was not much needed, except as adviser in hard places. She sat in the room with them, doing some sewing of her own, so quiet that half the time they forgot she was there. It was great fun, sewing all together and chattering as they sewed.

Much of the time they talked about how splendid it was of them to be so kind to little 'Lias. "I don't believe most girls would put themselves out this way for a dirty little boy," said Stashie, **complacently**.

"No, *indeed!*" chimed in Betsy. "It's just like a story, isn't it?—working and sacrificing for the poor."

"I guess he'll thank us for sure," said Ellen. "He'll never forget us as long as he lives."

Betsy's imagination was fired by this suggestion. "I guess when he's grown up, he'll tell everybody about how, when he was so poor and ragged, Stashi Monahan and Ellen Peters and Betsy Ann..."

"And Eliza!" put in that girl hastily, afraid she would not be given her share of the glory.

Cousin Ann sewed and listened and said nothing.

Toward the end of May two little shirts, two pairs of trousers, two pairs of stockings, two sets of underwear (from the teacher), and the pair of shoes Uncle Henry gave were ready. The girls handled the pile of new garments with inexpressible pride and debated which way of bestowing them was sufficiently grand to be worthy of the occasion.

Betsy was for taking them to school and giving them to 'Lias one by one, so that each child could have her thanks separately. But Stashie wanted to take them to the house when 'Lias's stepfather was there and shame him by showing that little girls had done what he ought to have done.

Cousin Ann broke into the discussion, asking in her quiet voice, "Why do you want 'Lias to know where the clothes came from?"

They had forgotten that she was there and turned quickly to stare at her. Nobody could answer her strange question. It had not occurred to anybody that there could be such a question!

Cousin Ann asked another: "Why did you make these clothes anyhow?"

They stared again, speechless. Why did she ask that? She knew why.

Finally little Molly said, in her honest way, "Why, *you* know why, Miss Ann! So 'Lias Brewster will look nice, and Mr. Pond will maybe adopt him."

"Well," said Cousin Ann, "what has that got to do with 'Lias knowing who did it?"

"Why, he wouldn't know who to be grateful to," cried Betsy.

"Oh," said Cousin Ann. "Oh, I see. You didn't do it to help 'Lias. You did it to have him be grateful to you. I see. Molly is such a little girl, it's no wonder she didn't really take in what you girls were up to." She nodded her head wisely.

Little Molly had no idea what everybody was talking about. She looked from one downcast face to another rather anxiously. What was the matter?

Apparently nothing was the matter, she decided, for after a minute's silence, Cousin Ann got up with her usual face of cheerful gravity and said, "Don't you think you girls ought to top off this last afternoon with a tea party? There's a batch of fresh cookies, and you can make yourselves some lemonade if you want to."

They had refreshments on the porch, in the sunshine. Nobody said another word about how to give the clothes to 'Lias, till, just as the girls were going away, Betsy said, "Say, don't you think it'd be fun to go some evening after dark and leave the clothes on 'Lias's doorstep and knock and run away before anybody comes to the door?"

She spoke in an uncertain voice.

"Yes, I do!" said Ellen. "I think it would be lots of fun!"

It was a warm, dark evening in late May, with the frogs piping their sweet, high note and the first fireflies wheeling over the meadow near the tumbledown house where 'Lias lived. The girls took turns carrying the big paper-wrapped bundle and stole along in the shadows, full of excitement, pressing their hands over their mouths to keep back the giggles.

One window of the small house was dimly lighted, and they thrilled with excitement and joyful alarm. Suppose 'Lias's dreadful stepfather should come out and yell at them!

Nobody stirred inside the room with the lighted window. They crept forward and peeped cautiously inside . . . and stopped giggling. The dim light coming from a little kerosene lamp with a smoky chimney fell on a bare, greasy wooden table and two broken-backed chairs, with little 'Lias in one of them.

He had fallen asleep with his head on his arms, his pinched, dirty, sad figure showing in the light from the lamp. His feet dangled high above the floor in their broken, muddy shoes. A piece of dry bread had slipped from his bony little hand, and a tin dipper stood beside him on the bare table.

Nobody else was in the room, nor evidently in the dark, empty house.

Betsy never forgot what she saw that night through that window. Her eyes grew very hot and her hands very cold. Her heart thumped hard. She reached for little Molly and gave her a great hug in the darkness. Suppose it were little Molly there, all alone in the dirty, dismal house, with no supper and nobody to put her to bed. Ellen, next to her, was crying into the corner of her apron.

Nobody said a word. Stashie walked around soberly to the front door, put down the clothes bundle, and knocked loudly. They all darted away noiselessly to the shadow of the trees and waited until the door opened. A square of yellow light appeared, with 'Lias's figure, very small, at the bottom of it. They saw him stoop and pick up the bundle and go back into the house. Then they went quickly back, separating at the crossroads with no good-bye.

Molly and Betsy began to climb the hill toward home. It was a very warm night for May, and little Molly began to puff for breath. "Let's sit down on this rock awhile," she said.

They were halfway up the hill now. From the rock they could see the lights in the farmhouses scattered along the valley road and on the side of the mountain opposite them, like stars fallen from the multitude above. Betsy lay down and looked up at the stars. After a silence, little Molly's chirping voice said, "Oh, I thought you said we were going to march up to 'Lias in school and give him his clothes. Did you forget about that?"

Betsy gave a wriggle of shame as she remembered that plan. "No, we didn't forget it," she said. "We thought this would be a better way."

"But how'll 'Lias know who to thank?"

"That's no matter," said Betsy. She meant it too; she was not even thinking about what she was saying. Between her and the stars, thick over her head in the black soft sky, she saw again the dirty, disordered room and the little boy, all alone, asleep in a broken-backed chair.

She looked hard and long at that picture, all the time seeing the quiet stars through it. And then she turned over and hid her face on the rock.

Every night since Betsy could remember, she had said her "Now I lay me," but she had never really prayed till she lay there with her face on the rock, saying over and over, "Oh, God, please, please, *please* make Mr. Pond adopt 'Lias."

If I Can Live

If I can live
To make some pale face brighter and to give
A second **luster** to some tear-dimmed eye,
　Or e'en **impart**
One throb of comfort to an aching heart,
Or cheer some wayworn soul in passing by;

If I can lend
A strong hand to the falling, or defend
The right against one single envious strain,
　My life, though bare,
Perhaps, of much that seemeth dear and fair
To us of earth, will not have been in vain.

The purest joy,
Most near to Heaven, far from earth's **alloy**,
Is bidding cloud give way to sun and shine;
　And 'twill be well
If on that day of days the angels tell
Of me, "She did her best for one of Thine."

– Author Unknown

153

If I Can Stop One Heart

If I can stop one heart from breaking,
I shall not live in vain:
If I can ease one life the aching,
Or cool one pain,
Or help one fainting robin
Unto his nest again,
I shall not live in vain.

– Emily Dickinson

Emily Dickinson (1830-1886) was an American poet. After attending college, she became a recluse, seldom seeing anyone but her family and never traveling. She wrote poetry all of her life, but only a few of her nearly two thousand poems were published in her lifetime.

"For to their power, I bear record, yea, and beyond their power they were willing of themselves." – 2 Corinthians 8:3

The Rich Family in Our Church

Eddie Ogan

I'll never forget Easter 1946. I was fourteen, my little sister Ocy twelve, and my older sister Darlene sixteen. We lived at home with our mother, and the four of us knew what it was to do without many things.

My dad had died five years before, leaving Mom with seven school-children to raise and no money. By 1946 my older sisters were married, and my brothers had left home.

A month before Easter, the pastor of our church announced that a special Easter offering would be taken to help a poor family. He asked everyone to save and give sacrificially. When we got home, we talked about what we could do. We decided to buy fifty pounds of potatoes and live on them for a month. This would allow us to save twenty dollars of our grocery money for the offering.

Then we thought that if we kept our electric lights turned out as much as possible, we'd save money on that month's electric bill. Darlene got as many house- and yard-cleaning jobs as possible, and both of us babysat for everyone we could. For fifteen cents, we could buy enough cotton loops to make three pot holders to sell for one dollar. We made twenty dollars on pot holders.

That month was one of the best of our lives. Every day we counted the money to see how much we had saved. At night we'd sit in the dark and talk about how the poor family was going to enjoy having the money the church would give them. We had about eighty people in church, so we figured that whatever the amount of money we had to give, the offering would surely be twenty times that much. After all, every Sunday the pastor had reminded everyone to save for the sacrificial offering.

The day before Easter, Ocy and I walked to the grocery store and got the manager to give us three crisp twenty-dollar bills and one ten-dollar bill for all our change. We ran all the way home to show Mom and Darlene. We had never had so much money before.

That night we were so excited we could hardly sleep. We didn't care that we wouldn't have new clothes for Easter; we had seventy dollars for the sacrificial offering. We could hardly wait to get to church!

On Sunday morning, rain was pouring. We didn't own an umbrella, and the church was over a mile from our home, but it didn't seem to matter how wet we got. Darlene had cardboard in her shoes to fill the holes. The cardboard came apart, and her feet got wet. But we were joyful as we sat in church.

I heard some teenagers talking about the Smith girls having on their old dresses. I looked at them in their new clothes, but I felt rich.

When the sacrificial offering was taken, we were sitting on the second row from the front. Mom put in the ten-dollar bill, and each of us girls put in a twenty. As we walked home after church, we sang all the way. At lunch Mom had a surprise for us. She had bought a dozen eggs, and we had boiled eggs with our fried potatoes!

Late that afternoon the minister drove up in his car. Mom went to the door, talked with him for a moment, and then came back with an envelope in her hand. We asked what it was, but she didn't say a word. She opened the envelope, and out fell a bunch of money. There were three crisp twenty-dollar bills, one ten-dollar bill, and seventeen one-dollar bills.

Mom put the money back in the envelope. We didn't talk; we just sat and stared at the floor. We had gone from feeling like millionaires to feeling like poor folks.

We had had such a happy life that we felt sorry for anyone who didn't have our mom and dad for parents and a house full of brothers and sisters and other children visiting constantly. We thought it was fun to share silverware and see whether we got the fork or the spoon that night. We had two knives which we passed around to whoever needed them.

I knew we didn't have a lot of things that other people had, but I never thought that we were poor. That Easter Day I found out we were. The minister had brought us the money for the poor family, so we must be poor.

I didn't like being poor. I looked at my dress and worn-out shoes and felt so ashamed that I didn't want to go back to church. Everyone there probably already knew we were poor! I thought about school. I was in the ninth grade and at the top of my class of over one hundred students. I wondered if the others at school knew we were poor. I decided I could quit school since I had finished the eighth grade. That was all the law required at that time.

We sat in silence for a long time. Then it got dark, and we went to bed. All that week, we girls went to school and came home, and no one talked much. Finally on Saturday, Mom asked us what we wanted to do with the money. What did poor people do with money? We didn't know. We'd never known we were poor.

We didn't want to go to church on Sunday, but Mom said we had to. Although it was a sunny day, we didn't talk on the way. Mom started to sing, but no one joined in, and she sang only one verse.

At church we had a missionary speaker. He talked about how churches in Africa made buildings out of sun-dried bricks, but they needed money to buy roofs. He said one hundred dollars would put a roof on a church. The minister said, "Can't we all sacrifice to help these poor people?"

We looked at each other and smiled for the first time in a week. Mom reached into her purse and pulled out the envelope. She passed it to Darlene, Darlene gave it to me, and I handed it to Ocy. Ocy put it in the offering.

When the offering was counted, the minister announced that it was a little over one hundred dollars. The missionary was excited. He hadn't expected such a large offering from our small church. He said, "You must have some rich people in this church."

Suddenly it struck us! We had given eighty-seven dollars of the "little over one hundred dollars." We were the rich family in the church! Hadn't the missionary said so?

From that day on I've never been poor again.

Storing Up
Treasures

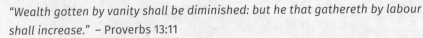

"Wealth gotten by vanity shall be diminished: but he that gathereth by labour shall increase." – Proverbs 13:11

The Farmer's Treasure

Aesop

Aesop (ē' săp') is the supposed author of about two hundred Greek fables. Various legends give various stories about him: one says he was a slave, another that he was adviser to an ancient king, a third that he was a riddle solver for a king of Babylon. Other people say Aesop never existed, and his name was merely invented to give an author to various fables—so that, after a time, "a story by Aesop" meant "a fable."

Many of the Aesop fables contain talking animals. This one is different.

A farmer who had come to the end of his life desired that his sons should not fail to make profitable the land which he would leave them. So he said to them:

"My sons, when I am dead you may have the treasure that is hidden in our vineyard."

They thought that there must be a pot of gold buried there. So, as soon as they came into possession of the farm, they took spades and dug up all the soil in the vineyard. They did not find any pot of gold, but the vineyard was so well dug over that it bore ten times more grapes than ever before.

"If ye abide in me, and my words abide in you, ye shall ask what ye will, and it shall be done unto you." – John 15:7

When Tata Prays

Harvey Yoder

Silvia Tarniceriu grew up in a large, poor, Christian family in the country of Romania. The government of Romania was then Communist, and the schools taught that there was no God. But in this story, Silvia finds proof that there is a God who hears when His people pray. You can read more about Silvia's life in the book God Knows My Size.

Once when Mama had taken her mending to spend the evening with her parents, Tata[1] turned the preparations for our sparse supper into a special event. Scarcely had the yard gate closed behind Mama when Tata wondered who would find the biggest cooking pot and fill it with water? Who would bring some kindling in to start the fire in the mud brick stove? And would anyone be interested in going to borrow just a little bit of sugar from a generous neighbor?

Victor ran out the door to fetch the water. Five-year-old Stefan[2] – *Fanel,*[3] we called him—went to gather the chips, and I brought back sugar in a cracked cup. With excitement, we crowded into our lean-to kitchen. We watched as the fire crackled into a bright flame and as the oven plate was removed so the cooking pot could be set right over the glowing coals. Then we eagerly waited for the water to boil. What special food was Tata going to make? I had heard Mama say despairingly that we had only a little bit of flour left and she did not know what to make for supper. The **meager** wages that the state-run **foundry** paid Tata were never enough to provide for our needs, and sometimes there simply was not enough money to buy food. That was when Mama's voice quivered and her brow

---

1 Tata (tä′ tä): Daddy
2 Stefan (ste fän′)
3 Fanel (fə nel′): nickname for *Stefan*

wrinkled up like a freshly furrowed field. But now, Tata was going to make supper for us! What could it be?

We crowded around the stove as Tata heated some water in a saucepan. Then he took some flour, found a little bit of oil, and stirred the mixture together to make a batter.

"Is the water boiling yet?" he asked as he leaned over to peer into the pot at the back of the stove. His skinny frame made a sort of arch over the stove.

He spooned the flour batter slowly into the hot water, and as the mixture cooked, it formed into small dumplings. The aroma of something cooking filled our simple kitchen, and we all realized just how hungry we were. I gave a little giggle as I felt my insides rumble. I patted my middle and waggled my finger at my stomach. "Shh," I admonished.

"Let's take one and put a little sugar on it." Tata dished up a plump noodle shaped like a fat pillow, and carefully I sprinkled a teeny bit of the precious sugar on it. Then Tata broke the small dumpling into tiny pieces and gave each of us a crumb to taste.

With what delight we each took our tiny portions and placed them in our mouths. How we gently munched the slightly sweet dumpling and carefully savored each bit before we reluctantly swallowed. When a crumb clung to a corner of three-year-old Ana's[4] lips, I gently took my forefinger and pushed the crumb into her mouth. I felt my own throat tremble and I swallowed too as I watched Ana, or *Nuti*[5] as we called her, swallow the last teeny bite.

So it is no wonder that I thought Tata was like God, because as we sat around the table and ate the delicious warm dumplings that evening, I was vividly reminded of the time when Jesus fed the five thousand with a small boy's lunch. My father could do miracles too!

I gave another experimental pat to the saucer I was making. The clay had been just right to make a set of play dishes. Victor, even though he was nine and sometimes thought he was too old to play with clay, had looked with interest at the cups and bowls that Fanel and I were making. Soon we three children were busily making pottery. Even Nuti had her own lump

---

4 Ana (ä' nə)
5 Nuti (nüts' ē): nickname for *Ana*

of clay and tried to make a bowl, but spent most of the time watching the wet clay squeeze out from between her fingers.

"I will make a teapot," I announced as I set the saucer on a board to dry. In my mind, I could picture the spout gracefully curving from the squat body, just like the teapot Mama used. I frowned thoughtfully for a moment at my lump of clay. "I need to look at the big one," I decided, and with a quick spring to my feet, I was up and running across the yard. Barefooted, I crossed the hard mud floor of the porch and went into the entry.

Oh, we must have guests, I thought to myself when I saw that the door to one of the rooms was closed. I could hear the murmur of voices, first Mama's voice, then Tata's. Even though I knew it was Mama, there was a different tone to her voice, almost as if she were crying.

I didn't like when Mama cried. Mama had cried too when, instead of bringing a baby home from the hospital as we all expected she would, only Mama came home. And when Mama cried, it made me feel as if somehow our home had a crack in it. A big black crack that ran down one of the sturdy white walls and allowed some unknown threat to come in and destroy our happiness. So the sound that came from behind the door stopped me from going into the kitchen to look at the teapot.

Then I heard Tata's voice again. A rush of warmth swept through my being as I heard my beloved Tata's steady and calm tones. But there was also something different about his voice that was not quite his everyday voice. I didn't really mean to **eavesdrop**, but with my usual directness, I wanted to know what was happening. I stepped closer and pressed my ear against the door.

"You know we have no food in the house. You gave us these dear children, and we love them all. But You also know we have no food. And suppertime is coming, and we need to feed our dear children."

Tata's voice came quite clearly through the door. In my mind, I could see him kneeling beside the cot that doubled as our bed at night, work-worn hands folded in prayer, talking with God.

"God, I know that You love us. You have promised us that You will never leave us nor forsake us. You fed Elijah in the wilderness. You helped the widow and her boy. And now we ask You to help our children. We have borrowed from the neighbors, and we are ashamed to beg from them again. Please, God, help us. Strengthen our faith."

Tata was pleading for food! I suddenly realized how desperate our situation was. We almost always had *mamaliga*,[6] the poor man's staple. Even if we got tired of it, there always had been enough mamaliga to take away the emptiness from our stomachs. And now we didn't have mamaliga either?

As I heard the kind, yet pleading voice of my Tata, my whole being longed to comfort him. "I am not hungry," I whispered to myself. "I will not need to eat. I can do without food." I so desperately wanted to do something to fulfill the longing I heard in my father's voice. "I can just wait until..." my thoughts went in circles. Until when? I suddenly realized that we would need food sometime. The voices of the children playing outside were real voices. They would need food. Even the older children needed food so they could go to school or go to work. Everyone needed at least some food!

The hinges of the yard gate squeaked. Someone was coming! I suddenly realized that I was eavesdropping and Tata must not find me here. I quickly turned and went back outside.

"Silvia!" It was our neighbor, Mosu Lolu,[7] who lived in the house behind ours. Mosu sometimes would stop me on the way home from school and give me a cup of milk or maybe a slice of white bread. That is, if his wife did not see us. She never shared willingly with our noisy, happy family, even though we were neighbors. I had heard her sharp remarks about people who had children in litters like animals. Once I even heard her say that "the Tarniceriu[8] family is no different from the uncivilized Chinese who have huge families." They themselves had successfully raised their family, and living next door to such a large family was disturbing to her.

But Mosu Lolu always liked me. And now, his kind face was relaxed and smiling. "Where is your Tata?" his hearty voice boomed out.

"Tata!" I called, running into the house. The closed door opened, and I eagerly seached my father's face for any sign of turmoil. But his face shone as bright as the sun that was now dipping toward the western horizon. There was not a trace of worry, just a calm trust.

---

6 mamaliga (mä mä lē' gə): cooked cornmeal mush
7 Mosu Lolu (mō' shü lō' lü): *Mosu* is a term of respect for an older man.
8 Tarniceriu (tär ni cher' yü)

"Do you have anything for supper?" Mosu Lolu asked in a friendly way. "My wife is visiting her sister, and I have a big bucket of milk from our cow. Do you need it?"

Need it? I could scarcely believe my ears! How could Mosu Lolu know how desperately we needed that milk? How was it possible that tonight his wife was gone and that he had thought about the large family next door?

But Tata's voice was calm and he said that, yes, we would be glad for the milk. And no, we didn't have any bread in the house. But we would be thankful for the milk.

"Give Silvia a pail and we will go for the milk," Mosu Lolu said as he turned to leave.

I returned not only with the pail of foamy milk, but I also clutched a handful of coins with which to buy bread.

Bread! Sometimes for a treat we might have bread on Sunday mornings. But this time, Tata sent Victor to the bakery right away for a delicious loaf.

As our large family gathered around the table for this unexpected feast, Tata led in a prayer of thankfulness and praise to God who answered our prayer and loved us in such a wonderful way. I didn't mind that the prayer was long, but every once in a while I opened one eye and peeped at the bread. Yes, it was true. And there was a big pitcher of milk on the table. Bread and milk. Manna from Heaven.

"We thank You that You hear our prayers. And we thank You that You moved in Mosu Lolu's heart to share with us in such a wonderful way. We bless Your name and praise You!"

The words flowed from Tata's mouth. It was more than a prayer. It was a hymn of praise.

I wiggled with slight impatience, but the words of Tata's prayer were now also echoed in my heart. Now I realized that when Tata prayed, God answered. Prayers were more than just something people said. Prayers were talks with God. Talks about needs. And God was Someone who heard when Tata had needs.

In my heart, I prayed too. I didn't know where we would get food for the coming days, but I did know that Someone loved and cared for the Tarniceriu family! God did!

*"And he said, Blessed be the L*ORD *God of my master Abraham, who hath not left destitute my master of his mercy and his truth: I being in the way, the L*ORD *led me to the house of my master's brethren." – Genesis 24:27*

Eliezer's Prayer

Genesis 24:1-28

And Abraham was old, and well stricken in age: and the LORD had blessed Abraham in all things.

And Abraham said unto his eldest servant of his house, that ruled over all that he had, Put, I pray thee, thy hand under my thigh: and I will make thee swear by the LORD, the God of heaven, and the God of the earth, that thou shalt not take a wife unto my son of the daughters of the Canaanites, among whom I dwell: but thou shalt go unto my country, and to my kindred, and take a wife unto my son Isaac.

And the servant said unto him, Peradventure the woman will not be willing to follow me unto this land: must I needs bring thy son again unto the land from whence thou camest?

And Abraham said unto him, Beware thou that thou bring not my son thither again. The LORD God of heaven, which took me from my father's house, and from the land of my kindred, and which spake unto me, and that sware unto me, saying, Unto thy seed will I give this land; he shall send his angel before thee, and thou shalt take a wife unto my son from thence.

And if the woman will not be willing to follow thee, then thou shalt be clear from this my oath: only take not my son thither again.

And the servant put his hand under the thigh of Abraham his master, and sware to him concerning that matter.

And the servant took ten camels of the camels of his master, and departed; for all the goods of his master were in his hand: and he arose, and went to Mesopotamia, unto the city of Nahor. And he made his camels to kneel down without[1] the city by a well of water at the time of the evening, even the time that women go out to draw water.

---

1 without: outside

And he said, O Lord God of my master Abraham, I pray thee, send me good speed this day, and show kindness unto my master Abraham. Behold, I stand here by the well of water; and the daughters of the men of the city come out to draw water. And let it come to pass, that the **damsel** to whom I shall say, Let down thy pitcher, I pray thee, that I may drink; and she shall say, Drink, and I will give thy camels drink also: let the same be she that thou hast appointed for thy servant Isaac; and thereby shall I know that thou hast showed kindness unto my master.

And it came to pass, before he had done speaking, that, behold, Rebekah came out, who was born to Bethuel, son of Milcah, the wife of Nahor, Abraham's brother, with her pitcher upon her shoulder. And the damsel was very fair to look upon, a virgin, neither had any man known her; and she went down to the well, and filled her pitcher, and came up.

And the servant ran to meet her, and said, Let me, I pray thee, drink a little water of thy pitcher.

And she said, Drink, my lord: and she hasted, and let down her pitcher upon her hand, and gave him drink.

And when she had done giving him drink, she said, I will draw water for thy camels also, until they have done drinking.

And she hasted, and emptied her pitcher into the trough, and ran again unto the well to draw water, and drew for all his camels.

And the man, wondering at her held his peace, to wit whether the Lord had made his journey prosperous or not. And it came to pass, as the camels had done drinking, that the man took a golden earring of half a shekel weight, and two bracelets for her hands of ten shekels weight of gold;

And said, Whose daughter art thou? Tell me, I pray thee: is there room in thy father's house for us to lodge in?

And she said unto him, I am the daughter of Bethuel the son of Milcah, which she bare unto Nahor. She said moreover unto him, We have both straw and **provender** enough, and room to lodge in.

And the man bowed down his head, and worshipped the Lord.

And he said, Blessed be the Lord God of my master Abraham, who hath not left **destitute** my master of his mercy and his truth: I being in the way, the Lord led me to the house of my master's brethren.

And the damsel ran, and told them of her mother's house these things.

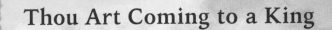

Thou Art Coming to a King

Thou art coming to a King,
Large petitions with thee bring.
For His grace and power are such
None can ever ask too much.

– John Newton

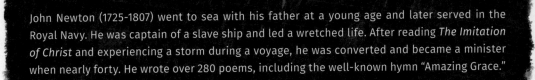

John Newton (1725-1807) went to sea with his father at a young age and later served in the Royal Navy. He was captain of a slave ship and led a wretched life. After reading *The Imitation of Christ* and experiencing a storm during a voyage, he was converted and became a minister when nearly forty. He wrote over 280 poems, including the well-known hymn "Amazing Grace."

The God of the Exodus

This psalm speaks about the time Moses led Israel out of Egypt and refers to the dividing of the Red Sea and the River Jordan, as well as the time God provided Israel with water from a rocky hillside in the desert. This psalm is a good example of Hebrew poetry.

1 When Israel went out of Egypt,
    the house of Jacob from a people of strange language;
2 Judah was his [God's] **sanctuary**,
    and Israel his **dominion**.
3 The sea saw it, and fled;
    Jordan was driven back.
4 The mountains skipped like rams,
    and the little hills like lambs.
5 What ailed thee, O thou sea, that thou fleddest?
    thou Jordan, that thou wast driven back?
6 Ye mountains, that ye skipped like rams;
    and ye little hills, like lambs?
7 Tremble, thou earth, at the presence of the Lord,
    at the presence of the God of Jacob;
8 Which turned the rock into a standing water,
    the **flint** into a fountain of waters.

– Psalm 114:1-8

"But my God shall supply all your need according to his riches in glory by Christ Jesus." – Philippians 4:19

The Richest Prisoner

Pyotr Rumachik, as told to Georgi Vins

Pyotr (Peter) Rumachik was arrested and imprisoned in Soviet Russia five times. Accused of speaking out against the Soviet government, a common charge against Christian ministers, he has always denied this charge, saying, "As a Christian, a church minister, I have no involvement in political activities." He tells the following story about his fifth term in prison, which lasted from August 1980 until February 5, 1987. Later he pastored an independent Baptist church in Dedovsk, Russia, near Moscow.

For me, life as a prisoner was quite hard in 1981 and a large part of 1982 and 1983, but the year 1984 was a year of especially great trials. In that year my mail was stopped. I was told that I would not be allowed to send any more letters because my wife was spreading them around the country. So this door of communication was slammed shut. I could write back to no one, but could only give thanks in my prayers for the letters I received.

I experienced times of imprisonment in the punishment cells, in concrete and iron, sometimes in crowded cells, sometimes in **solitary confinement**. All of this was very hard and certainly gave no comfort to the outer man. But, through it all, the Lord gave me strength to endure and "be of good cheer," as the Apostle Paul put it.

In the hard times I spent many days in prayer and fasting before the Lord. I suppose those days would add up to weeks. Sometimes I hardly got any sleep for up to fifteen days, because the guards would keep me in cells where the windows had been knocked out, and I was shivering all the time. After one such spell, I ended up in the hospital. As I said, this was a great hardship for the physical man, but the inner man was strengthened and comforted by God. During those long periods of prayer and fasting in solitary confinement, my heart enjoyed the presence of God. Like the Apostle Paul, I would spend many hours singing hymns.

The men in the next cells listened to me sing. I would call out, "Do you like these songs? Do you want me to sing some more?"

"Yes, keep singing. We've never heard such songs before. If you have strength, sing some more," they would answer.

Many of these men were criminals. They had done all sorts of terrible things. But the Lord softened their hard, black hearts. As I had opportunities to talk to them, some repented. The Lord sowed His seed in their hearts; and there, in those very hard circumstances, people were saved. Sometimes people tried to keep me from talking about Christ, but the Lord again showed His mighty hand, and those whose hearts had already received the message stood by me. They were able to influence others, and through them the Lord gave a greater opportunity to witness about Christ.

When my circumstances were extremely hard, I was more aware than ever that my brothers and sisters in Christ were praying for me. I could feel their prayers. I knew that the church was not indifferent to me and the other Christians in bonds, but rather was crying out to the Lord on our behalf. I knew this with certainty even during periods when I was in **isolation** and received no mail.

There were other times though, especially before holidays, when I received thirty to fifty letters a day and telegrams as well. The young people sent so many bright, colorful, beautiful cards. I was the happiest, richest man. God's children poured out their souls in the letters, and I knew that the church was alert and praying. Many men in the camp never received any mail at all from family or friends. When they saw how much mail I received, they would say to me, "You're the richest man among us." Sharing my letters with them was always a wonderful opportunity for me. The other prisoners were surprised to read the greetings from people who had such a deep compassion for those who suffer. Never in their lives had they heard of such care. The letters and cards provided a natural opening to talk to these people about Christ, His truth, His love for sinners, and His compassion for those who have been forsaken and forgotten by everyone else.

Many men asked me, "When we leave, will we be able to hear the Word of God somewhere?"

"Of course," I answered. "Just don't let God's Word depart from your heart. Anywhere you go, you'll be able to find God's people. Tell them what happened to you while you were in bonds. Tell them you know me, and they'll help you. They'll give you God's Word. Just keep seeking God; seek Him, His truth, and His ways. Keep seeking that salvation that He offers to every man."

Amazingly, I was able to keep my Bible from 1980 up to February of 1987. It has been in many places, including solitary confinement cells. A number of times the authorities took it away, once for more than a year, but the Lord returned it to me. Whenever I got it back, my joy was indescribable. Sometimes I knew that within a few hours or days they would take my Bible away again, so I would read chapter after chapter, whole books, in the semi-darkness of my cell, feeding on the heavenly bread that gave life to my soul and, through me, to others.

Once the guards tried to steal my Bible. They searched my cell, and one of them secretly sneaked the Bible out in his pocket.

"Where did you get that Bible, anyway?" the old **warden** demanded when he got my complaint.

"I was given permission to have it, so either you or one of your guards must know where I got it," I answered.

After threatening to lock me in solitary, he finally gave it back. Then, for the next forty minutes, he asked me all kinds of questions about God. At the end of our talk, as I was leaving his office, he slapped me on the shoulder and said, "I guess I don't have many years left myself."

"That's all the more reason you should think about your soul. Otherwise, you may end up a most unfortunate man."

Thus we parted.

During one of those times when I was without my Bible, I was writing a letter to my family when another prisoner walked over and held out a notebook to me. "Here, read this poem," he said.

"I'm right in the middle of a letter," I said. "If you'll let me keep it, I'll look at it as soon as I'm finished."

He realized I was not really in the mood to look at his notebook, but he insisted, "Please, just read this one poem."

Looking up, I couldn't believe what I saw. There was a poem about Christ's sufferings on Calvary. My spirit was strengthened and revived as I read it. I started flipping the pages, discovering other poems and some passages from Scripture.

The man stood to the side, watching and smiling as I turned the pages. "It's yours. You can keep it," he announced.

After finishing my letter, I spent the rest of the evening poring over the notebook. It was full of beautiful verses about Christ and the church, about how Christ calls the church His beloved, encourages us, and never forsakes the prisoners.

That notebook stayed with me for years and was especially precious during those times when I did not have my Bible. I managed to keep it through many searches, and I had hoped to bring it home with me, but last September the authorities took it away, supposedly to examine it, and in spite of all my pleas, they didn't give it back.

So who was the man who gave me that notebook? He was far from being a Christian. He is one of the Buryat people from Zabaikal, descendants of the Mongols.[1] The Buryat people know almost nothing of Christ. Some of them are religious people, Buddhists. The man who gave me the notebook, though, was not a Buddhist. He said that though he did not really believe in God, he used to listen to Christian radio programs late at night when he was shepherding. He taped the programs onto cassettes and later copied parts of them into the notebook. Somehow he managed to hang on to the notebook and get it into the camp.

I often compare this man to the raven that brought food to the Prophet Elijah in the wilderness. People might say, "What good could a raven bring?" But, like the raven, this unbelieving man brought me food from the Lord, and for a long time I fed on the notebook that he had written with his own hand. God heard the prayers of His child and answered them in this amazing way.

---

1 The Buryat people live mostly in the area around Lake Baikal (Zabaikal), the largest freshwater lake in the world. Lake Baikal is in Russian Siberia, directly north of Mongolia. The Mongols are the nomadic, shepherding people of Mongolia.

Oh, Father, in My Testing Hour

Many Christians have suffered in prison as Pyotr Rumachik did. One of them was Leonard Sommer, who died in prison on Christmas Day in 1573.

Oh, Father, in this testing hour, sustain my fainting heart.
While pride must be full overthrown, let mercy have her part.

Here lay I in sore prison chains, by enemies beset,
Who rail against Thy Holy Word, their hearts on evil bent.

Long as thy grace lays hold on me, my heart will sing for joy—
In dismal dungeons, fire, and rack—through Satan's cruelest ploy.

For through Your grace I shall be found worthy my cross to take;
United ever to my Lord, and suffering for His sake.

– Leonard Sommer

"Give, and it shall be given unto you; good measure, pressed down, and shaken together, and running over, shall men give into your bosom. For with the same measure that ye mete withal it shall be measured to you again." – Luke 6:38

Flor Silin's Gift

Nikolai Karamzin

Every time I think back on the misery of the "famine year" in the regions of the Lower Volga,[1] I feel again the horror of drought. The summer's scorching heats dried up all the fields, and there was no relief from the drought except the tears of the ruined farmers. During the cold, comfortless autumn, the despairing country folk crowded around their empty barns with folded arms and sad faces, pondering on their misery instead of rejoicing as usual in the golden harvest. At last the winter came, bringing with it terrible agony, and whole families left their homes to become beggars on the highway. At night the canopy of heaven served them as their only shelter from the piercing winds and bitter frost.

Even though I was only a child at the time, I cannot forget the images of the **calamity** which was all around us. But if I should try to describe these scenes in detail, I am afraid I would harm the feelings of my readers. So I will go on to the tale I have to tell you.

In those days I lived on a farm not far from Simbirsk.[2] In a nearby village there lived a man named Flor Silin, a poor, laboring peasant who was a remarkably diligent, skillful, and wise farmer. Flor had been blessed with abundant crops, and because his wants were few, his granaries were full of corn even during the famine year. Everyone in the village was reduced to begging except Flor Silin. Here was a perfect opportunity to grow rich! Watch how Flor Silin acted.

Flor called his neighbors to his farm, and he addressed them in this way: "My friends, you need corn to stay alive. God has blessed me with an

---

1 The Volga River forms north of Moscow, capital of the Federation of Russia, and runs east, then south. The "lower Volga" is the area of the Federation of Russia that lies along the southern part of the Volga River.

2 Simbirsk: the former name of modern Ulyanovsk, which lies southeast of Gorky on the Volga River

abundance. Help me to thrash out a quantity of corn, and each of you take what he wants for his family."

The peasants were amazed. After all, greed exists just as much in the countryside as it does in the city. The fame of Flor Silin's **benevolence** reached other villages; **famished** peasants from near and far presented themselves before him and begged for corn. Flor received them as brothers, and while his store of grain remained, he gave to all who asked him.

Thinking there would be no end to his generosity, Flor's wife finally reminded him that it was necessary to think of their own needs too.

"Hold your **lavish** hand before it is too late, Flor," she begged.

In answer, Flor told his wife, "In the Scriptures it is written, 'Give and it shall be given unto you.' "

The following year God heard the prayers of the poor, and the harvest was abundant. The peasants who had been saved from starving now gathered around Flor Silin.

"Here," they said, "here is the corn you lent us. You saved our wives and children. We should have been famished, but for you. May God reward you; He alone can! All we have to give is our corn and grateful thanks."

"I need no corn at present, my good neighbors," he replied. "My harvest has exceeded all my expectations—thank God. As for last year, let us thank God for meeting all of our needs—I was only His humble instrument."

They urged him, but it was in vain. He would not accept their corn.

"If you have excess, share it among your poor neighbors. There were many who could not sow their fields last autumn and are still in need. Let's help them, dear friends. Almighty God will bless us for it."

"That is a good idea!" the peasants said. "Our poor neighbors shall have this corn. But they shall know that they owe this timely gift to you, Flor Silin. They, too, will tell their children that they owe their debt of gratitude to your generous heart."

Nicolai Michalovich Karamzin (1766-1826) was a Russian writer and historian who wrote *Letters of a Russian Traveler* and *History of the Russian State*. He tried to make literary Russian easier to read.

"I have showed you all things, how that so labouring ye ought to support the weak, and to remember the words of the Lord Jesus, how he said, It is more blessed to give than to receive." – Acts 20:35

The Sweater

Mark Hager

Mr. Conway sent for me to come down to his house. He was our neighbor, and he was old, and I guessed it was just another of the ordinary chores Mom had been sending me to do for him ever since I had been big enough.

When I got there, the old gentleman wanted me to take his shoes across town to Mr. Gentile's shoe shop and get them mended.

While I was waiting for him to pull off his shoes, a car drove up, and a man and a boy got out and asked for a drink of water. Hunters, they looked like, probably on their way up the mountain. I led them down to the spring and showed them where the tin cup hung, Mr. Conway's two puppies following us.

While I waited, I couldn't help noticing the boy's pullover. He looked about fourteen, which was my age, and the sweater was my size, and it was the most beautiful sweater I had ever seen—thick and warm, a deep splotchy gray-green. Mom and I had just been talking about sweaters. She had said that I would need a new one soon because I'd outgrown my old one, and the weather was turning cooler.

While the boy was getting a drink, the puppies started gnawing at his shoestrings. He stooped and started playing with them. After the boy was friendly like that with the puppies, I ventured to ask him where he got his sweater and how much it cost. He said it cost nineteen dollars and told me the store in town where he'd bought it. He said they had a whole rack full of them.

As the boy and his father went back to the car, I heard the boy ask his father to buy him one of the puppies, but it seemed as if the father wasn't paying attention.

After they drove off, Mr. Conway wrapped his old shoes in a newspaper. Then he dug in a ceramic vase until he found six and a half dollars.

"Sorry, Marc," he said, "that I ain't got none extra for you to spend. The truth is, that is the last cent between me and the Judgment Day."

I knew that was true. I had asked Mom more than once why old Mr. Conway lived alone when he had children who could take him home with them.

Then she'd explain that he didn't want to go home with them. She'd say the old gentleman loved his little house, and I would tell her I didn't see anything about it to love. She would say that was because I was a boy yet and couldn't understand the minds and hearts and feelings of older people. She said he could love the cracks in the windowpanes and the saggy, mossy roof; that he could love the sigh of the wind in the weeping willow tree and the laugh of the spring that giggled as it came from the red bank.

"Why, to him," my mother would say, "the old place is drowsy with dreams and moldy with memories dear to his heart."

But all that made no sense to me. My fingers ached when I chopped his wood, and doing chores around his **deteriorating** old house frustrated me.

As I took Mr. Conway's shoes under my arm and started down the road, he called from the door.

"Tell him to fix 'em while you wait," he called. "Tell him I'll have to sit by the fire in my sock feet till you get back."

As I went down the road, I kept thinking of the sweater. I went by our house on the way to town, so when I got there, I slipped into the kitchen and felt in the money cup on top of the cabinet. I always remembered to feel in the cup first, because I could tell it hurt Mom to ask her for money when she didn't have it. But this time I felt bills in the cup.

I got what money I had out of my sock drawer and ran to Mom. I told her about the boy with the sweater, and after a while she gave me three more dollars, and I had enough to buy the sweater.

When I got into town, I went first to the big store the boy had told me about and searched along the rack of sweaters until I came to the same kind of sweater the boy had worn. I bought it. Outside I put it on, and I walked slowly toward Mr. Gentile's shop, enjoying my new sweater.

Inside Mr. Gentile's shoe shop, I laid the old shoes on the counter. He unrolled them from the paper. He examined the old shoes. Then he looked at me and shook his head.

"Can't be fixed no more," he said. "Nothing left to sew the soles to." He pushed them back. I took the old shoes under my arm and walked out.

For a little while I stood on the street corner with the old shoes under my arm. I could see Mr. Conway waiting in his sock feet in the little house in the bend of the creek, his socks worn and **threadbare**. I glanced down at the tattered shoes that bore the shape of his feet and wondered if these old shoes hadn't been even closer to him than his best friends on earth.

I began to walk slowly around the block. In front of the big store, I stopped again. I felt the six and a half dollars in my pocket. Then I pulled off my new sweater and went inside the store again.

"I decided I don't want the sweater," I told the man who had sold it to me. "I was just wondering, do you have a pair of shoes about the size of these old shoes that you would trade me for the sweater and six and a half dollars?" I even explained to the man who I wanted the shoes for, and how his old shoes could not be fixed anymore.

"Why, I know that old gentleman," the salesman said. "He's been in here several times. He always looks at a particular pair of shoes. I still have them."

He went back and pulled down a shoe box. I saw $29.50 on the end of the box.

"I just have this sweater and six and a half dollars," I said.

The man didn't answer. He just reached up and jerked down a pair of heavy long socks, stuck one in each shoe, and wrapped the new shoes in the old newspaper. I went out of the store, leaving my sweater lying on the counter, but I had a curious feeling inside.

When I got back in sight of the little old house, I slowed down and considered. I thought of some of Mom's sayings. I remembered her saying the sunshine always seemed brighter just after a dark storm cloud, and how she said dark hollows were good places to look at the stars from, and how happy you could be just after a streak of sorrow.

I thought I might make Mr. Conway happier by first making him a little more unhappy.

I recollect to this day how I found him waiting in his sock feet in his big old easy chair by the fire.

"Mr. Gentile couldn't fix your old shoes," I said. "He said there was nothing left to sew the soles to."

What puzzled me was that what I said did not dim a curious gay twinkle I saw in Mr. Conway's blue eyes.

"That's all right," he said, "just give 'em here. I can manage in 'em a little while longer."

He took the old newspaper and unrolled the new shoes. I recollect how he felt them with his old hands, and then some water came down his cheeks, and he got up. He walked over to his bed and from under a pillow he got out a sweater, just like the sweater I'd bought and then returned in town.

"I saw you eyein' this sweater this mornin'," he said. "When those hunters came back, I hit that boy up for a trade. I traded him one of the puppies for his sweater."

I gave Mr. Conway's neck a long hard hug, and then I broke for home with my sweater on to show it to Mom.

"To every thing there is a season, and a time to every purpose under the heaven."

– Ecclesiastes 3:1

A Time to Talk

When a friend calls to me from the road
And slows his horse to a meaning walk,
I don't stand still and look around
On all the hills I haven't hoed,
And shout from where I am, What is it?
No, not as there is a time to talk.
I thrust my hoe in the mellow ground,
Blade-end up and five feet tall,
And plod: I go up to the stone wall
For a friendly visit.

– Robert Frost

There Is a Season

¹ To every thing there is a season,
And a time to every purpose under the heaven.

² A time to be born,
And a time to die;

A time to plant,
And a time to pluck up that which is planted;

³ A time to kill,
And a time to heal;

A time to break down,
And a time to build up;

⁴ A time to weep,
And a time to laugh;

A time to mourn,
And a time to dance;

⁵ A time to cast away stones,
And a time to gather stones together;

A time to embrace,
And a time to refrain from embracing;

⁶ A time to get,
And a time to lose;

A time to keep,
And a time to cast away;

⁷ A time to **rend**,
And a time to sew;

A time to keep silence,
And a time to speak;

⁸ A time to love,
And a time to hate;

A time of war,
And a time of peace.

– Ecclesiastes 3:1-8

"But godliness with contentment is great gain. For we brought nothing into this world, and it is certain we can carry nothing out." – 1 Timothy 6:6, 7

The Way It Is

John Ruth

My name's Sam Blair. We live on a farm on a dirt road along Simpson Creek, two miles out of Greenville. We are poor folks because there's a mortgage[1] on our farm—but we get along all right.

Sometimes when I didn't have anything special to do, I wished and wished for a bike. I'd just sit down somewhere and want a bike. And I'm telling you, I really wanted it! But you see, a family has to have money to have something like a bike.

It's like this. Some people have money. Their children have all kinds of things they don't need. But then there are folks like us. We walk to school. If we go on an errand, we use our legs. We poor children can't see how it is fair that other children can have spending money and bicycles and baseball mitts and a whole lot of other things we don't even know about, and we can't have any. Sometimes we borrow their things to use, but that isn't like having them yourself.

But what I wanted to tell you about was the bike contest I was in once. One night after school, I was walking home and I noticed a new sign in Pop Martin's hardware store window. I was late but I stopped to read it because anything in Martin's store window was sure to interest us boys. The next minute shivers were chasing up and down my spine. This is what the sign said:

Contest!
Martin's Hardware Store
will award this bicycle to the boy who catches the largest number
of muskrats in the coming season with *Martin's Animal Traps*
Ages 10-16 eligible
Contest closes February 1

---

1 A person who lends money often has a mortgage on the borrower's property. The mortgage is the lender's claim to own part or all of the property in exchange for the money he has lent.

And right beneath the sign was the most beautiful bike you ever saw! It was all shiny and red and had a horn and lights and balloon tires and everything you could wish for. And I had the chance of winning it. I could hardly believe my eyes. If I won it, I could ride back and forth to school just like the other boys. I must have been acting sorta excited because Pop Martin was standing inside the store looking at me as if something was wrong with me. I heard the rest of the boys coming down the street, and I knew they would kid me about winning the bike, and anyway it was getting late; so I started home. I have two miles to walk home every night, and Dad wants me home by 4:30 to help with the milking, so I have to step pretty lively.

I ran almost the whole way home that night. I wasn't tired. I was thinking about the bike all the time. It seemed too good to be true that I, a poor boy, had a chance to have a new bike. Why, I would be just like the other boys. They all had bikes. I was the only one that didn't have one. People would think I came from a rich family. Dad would be proud of me. I knew he would have liked to give me a lot of things, but he just didn't have the money.

I got to thinking about my traps. I had forty-two of them. They were old ones that Pop used, but they were pretty good. I hoped they were Martin's brand. I was a pretty good trapper, and each season I usually caught about thirty-five "mushies"—that's our nickname for muskrats around here.

I felt good that night and milked fast. Dad seemed sorta worn-out and tired. Sometimes I pitied him. He was always worrying about the mortgage on our farm, and he had a whole lot of wrinkles in his forehead. They made him look older than he really was. Dad and Mother had a pretty good start before the Depression[2] came and set them back. Grandpa had been able to help Dad get started. That was all gone now though, and I never found out much about it.

One night after supper, Dad came into the living room and sat down. I was in the next room, but he didn't know it, and he started talking about the mortgage. We didn't get the evening paper anymore because Dad was afraid ten dollars a year for something we didn't really need was too much.

---

2 Great Depression: the years from 1929 to 1939 in the United States, a time of severe hardship

So he just settled down farther in the creaky old cane-bottom chair and said, "Well, Mother, it doesn't look too good."

He edged and the chair started creaking again as he shifted. "It wouldn't make me feel so bad, but it's the children I pity. They never have much. Take Sam, now, he's never even had a bike. What other boy his age around here doesn't have one? He really works hard for me and I appreciate it, but I need every cent we can get right now. I hope he gets a good catch of muskrats this year. With the money from the furs, we should be able to pull through the winter, but it will take some **scrimping**."

Mother didn't say much and that was the last I heard Dad talking anymore that night, but, by the way they looked when I went to bed, I guessed they were still thinking about it.

After that I didn't ask Dad for anything I didn't really need. I think he knew that I was trying to help out, and it made him sad that he couldn't give me the things other people gave their children. I didn't mind though, because that's the way it is when you're poor, and you get used to it.

I looked at my traps the first chance I got and found out only twenty-five of them were Martin's brand. I felt pretty glum for a while after that, but I didn't let on. I acted real hopeful when anybody said anything to me about the contest. I couldn't hope to do much, though, with only twenty-five traps. Bill Sheldon, a boy in my grade at school, had a whole lot of traps and had plenty of money to buy more. His father owned the grocery store in town, and Bill had just about anything he wanted. I even heard one of the boys saying he could have a whole ice cream cone every day if he wanted one. I just wished I could have taken his place for a couple of days!

Trapping season started the first day of December, and I could hardly wait. It happened to be a Saturday—I was glad for that, because I could set my traps in the morning instead of having to wait until after supper. The weather was good for mushy trapping, and I hoped for a good catch the first night. I set all the Martin traps in the best trails because I wanted to catch the most with them. It took me all morning to finish the job, and I was real hungry when I came into the house at dinner. My spirits were pretty high, and Mother noticed I was feeling good. She said something about a trapping contest Pop Martin was running for the boys, but I didn't show my interest.

I kept thinking about the bike all afternoon. It seemed to me it wasn't only for my sake that I wanted to win it, but maybe Dad would feel better if I did. I even got to thinking it was almost my duty to win it.

I went to look at my traps for the first time at ten o'clock that night. The first half dozen were on the banks of the little run behind the orchard. I was real pleased to see two big fellows in the traps. Neither trap was a Martin's, so I couldn't count them toward the bike. I kept on toward the creek, shining my old flashlight and whistling to Sport, our collie, because it gets pretty scary out there along the creek after dark. I noticed a great big light swinging around farther up the creek on our neighbor's land. It was probably Bill Sheldon and his new spotlight his father gave him. I heard voices and guessed he had brought some of the boys along.

Well, I had eleven muskrats hanging by their tails in the shed when I went in that night. I went straight to bed since I was pretty tired that night and there was milking to do in the morning.

The next time I checked, there were eight more mushies in the traps. That made nineteen altogether, and nine of them were caught in Martin traps. I was hoping I'd catch more in them, but it didn't turn out that way. I skinned them all on Monday evening after school. I had to make my own stretchers out of shingles because the store-made ones cost too much. The shingles did pretty good though.

All through the week the weather was good for mushy trapping. The boys were always talking about the new bike in the hardware store window. I never said much about it, and I hoped they wouldn't ask me if I was going to try to win it. I kinda thought it belonged to me, me not having a bike and they all having one. They didn't need any, but I should have one for going back and forth to school. Bill Sheldon was pretty sure he would get it. I heard him telling some of the boys he was going to buy more traps. I knew he had plenty of money to do it if he wanted to.

Then, on the fifteenth of December, the weather went bad. It was the second Saturday after the beginning of the season. It snowed from ten o'clock in the morning to six that night. The snow covered all the traps, and the mushies stayed in their dens. The snow had just started to melt a few days later when we had a blizzard. This time it was really a deep snow. There was almost sixteen inches of snow on the ground when it stopped snowing.

The next day in school, the boys were telling each other how many mushies they had caught. I had just gotten in the room and was warming my hands at the radiator, and I didn't hear much; but Bill Sheldon, he always talks so loud, I could hear him saying he caught twenty-eight. I had caught thirty-seven, but only twenty-three of them in Martin's traps. I got a little bit afraid Bill would win the bike, but I just couldn't think of it. If only the snow would melt soon, but it hung on.

Finally, with fourteen more days in that trapping season, it rained, and the snow melted. I shifted my traps around some because the water was pretty high.

Bill Sheldon was pretty confident. He wasn't trying to win the bike because he needed it, like I did, but because he wanted to show the rest of the gang that he was leader. That's what made it so hard for me. I couldn't understand why boys that didn't need things could have them when fellows like me should have had them; but I did my best.

I thought about the bike when I went to sleep at night. I thought about it when I was milking. Dad got a little ruffled about the way I didn't keep my mind on what I was doing. Once I almost poured a whole bucket of milk down the drain in the milk house. That was just about too much for him. He looked at me as if he had taken all he could stand and wouldn't take any more. I tried to do a little better after that, but I kept thinking about that bike.

One night Dad asked me what was on my mind. He smiled when I told him about the contest and the wonderful new bike. I musta got excited. He probably remembered how he felt when Grandpa promised him a new horse and buggy. Of course, they had more money then and could afford things like that.

I noticed Dad was feeling better the next morning. When I came around to the shed, he was counting the mushy skins I had hanging there. He asked me how many I had caught in all, and I told him. There were fifty-four of them in all, and thirty-six of them were caught in Martin's traps. Maybe you wondered why I didn't use the muskrat money to buy a new bicycle, but you see, Dad always needed money and I gave it to him. That's the way it is when you're poor. All the money goes to the family. It helps out a lot that way. Anyway, Dad seemed pretty happy about my big catch, but when I told him only thirty-six counted toward the bike, he seemed a little sad. I didn't feel so good for a while either, but my spirits gradually rose toward evening.

We boys were all supposed to come together on the fifth of February at Pop Martin's store to see who would get the bike. I came to town early to mail a letter for Mother. The bicycle was to be given away at nine-thirty. I was there at nine.

In about fifteen minutes the boys arrived with Bill Sheldon in the lead. Pop Martin came around the counter with a big smile on his face and took out his notebook. We were all looking at each other, and nobody asked anybody else how many he had caught. Every boy in the store wanted that bike, but I was the one who really needed it. I was so nervous my knees felt like wet strings.

Well, Pop started down the line in alphabetical order. I was second. "Sam Blair!" said Pop sorta loud. I said, "Thirty-six," and my voice was shaking when I said it. I thought everybody looked at me then. Bill Sheldon was sitting on the counter, and he turned right around and stared at me. I tried to figure out if he had more than I did or not, but I couldn't tell by his expression. I was getting more and more nervous as Pop went on. He was down to "L" now, and I still had the most. I put out a hand to steady myself and knocked a shovel over. Everybody looked again, and I got red all over. Pop Martin glanced over at me with a funny look in his eye.

Finally he got to the letter "S." "Bill Sheldon," Pop said. Bill looked around and said triumphantly, "Thirty-nine!" All of a sudden I felt hot all over. Why should Bill, who never needed anything in his life, have this new bike, when I was the one who really needed it?

He never knew how I wished for it. I earned it more than he did. It just wasn't fair. It wasn't fair to Dad and Mother. They had done as much as they could for me. Their boy was as good as Bill Sheldon. Then why couldn't I have won the prize? Why did the rich people get all the breaks? I almost bawled right there in the store, but I managed to say, "Say, Bill, you really won a neat bike. I hope you'll have fun with it." Bill said,

John Ruth was born in 1930 on a Pennsylvania farm. He was a minister at the Salford Mennonite Church and wrote many books about Mennonites and their history.

"Thanks. I hate to beat you, but that's the way it is."

Yes, that's the way it is. The rich people have what they want, and we must get along without. I went to the front door and took one long look at the bike, all shiny and red, and then Bill came to take it out of the window, and I trudged home in the slush.

What a different return I made that morning than I had hoped for. I was going to wave gaily at Pop and Mom when I rode right up to the kitchen door. Dad would come running from the barn, and he and Mother would talk about how their boy won the prize all by himself. Then they would say how useful it would be. Now everything was changed. Maybe they didn't think it was as important as I did. Oh, well, that was over. I might as well forget about it.

I came walking slowly in the lane. Dad came around the barn and saw me coming home without the bike. He stepped out of sight when I looked up, but he seemed hunched up, and more like an old man when he went back. Mother looked out of the window. I tried to cheer up and step lightly, but it was no use. I petted Sport when he came to me.

That night after supper, Dad asked me who won the bike, acting as if he was only half-interested. I told him it was Bill Sheldon. He said, "Now see here, Sam, Mother and me were thinking about giving you some of that muskrat money to buy a secondhand bike with. Tell me how much you think you'll need, and I'll let you have it."

All at once I was mad at myself. Here I was getting my parents worried about a little thing like a bicycle, when I didn't even need one.

"No, sir," I said to Dad. "I don't want it. Bill Sheldon can have that bicycle. I don't even need a bike, and I wouldn't want to spend money on something that isn't even necessary. That's just the way it is—you have to use your money wisely."

Dad's face got a sudden sort of softness all over it—like I'd never seen before. He smiled. "Sam, I'm very proud of you—proud because you're so ready to deny yourself. And you know what, working together like we are, we're going to pull through."

Since that time I've given up wanting a bike somewhat. Because that's the way it is; we can't have everything we want.

All Things Are Thine

All things are Thine; no gift have we,
Lord of all gifts, to offer thee;
And hence with grateful hearts today,
Thine own before Thy feet we lay.

Thy will was in the builder's thought;
Thy hand unseen among us **wrought**;
Through every motive, **scheme**, and plan,
Thy wise eternal purpose ran.

O Father, stoop, these walls to bless;
Fill with Thy love their emptiness;
And let their door a gateway be,
To lead us from ourselves to Thee.

– *John Greenleaf Whittier*

John Greenleaf Whittier (1807-1892) was a Quaker poet and abolitionist. He had little formal schooling. A schoolmaster gave him a volume of Burns' poems, which inspired him to write poetry. He often wrote about rural life. "Snow-Bound" was his best-known poem. In the latter part of his life, Whittier wrote religious verse. Some hymns we sing today contain parts of his poems.

> *"Not that I speak in respect of want: for I have learned, in whatsoever state I am, therewith to be content."* – Philippians 4:11

Dots and Dashes

••• ——— •••

Lois Trimble Benedict

The cold wind from the Arctic Ocean caught one end of Eric Svenson's red scarf and blew it out behind him. Dark clouds were scudding across the last blue patches in the sky. Under his arm, Eric carried two glass jars containing a mild **solution** of sulfuric acid.

Eric braced himself so the wind wouldn't blow him over. For him, walking consisted of teetering along on his toes, because Eric had cerebral palsy.[1] There was no other way to put it—Eric was a cripple.

Fourteen years ago, when Eric had been born, his father had been so delighted for a son that he had named him Eric and bragged about his strength. He was counting on Eric's growing into a big strong fisherman, brave and fearless—a real Icelandic Viking! But a year later the doctor had told his father that Eric would never walk like other boys.

Inside Eric felt as brave as any other Icelander. But all the bravery in the world would never make it possible for him to put down his heels when he walked. Eric would never be able to take his place on the fishing crew of the *Husavik,* the fishing boat owned by the men of Husavik, Eric's hometown. How could he manage to walk on a slippery, jostling deck in a storm? Even this afternoon he was walking home alone because he could not go skiing with the other children.

One glass jar shifted under his arm. Eric slid it more tightly into the crook of his elbow and tightened his hold. Little fluffy snowflakes blew along on the wind now. It was almost dark, even though it was only three o'clock on a January afternoon.

As he hung his cap and heavy coat on a peg in the hall, his mother

---

1 cerebral palsy: loss of the use of certain muscles and coordination because of brain damage

called from the kitchen, "Did you see any sign of Father's boat coming in the fjord?" Eric thought her voice trembled.

"No." He sat down to pull off his outdoor shoes—heavy cripple's shoes. He wiggled his toes inside his heavy, woolen socks. "They've been gone four days, haven't they?"

"Last trip out they had to go to Siglufjördur[2] to find fish. They must have had to go quite a way this time too." Mother closed a cupboard door.

Eric carried his jars into his room. At the back of the worktable stood a row of glass jars, all alike and all containing sulfuric acid. Eric took the lids off the two he had brought home from school, inserted a strip of zinc in one and put it beside the other jars on the right. He put a strip of copper in the other and set it with the jars on the left. The wire to connect all these cells hung from the light over his table. Carefully he connected the wires along from cell to cell in series, so he would have ten volts of electricity when he finished. The receiver came to life with a series of chattering, clicking sounds from the loudspeaker. But Eric paid no attention to it.

He still had a happy, glowing feeling as a result of his demonstration in science class at school that afternoon. Even when he had been a small child, Eric had had to learn that he could not do many things. He had never had a bicycle, and when he was in the lower grades in school, the other children had gone out to the slopes of the Tunguheioi for skiing, but not Eric Svenson. Many times he had been lonely; many times he had been discouraged.

Then one day his father had brought him a set of glass beakers and jars with some chemicals. Eric had liked mixing the powders together to get chemical reactions. Doing that almost made him forget his frustration and disappointments because he was crippled. Mother had ordered a magazine for him from America. Long before he started studying English in school, Mother had sat with him long hours translating the technical articles into Icelandic. Eric had learned how to make this battery from an article in that magazine.

He had taken only two jars with him to school because it was hard to carry them. Before he had started his experiment, the other boys had been laughing and joking about the things they would do out on the ski slopes

2 Siglufjördur (sā' ləf yúr dər)

after school. Only the teacher had paid much attention while he was setting up. But when he hooked the loudspeaker to the wires, clicking sounds had come immediately.

The boys were so surprised that they stopped laughing and talking. Every eye in the class had turned on him. Even Jons, the best skier in the class, had listened intently.

•—•• •• ••• — • —• Then Eric had turned it off while he explained about the chemical reaction between the sulfuric solution and the metal strips. He told them that he had produced one volt of electricity, but that at home he had lots of jars and produced enough current to send and receive messages from quite a distance. —— — ••• — • •—• Once again the loudspeaker gave out sounds as he turned it back on.

Now Eric had the two jars he had brought home from school hooked into the series, and the regularity of the sounds coming in over the loud-speaker here on his worktable attracted his attention. There was a definite sequence to them, a regularity and even spacing. He bent forward, listen-ing. ••• Three dots. Eric held his breath. What would the next letter be? ——— Three dashes. Eric's throat tightened, and he could hardly swallow. By now he felt sure he knew what would come next. Yes, ••• three dots again! The distress signal!

Eric put on his headphones and adjusted them so they were tight against his ears. He must get every dot and dash correct, and he must be sure the sounds from the house didn't interfere. As he was doing that, he remem-bered the homemade battery set he had given his father for Christmas. It was on his father's fishing boat. He had set the twelve glass jars firmly in a wooden tray so that they could be put on the back of the radio table in the boat, where they couldn't shift around in a storm. Was this his father now?

Eric was leaning over his set, listening intently, when his mother opened the door and came in. She put socks in one drawer, shirts in another. She banged the last drawer shut, and Eric could hear it even with the head-phones clamped tightly against his ears.

Then she went to the window. By now the snow was falling fast, and as usual in Iceland, there was a strong wind with it. White caps dotted the waves in the fjord.

"I wish Father were home," she said. She put her hands up to the window, as if holding them there she could stop the rattling, as if she might even stop the storm outside.

Just then the key began clattering again. Clicking, loud and regular, came through his headphones. His homebuilt receiver was **monitoring** 2182, the channel used by ships in distress. "Shh," he said to his mother.

Next the ship would give its name and location. Before the name came, Eric knew what ship it would be. But he wanted to get it from them. And most important of all, he must know its exact location. Automatically he reached toward the back of his worktable and pulled the radio set nearer where he could turn to it quickly. He would use the radio to contact other fishing boats that might be able to help.

Mother sensed that Eric was listening to an important message, and she went out. *TF 4675:* that was the fishing boat code for Iceland. Then more dots and dashes. •••• ••— ••• •— ••—•— •• —•— *Husavik,* Father's boat! The *Husavik* belonged to the men of the town. Most of the fathers and grown sons of the village were on that boat. They gave their position. Eric stood, running his finger over the map on the wall. They had gone quite a way for their fishing, but they were only about a mile offshore, north of Siglufjördur on the northern coast of Iceland. But in January, in an Icelandic storm, a mile could be as far away as another planet.

He pushed his headphones up on his head so he could use his radio **transmitter** better. He turned it to the ship-to-shore frequency—2638. The wind howled around the corner of the house as he sent out a call for help. He hoped his voice was loud enough and strong enough to carry to another boat. There was an extra loud whine of the wind as he gave out the signal. While he waited for a reply, the wind screeched and dashed a blinding curtain of snow against the windowpane. He spoke into the transmitter again, trying to say his words slowly and clearly.

There was a click! Then a voice! Eric strained to listen. It was the boat *Dalvik,* and it was at the northern end of the fjord, near the ocean. Eric checked its position on his map. It was nearly ten miles from Father's boat. If the trouble was serious—and it must be if Father was using his battery set rather than his regular radio—the *Dalvik* might not be able to get to him in time.

Eric sent out another call before he gave the position of the *Husavik.* Another voice, somewhat fainter, came in. It was from the *Siglufjördur,* on its way home. Plotting its position, Eric found that the boat was only half a mile from his father's. They should be able to reach the *Husavik* in ten minutes. They might be able to help in time. He turned all the voltage he could on the radio transmitter and directed the boat to sail east, giving the *Husavik*'s location again.

Before he turned back to his homemade set, Eric tried to contact his father on the radio. But he got no response. He didn't know what had happened, but it must have been something serious. Evidently Father's radio was gone. Back to the dot-and-dash method—and he was thankful he could tell them that another boat was close and on its way.

There was nothing to do now but wait for the *Siglufjördur* to get near the *Husavik*. Eric went to the window to look out. The waves in the fjord were higher than the mast of a fishing boat. If they were that high in the fjord, what would they be like out on the Arctic Ocean? As he stood there, Eric realized that the only person on Father's boat who knew Morse code was his own father. He and Father often had sent signals from one part of the house to another, just for fun. None of the other men had any reason to learn the code, not even Karl, the radio operator.

Eric heard his older sister come in the door from skiing, talking and laughing. He closed the door to shut out the noise and turned to the radio. The *Siglufjördur* was back on the air, saying they could see Father's boat dimly through the heavy snow. It was listing[3] badly, and they were hurrying to get to them on time.

"Eric," his mother called. "Come. Coffee time."

Eric didn't even answer. He couldn't leave his radio and telegraph set now. Kris, his sister, came bursting into the room just as he was getting the last of the message from the *Siglufjördur*.

"Shh," Eric said. He wanted to know how badly Father's boat was listing.

Kris didn't realize this was important, that this was a time she should keep still. Impatiently she said, "Eric, coffee time!"

"Please keep still," he said in a low voice. "There's a boat in trouble."

"Boat in trouble" was enough to make a girl in a fisherman's family keep still. She left the room and in a few minutes was back with a drapa bread sandwich, some pickled herring, and a glass of milk. Without saying

---

3 list: lean over on its side in the water

a word, she set everything on the worktable where he could reach it when he had time.

Over the homemade set came the message, "Won't inflate." That must mean that at least one of the rubber lifeboats was useless. Father carried four on his boat.

Mother rapped at the door lightly, pushed it open, and came in. Between messages she asked Eric, "Is Father's boat in trouble?"

Eric nodded, only half listening—another set of dots and dashes was coming in.

"There must be trouble; it must be dangerous if Father is using that dot-and-dash set. What's the matter with his radio?"

Eric, too, wished he knew what was wrong with Father's radio, but he couldn't explain just then. With Mother looking over his shoulder, he translated the dot-and-dash combinations into words. Mother could see for herself: "Lifeline ready."

"Lifeline. Oh!" She turned away. All her life she had known what using the lifeline meant. Her father had been a fisherman, and his father before him. The lifeline was the fisherman's last resort. Mother pressed her hand against her mouth to stifle any sounds. Straight, stiff, and tense, she stood behind Eric's chair, gripping it so tightly that her knuckles showed white and sharp. Kris was silently listening, waiting too.

The first time there was a lull, Eric turned and told them what he knew—the *Siglufjördur* was near Father's boat and standing by to help. He didn't tell her the boat was listing badly and that at least one of the lifeboats was useless. But Mother was a true fisherman's wife; she had to be brave, just as brave as the men on the boat.

The clicking sounds came in again. The third life raft had been swept off the deck by a big wave. The third life raft! Eric didn't write that message out. There was only one lifeboat left—one twenty-four-man boat for a crew of twenty-eight men! And the unbreakable rule of the sea was that the captain was the last to leave his boat.

More dots and dashes. The life gun was set up, preparing to shoot it toward the *Siglufjördur*. Mother paced up and down across the floor in Eric's room. Eric himself was tense and nervous, but for Mother's sake he tried to be calm.

"Don't worry, Mother. You know Father is good at shooting a lifeline."

Even though they both knew that, Eric felt apprehensive. If the boat was listing more and more, as the *Siglufjördur* had reported, there wouldn't be time for more than one shot. Father would have to gauge this strong wind with its unexpected gale force gusts. The waves would be high. At times probably the boat would be between two high crests of waves and neither boat could see the other one.

Then a loud voice came over the receiver from the *Siglufjördur:* "Lifeline received; we're fastening it."

Mother sank down onto the bed with relief. But there was no relief for Eric. He knew there were twenty-eight men with only one lifeboat. Was there time for two trips across? He was afraid not.

"We see the boat coming. It's very full."

Mother was breathing heavily. Eric sat tense and stiff, and Kris paced up and down in the hallway.

"The boat is really crowded. Many of the men are holding the lifeline. They are coming fast because they are pulling the boat along the lifeline!"

Eric could picture them—massive, strong hands tightly grasping the lifeline above them. Could all twenty-eight men have gotten into the boat if half of them lifted themselves on the line and hoisted the boat along? The silence in the room almost hurt. Eric pushed the jars of acid back on his table. He wouldn't need them again. He pulled the radio receiver nearer, as if that would bring Father closer. Suddenly the voice spoke again: "All the men from the *Husavik* are in the lifeboat. We've counted twenty-eight heads. We put our rope ladder over the side for them. They're all safe, and barely in time too."

Eric sank back into his chair, his tense muscles slowly relaxing. On the bed, Mother burst into grateful tears.

Late that night Father sat at the kitchen table with a mug of steaming coffee. He looked at his family, sitting with him. "Now I suppose you want the whole story." All three of them nodded.

"Well." Father paused, wearily pushing his hair back from his face. "It was late this afternoon. The wind had been picking up, and the waves were coming high. But we were all right until a big wave smashed into us.

Not just big—it was a mountain. Snapped the main mast and rammed us against a rock. We knew we were in trouble—the boat was taking on water, and we weren't sure how much time we had.

"Of course, I wanted Karl to radio for help right away. But he couldn't—when the boat had lurched, it threw Karl off balance so that he fell and hit his head on the table."

Father paused, sipped his coffee. "Well, things just kept right on happening. Karl banging against the table upset the microphone and knocked it over; it rolled off the table and out the door of the operator's cabin—and there it was washed away. The only thing we had left was the set Eric had given me for Christmas. There was nothing to do but use it, and hope and pray he would be listening."

He glanced at Eric, a smile brightening his haggard face. "How does it feel to know that the set you made me saved our lives?"

Eric grinned. He didn't need to answer.

Your Place

Is your place a small place?
Tend it with care!—
He set you there.

Is your place a large place?
Guard it with care!—
He set you there.

Whate'er your place, it is
Not yours alone, but His
Who set you there.

– John Oxenham

John Oxenham (1852-1941) was an English publisher,
poet, and novelist. His real name was William Arthur
Dunkerly; he used John Oxenham as a pseudonym
when he began to write. His works include over forty
novels and several volumes of prose and poetry.

Stooping
Gracefully

"When pride cometh, then cometh shame: but with the lowly is wisdom."
– Proverbs 11:2

Stoop!

Author Unknown

When he was young, Benjamin Franklin visited Cotton Mather, the Massachusetts minister. They spoke for a while, and when the interview was over, Cotton Mather showed Benjamin Franklin out of the house by a back way. As they were walking through a low narrow passage, the minister said to Franklin, "Stoop! Stoop!"

Franklin did not immediately understand the meaning of the advice, until he took another step and smacked his head sharply against a beam projecting over the passage.

"My lad," said the old minister, "you are young, and the world is before you; learn to stoop as you go through it, and you will save yourself many a hard thump."

This is not an easy lesson to learn: to stoop gracefully and at the right time.

When another young person stands before you in a **passion**—fuming and foaming—even though you know he is both unreasonable and wrong, it is folly to stand just as **rigid**, and stamp just as hard, and talk just as loud as he does. This only places two madmen face-to-face.

Stoop, as you would if a tornado were passing. It is no disgrace to stoop before a heavy wind. It makes just as much sense to bellow back at a mad bull as it does to answer a madman's **ravings** by raving in return. Stoop gracefully and, amid the pauses of the wind, throw in the soft words that turn away wrath.

When you are **reproved** for an error you have committed, for a wrong you have done, or for being neglectful, stoop! Do not try to **justify** or excuse your faults. Justifying yourself only increases your wrong and excites greater wrath against you. Stoop!

If you say mildly, "I know I was wrong; forgive me," you have stolen away all your enemy's thunder. One time, a friend came to me, his face black with frowns and with fury all bottled up inside, ready for an explosion because I had broken a promise I had made to him. I foresaw the storm. I took his hand in mine as he approached, simply saying, "I am very sorry; I forgot. Pardon me this time." What could the man say? He kept the cork in the bottle, and I escaped a terrible blast.

How much more easily and pleasantly we should get through life if we knew how and when to stoop!

However, when you are tempted to do something mean or wrong—when you are encouraged by your companions or by circumstances to do evil—then don't stoop! Give up your rights when you should. Give up "coat and cloak" to an unjust demand. Stoop in silence when you are treated unjustly. But never stoop to sin.

Mother to Son

Well, son, I'll tell you:
Life for me ain't been no crystal stair,
It's had tacks in it,
And splinters,
And boards torn up,
And places with no carpet on the floor—
Bare.
But all the time
I'se been a-climbin' on,
And reachin' landin's.
And turnin' corners,
And sometimes goin' in the dark
Where there ain't been no light.

So boy, don't you turn back.
Don't you set down on the steps
'Cause you finds it kinder hard.
Don't you fall now—
For I'se still goin', honey,
I'se still climbin',
And life for me ain't been no crystal stair.

– Langston Hughes

James Mercer Langston Hughes (1902-1967) was one of the most famous black poets and writers in the world. He was raised by his mother and grandmother, and much of his poetry expresses the black experience in America. He also wrote several books and plays, and was a newspaper correspondent during the Spanish Civil War.

"Behold, I have given you every herb bearing seed, which is upon the face of all the earth, and every tree, in the which is the fruit of a tree yielding seed; to you it shall be for meat." – Genesis 1:29

The Peanut Man and the Peanut Men

Part 1

Lawrence Elliot

The boll weevil is a dark, greedy little creature less than a quarter of an inch long. It feeds on the cotton plant and then **infests** it with millions of microscopic eggs. Around 1892 the boll weevil slipped into Texas from Mexico, and in the next twenty-five years, it laid waste field after cotton field across the South. Yearly crop damages soon exceeded $100 million, and no one can say how many families were blighted. By 1915, many southern farmers could not even pay their taxes.

This was just the type of problem George Washington Carver liked to solve. Dr. Carver was a teacher at the Tuskegee Institute in Tuskegee, Alabama.

"Burn off your infested cotton!" he encouraged cotton farmers wherever he went. "Plant peanuts!"

But no one listened. "Plant peanuts?" snorted a grizzled old sharecropper in response to Carver's pleas. "What for? Cotton's important—it makes clothes; everybody needs clothes! But peanuts! Why, give me 120 acres and I'll grow you enough peanuts for the whole state of Alabama!"

It was quite true. At the time, peanuts were a child's treat. Carver had not at first given much thought to finding other uses for peanuts; he only knew they were a nutritious food and that growing them would restore soils damaged by greedy farming.

Carver began to promote the peanut. He wrote farm bulletins that gave peanut recipes and the best methods for growing and harvesting peanuts, and lectured about peanuts. Slowly, pushed by the weevil and pulled by Carver, people began to plant peanuts. Here and there, in 20- and 40-acre fields, the velvety plant blossomed with tiny white flowers. Soon peanuts were the number one crop from Montgomery, Alabama, to the Florida border.

However, there was one problem. There were tons of peanuts but still not many uses for them. Carver made a short trip through the southern farmlands, where he saw barns and storehouses piled high with peanuts. He saw surplus peanuts rotting in the fields. He knew what he needed to do; he went for a walk in the woods.

In the woods, Carver had a conversation with the One who could solve any problem. As Carver told it later, that conversation went like this:

"Oh, Mr. Creator, why did You make this universe?"

The Creator answered, "You want to know too much for that little mind of yours."

"Well, dear Mr. Creator, what was man made for?"

"You are still asking for more than you can handle," the answer came.

Then I asked my last question, "Mr. Creator, why did You make the peanut?"

"That's better!" said the Lord, and He gave me a handful of peanuts and went with me back to the laboratory, and together we got down to work!

Carver began experimenting with peanuts. He ground, pressed, and heated them, discovering freely flowing peanut oil. He analyzed the elements of the peanut and found bundles of energy. He developed peanut butter, peanut ink, and peanut dyes. He made paper from peanut skins and soil conditioners from peanut hulls.

Quickly an industry grew up around the peanut. Within four years, the once-despised goober was putting money into the pockets of near-desperate southern farmers. Things went well until after World War I, when a new problem developed. Chinese peanut growers had begun to ship about thirty million bushels of peanuts a year to America. Thirty million bushels—half the amount of peanuts the country used. The Chinese might squeeze American farmers right out of the peanut business! The problem had become so serious that the United States Congress was going to consider placing a **tariff** on peanuts shipped from other countries.

In September 1920, the members of the United Peanut Association of America scheduled a meeting to discuss how they could convince Congress to do something about the Chinese peanuts. Some men wanted Dr. Carver, a black man, to address the meeting. The white farmers and businessmen heatedly debated whether or not to have Dr. Carver come and tell them about the things he had done with the peanut.

"If we need a Negro to tell us how to run our business, then we're in the wrong business," one Georgia farmer growled.

But most of the growers knew that Carver had practically created their business. He knew more about the peanut than anyone else. So they invited him, and early on Tuesday, September 14, he stepped off the train in Montgomery, Alabama, and asked the way to the Exchange Hotel, where the meeting was being held.

It was a brutally hot day. A glaring sun beat down on Carver as he walked along Jefferson Davis Avenue, his shoulders bent and his arms pulled taut by the weight of the suitcases he carried, each packed with specimen bottles.

Carver arrived at the hotel, and the doorman told him that the peanut men were over at City Hall. Dr. Carver slowly turned back downtown, his coat dark with sweat. At the City Hall he asked for the Peanut Association meeting and was led from office to office, until at last someone said that the Peanut Association was meeting at the Exchange Hotel, not at City Hall! He picked up his heavy cases and again went out into the searing heat. By now it was nearly midday.

Back at the hotel, the doorman refused to let Dr. Carver in. "Sorry, old uncle," he said, "no colored are allowed in here."

Carver set his cases down on the sidewalk, trembling with fatigue and frustration. There was no point in arguing. Finally he said, "My name is Carver, and I am expected at the United Peanut Association meeting. Would you be kind enough to tell them that I am waiting here?"

The doorman whispered to the bellboy. Together they snickered at the sad old figure and his battered suitcases. But eventually, the bellboy went inside. After a while, he returned and led Carver around to a service entrance to the hotel. Outside the meeting room, someone stopped Carver again and told him that the peanut men were just starting their lunch.

He would have to wait.

Years later, when Carver recalled this experience, he said it would have been very easy for him to simply pick up his cases and leave. "I am human, and this is what every instinct urged me to do. But as I stood there in the hallway, with people pushing by me as though I did not exist, God reminded me that I had not come all the way to Montgomery to pamper my personal feelings. I had not come to contribute to the wealth of the businessmen and big planters in that meeting room. I had come to help the thousands of sandy-land farmers I had persuaded to get into peanuts in the first place, and this organization was their instrument too."

It was nearly 2:00 p.m. before Carver was introduced to the assembly. Suddenly, the air was stiffly silent, but there wasn't a hint of resentment in Carver's manner as he opened his suitcases and tried to establish contact with his audience.

"Your Montgomery heat is hard on people," he said lightly, "but I hope you won't complain, since it is excellent for growing peanuts."

A few smiles broke out in the sea of lifeless faces. He addressed himself directly to the smiles. Soon he could feel the rest listening, his words changing their hostility to interest.

He showed them bottles containing leather and wood stains made from peanuts: tan and russet, black and green and blue. Here was soap, shaving lotion, and face powder; candy, and milk products ranging from ice cream to cheese. He told them that while one hundred pounds of cow's milk made ten pounds of cheese, the same amount of peanut milk made more than twenty.

The planters were soon wide-eyed, hanging on Dr. Carver's words. When he finished, the room rang with applause.

Men crowded forward. "It's hard to believe—all that from peanuts!" Some of the men even thought to thank Carver for his presentation. There was more applause, and then the planters clapped each other on the back and expressed their determination to fight for a tariff to protect the American peanut!

In the tumult and confusion that followed, Dr. Carver quietly put his bottles away, hefted his suitcases, and walked out. Scuffing along the hot, airless street as quickly as he could, he just caught the 4:00 p.m. train back to Tuskegee.

But the peanut men had not forgotten him. Alabama congressman Henry B. Steagall suggested that Dr. Carver should appear before the United States Congress when they discussed whether or not to charge the Chinese a tariff for their peanuts. Early in January, Carver received a telegram:

We want you in Washington, morning of 20th. Depending on you to show the Ways and Means Committee possibilities of peanut.

Carver wrote back that he would come, then he went back to his normal duties. For days, the dining hall at Tuskegee buzzed with the news that their Professor Carver would stand before Congress! The other teachers began to nag Carver about his clothes. His best suit was still the one his friends had bought for him twenty-eight years ago. "Surely you're not going to wear that to Washington!"

They repeatedly badgered him on this point, until Carver finally said, "Now look here! If it's a new suit the congressmen want to see, I can send them one in a box. But if it's me, why, I think they'll take me dressed as I am."

The Peanut Man and the Peanut Men

Part 2

Lawrence Elliot

Dr. Carver arrived, in his old suit, in Washington on Thursday, January 20 and went directly to the hearings in the House of Representatives building. Peanut Association officials were already on hand and very glad to see him! Different growers' associations had already presented arguments why the government should protect their products with tariffs.

The room rang with shouts and arguments. The congressmen were tired, irritated with the witnesses and with each other. Peanuts had not even been scheduled for discussion yet.

Carver listened for a while, and then, to the horror of the peanut growers, he left his cases in their care and said he would come back later. He went outside and found a taxi. He asked to be taken to the National Zoological Garden, where he walked slowly along, engrossed by the miracle of growth. He ran his fingers over the shrubs. All thoughts of the fight over peanut protection vanished.

He came upon an unusual Chinese arborvitae plant discolored with a rusty fungus. Kneeling on the damp winter earth, he searched the underside of the bush until he found what he was looking for. Then he called an attendant and pointed out a **parasite** growing on the plant. He explained how to treat it.

The matter of peanuts was not brought before the Ways and Means Committee that day, nor the following morning. The hearing room grew stuffy, and ragged tempers flared. By mid-afternoon, the Peanut

Association people were rigid with nervous agony. "We'll be lucky to get half an hour," one groaned. "We're sunk!"

"Somebody had better tell Carver what to say," urged Congressman Steagall.

"What's the use? It's too late."

It was past 4:00 p.m. when the first peanut spokesman was allowed to speak. The meeting was set to end at 5:00.

"Gentlemen, I'll try to be brief," the spokesman began.

"Please do!" retorted John Garner, the weary congressman from Texas.

The spokesman pleaded the Peanut Association's cause and was answered with a **brusque** "Yes, we'll consider it. Any other witnesses?"

The clerk called George W. Carver. Every head snapped around. Eyes gaped at the spectacle of the gray-haired black man in his worn suit, a sprig of arborvitae in his lapel, lugging two heavy suitcases toward the speaker's stand.

In the sudden hush, someone snickered, "Reckon if he gets enough peanuts to go with his watermelon, he'll be a right happy coon."

Carver heard it, but he had heard worse. When he reached the stand and began unpacking his cases, Chairman Fourdney said, "I think, considering how late it already is, that we can only allow you ten minutes."

Carver's heart sank. It would take ten minutes to gain their attention! He went on unpacking the bottles, groping for a way to begin.

"What do you know about the tariff?" Mr. Garner from Texas called out.

"Not a thing. I came to talk about peanuts!"

There was a ripple of laughter. Some congressmen sat up. Carver took a deep breath, held up a handful of chocolate-covered peanuts and said, "You don't know how delicious these are, so I will taste them for you." The congressmen laughed heartily.

He had their attention. Now if he only had some time.

"I am engaged in agricultural research and have given some attention to the peanut. It is one of the richest products of the soil. I'm just going to touch on a few highlights, because in ten minutes you'll tell me to stop. Here are a few products we've developed from the peanut. Here is a breakfast food developed from peanuts and sweet potato."

"What is that other stuff?" the committee chairman asked.

"Ice cream powder, here. Here, dyes made from the skin of peanuts. I have developed thirty different dyes from peanuts. This is a substitute for quinine, the drug that fights malaria. Peanuts can also provide various foods for livestock. Cattle fed on peanuts increase their milk production.

"I have several dozen other products here, but I see that my time is about up. Let me only say that the soil and climate of the South are particularly suited to growing peanuts. It would be a great pity if this crop were lost to us, and we came to depend on inferior foreign peanuts. Thank you," Carver concluded.

"Mr. Chairman," spoke up Mr. Garner from Texas. "All this is very interesting. I think his time should be extended."

"Very well," said the chairman. "Gentlemen, do you all agree?"

"Yes. Yes," several voices shouted.

"Will you continue, Mr. Carver? Your time is unlimited."

So Dr. Carver proceeded.

"Here is milk from peanuts. Here is instant coffee, which already has cream and sugar in it. Here is buttermilk made from peanuts, and meat sauce, pickles—"

"Did you make all those products yourself?" the chairman asked.

"Yes, sir," Carver answered. "I have developed 107 products made from sweet potatoes, and peanuts are going to beat the sweet potato by far. Here are oysters. I have made delicious meats from peanuts."

"So peanuts will put the livestock industry out of business!" quipped Congressman Rainey.

"No, sir. But peanuts can be eaten when meat can't. Peanuts are the perfect food. They are always safe."[1]

"Where did you learn all this?" asked Congressman Barkley.

"From a book."

"What book?"

"The Bible," Dr. Carver answered. "It says that God has given us everything for our use. In the first chapter of Genesis we are told, 'Behold, I have given you every herb that bears seed upon the face of the earth, and

---

1 Today, it is known that there are a few people who are allergic to peanuts. For them, peanuts are *not* safe.

every tree bearing seed. To you it shall be for meat.' There is everything there to strengthen, nourish, and keep the body alive and healthy."

"Mr. Carver, please go on," the chairman requested.

And he did. For nearly two hours he held the committee spellbound with his display of peanut products, his occasional stories, and kind humor.

When he had finished, Congressman Carew said, "You have rendered this committee a great service."

Every member rose and applauded vigorously. Someone called out, "Come again—and bring your other products with you!"

Later, the congressmen asked Dr. Carver to submit a summary of his presentation. This he did, closing his summary with these words:

"I have nothing to sell. I manufacture nothing. And I feel sure you gentlemen will put proper restrictions on every interest that arises in harmful competition with ours, without any suggestions of mine."

But the fact was that his presentation had persuaded the congressmen. The following year, Congress passed the Fordney-McCumber tariff bill, placing a tariff of three cents a pound on all unshelled, **imported** peanuts and four cents a pound on all shelled peanuts.

For a long time afterward, whenever Congressman Steagall told this story, he would always conclude by saying, "And to think, I wanted them to tell Dr. Carver what to say!"

"For he that is called in the Lord, being a servant, is the Lord's freeman: likewise also he that is called, being free, is Christ's servant." – 1 Corinthians 7:22

Escape From Slavery

Frederick Douglass

You mustn't expect me to tell you much about my family. A slave does not receive a genealogical tree from his master. In fact, I never met a slave from the part of Maryland where I lived who could tell me the exact day he was born. From the events I now know, I suppose I was born sometime in February 1817.

I remember my grandmother, who was held in high esteem by everyone. She was a good nurse, a famous fisherwoman, and an expert gardener. She was granted the privilege—I don't know why—of living in her own cabin, separate from the slaves' quarters; and it is life in that cabin that forms my first memories.

I only remember my mother from a few hasty visits that she made in the night, when she came on foot many miles to see me, to hold me just for a few minutes in the dark night before she had to flee home again to answer the driver's call to the early morning fieldwork. I had been taken from her when I was a baby so that we would not develop the strong ties that bind a family together and cause them to love their homes. Such was the nature of slavery.

Of my father I know nothing. Slavery did not recognize fathers or families. My mother was a slave—so I was a slave. My father might have been a white man, glorying in the purity of his Anglo-Saxon blood, but I was ranked with the blackest of slaves. Father he might be, but he would not be a husband to my mother, and he would sell his own child without a thought, if in its veins coursed one drop of African blood.

Grandmother's little cabin was like a palace to me, and for many years, I did not even know I was a slave. Like most children, I played, thought, and felt, charmed by the wonders and mysteries of life.

It was not long, however, before I learned that this house did not belong to dear Grandmother, but to someone I had never seen. I learned too the sadder fact that not only the house and land, but Grandmother herself and all the little children around her belonged to a mysterious person called "Old Master." And so, early, clouds and shadows began to fall on my path.

I soon learned that this old master only allowed the little children to live with Grandmother for a limited time, and that as soon as they were big enough, they were promptly taken away to live with the master. When the time came that I must go, Grandmother, knowing my fears, kindly kept me ignorant of the dreaded moment up to the morning (a beautiful summer morning) when we were to start. In fact, she kept the unwelcome truth from me through the whole twelve-mile journey.

It was afternoon when we reached the journey's end, and I suddenly found myself in the midst of a group of children of all sizes and many colors—black, brown, copper-colored, and nearly white. I had not before seen so many children. After laughing and yelling around me, the children asked me to go and play with them. I refused. Grandmother looked so sad, and I could not help feeling that our being there boded no good for me.

She affectionately patted me on the head and told me to be a good boy and go out and play with the other children. "They are kin to you." She pointed out to me my brother Perry and my sisters Sarah and Eliza. Brother and sisters they were to me, but slavery had made us strangers!

I really wanted to play with them, but I was full of fear that my grandmother might leave for home without taking me with her. Entreated to do so by Grandmother, however, I went to the back of the house to play with them, standing with my back against the wall watching the others play. At last, one of the children who had been in the kitchen ran up to me in **roguish** glee and exclaimed, "Fed! Fed! Grandmama gone!"

I ran into the kitchen to see, fearing the worst, and lo! She was indeed gone, clean out of sight. I fell upon the ground and wept a boy's bitter tears, refusing to be comforted. I had never been deceived before, and something of resentment mingled with my grief at parting with my grandmother, until I finally sobbed myself to sleep.

This was my introduction to the realities of the slave system.

Soon I was introduced to more. I was among the children left in the tender care of a certain "Aunt Katy." Ambitious of the old master's favor, ill-tempered and cruel by nature, Aunt Katy found many opportunities in her position to exercise her best qualities.

Lack of food was my chief trouble during my first summer there. The overseer allowed Aunt Katy to divide the food among the children as she saw fit. As cruel as Aunt Katy was, she did not lack motherly feeling, and it was her instinct to satisfy her own children's hunger before she gave food to the rest of us. She was frequently guilty of starving me. I was often so pinched with hunger that I disputed with old Nep, the dog, for the crumbs which fell from the kitchen table. Many times I followed, with eager step, the waiting-girl when she shook out the tablecloth, so that I could get the crumbs and small bones thrown out for the dogs and cats.

One time I offended Aunt Katy. I do not remember the offense, but she adopted her usual method of punishing me—namely, she made me go all day without food. As the day wore on, I found it impossible to keep up my spirits. Sundown came, with still no food. While she sliced heavy pieces of evening bread for the other children, Aunt Katy muttered savage threats against me. It was too much; I went out behind the kitchen and cried like a fine fellow.

At last, wearied of crying, I returned to sit by the fire. I was too hungry to sleep. While I sat in the corner, my eye caught sight of an ear of Indian corn on a shelf. I quietly shelled off a few grains and put the ear back. I placed the grains in the hot ashes to roast. When they were done, I eagerly pulled my roasted grains from the ashes and placed them in a little pile on the stool. I began to help myself, when who should appear but my own dear mother, who had come to snatch a few moments with her children.

I do not have the power to describe for you what happened then. I found myself in the strong, protecting arms of my mother. I told her of Katy's threat to starve the life out of me and saw the deep, tender pity arise in her face. She took the corn from me and in its place gave me a large ginger cake, and then gave Katy a lecture that was never forgotten. That night I learned that I was not only a child, I was *somebody's* child. I was grander upon my mother's knee than a king upon his throne.

But my triumph was short. I fell asleep on my mother's lap and awoke in the morning to her gone; and I was once again at the mercy of the Fury in my master's kitchen.

That night my mother had walked twelve miles to see me. She had the same distance to travel home again before the morning sunrise took her back into the fields to work. I do not remember seeing her ever again. Her death ended the little communication we had. To me it has always been a grief that I knew my mother so little and have so few of her words treasured in my memory.

I was not more than thirteen years old, when, in my loneliness and destitution, I really began to long for someone to whom I could go as to a father and protector. Through the preaching of a white Methodist minister, I discovered that in God I had such a friend. He said that all men, great and small, bond and free, were sinners in God's sight and must repent of their sins and be reconciled to God. For weeks I was a poor, brokenhearted mourner traveling through doubts and fears. But I finally found my burden lightened and my heart relieved.

Suddenly I loved all mankind, including slaveholders, though I **abhorred** slavery more than ever. I saw the world in a new light, and my great concern was to see everybody converted. My desire to learn increased. I gathered scattered pages of the Bible from the filthy street gutters, and washed and dried them, that in moments of leisure I might get a word or two of wisdom from them.

I became acquainted with a good old colored man named Charles Lawson. He prayed as he walked through the streets, at his work, on his dray—everywhere. His life was a life of prayer. Uncle Lawson became my spiritual father, and I loved him intensely.

I worked now and prayed with a light heart, believing that my life was under God's guidance. With all the other blessings I sought at His mercy seat, I prayed that God would someday deliver me from my bondage.

The years passed. I endured whippings and abuse. I was sold to another master, who employed me in his shipyards in Baltimore, where I learned to know ships from stem to stern and to talk and act like a sailor.

And then, at last, in 1838, my bondage ended. This is how it happened.

In those days the state of Maryland required free colored people to carry free papers at all times. These papers gave the name, age, color, height, and form of the free man, along with any scars or other marks on him that could further assist in his identification. Of course, more than one man could answer to the same general description given in the papers.

I did not closely resemble anyone I knew who had gained his freedom, but I had a friend at the time—a sailor—who owned a sailor's protection. This is something like free papers. It describes the owner's person and certifies that he is a free American sailor. At the head of the sailor's paper is a great American eagle, which gives it the appearance of an authorized document. I would take my friend's paper and flee by train to the shipyards of New York City.

My friend's paper did not describe me at all. It called for a much darker man than I, and close examination would have led to my immediate arrest. To avoid being scrutinized by a railroad agent upon boarding, I arranged with my friend to bring my baggage to the train just at the moment the train started off. I jumped upon the car as it was already moving.

The train was jostling and crowded, and the conductor was in a great haste to make his way through the crammed aisles. Though I was not a murderer fleeing from justice, I felt quite as miserable as such a criminal. The train was moving at high speed, but to my anxious mind it was moving far too slowly. Minutes were hours, and hours were days.

One thing was in my favor. In those days, a kind feeling toward sailors prevailed in all of Baltimore. I was wearing sailor's clothes, and possessed with my knowledge of sailing, I prepared myself to face the conductor—who would surely ask for my freedom papers.

Frederick Douglass (1817?-1895) was born in slavery, the son of a slave and a white father. In 1838, he escaped to the North, where he became famous for anti-slavery speeches. For two years he lived in Great Britain, earning money to buy his freedom. He founded *The North Star*, an abolitionist newspaper, and published it for seventeen years. In 1845 he wrote his autobiography, *A Narrative of the Life of Frederick Douglass*, from which "Escape From Slavery" is taken.

We were well under way when the conductor came into the Negro car to collect tickets and examine the papers of the black passengers. The critical moment had come. My whole future rested on the conductor. In a harsh and impatient tone, he examined the colored passengers before me. At last, he reached me.

Suddenly, his whole manner changed. Seeing that I did not readily produce my free papers, he said to me in a friendly way, "I suppose you have your free papers?"

"No, sir," I answered. "A sailor rarely carries his free papers to sea!"

"But you have something to show you are a free man, have you not?"

"I have a paper with an American eagle on it that will carry me around the world!"

With that I withdrew from my pocket the seaman's protection. The conductor hardly glanced at it, took my fare, and went on about his business.

But I was not yet out of danger. In fact, in the course of my escape from slavery, two men I knew crossed my path—Captain McGowan, for whom I had worked only a few days before, and a German blacksmith I knew well. Captain McGowan was traveling south on another train, and the two trains stopped so that he and I sat just across from each other for a moment. If the captain had looked over at me, he surely would have recognized me. The blacksmith was on my train. He looked at me intently as if he thought he had seen me before. I suspect he knew me, but had no heart to betray me. At any rate, neither of these meetings led to my arrest.

In the afternoon of that day, my train reached the Quaker city, Philadelphia. There I caught another train, bound for New York. The following morning I arrived there. In less than twenty-four hours, I had completed my journey and arrived at the end of my experience as a slave.

"And whosoever shall compel thee to go a mile, go with him twain."
– Matthew 5:41

The Second Mile

Betty Steele Everett

Marcus trudged along the dusty Judean road, trying not to look at the blazing sun that seemed to be concentrating all of its heat on his head.

"Why can't you find one of those worthless Jews when you want him to carry your pack?" grumbled his friend Gaulus. "I don't like lugging all this weight in the hot sun!"

Marcus shook his head. They had looked for some Jewish men to carry their packs before they started, but had seen none.

"Wait a minute," Gaulus said as he wiped the sweat from his forehead. "I think two are coming now."

Marcus glanced behind him—the two figures were obviously Jewish. "But they're hardly more than boys, Gaulus!"

"If their precious temple considers them men, so do I," laughed Gaulus. "Here!" He motioned to the two. "Over here!"

Marcus had been recently transferred to this area from Rome and had not learned much of the local language yet, but he knew enough to order one of them to carry his pack for the single mile Roman soldiers were allowed to demand of the conquered Jews.

The older of the two boys glared at Gaulus, but he picked up the pack. The other boy glanced at Marcus and then took the gear.

Marcus knew that the Jews would not speak to them as they walked—something about **defiling** themselves if they spoke to a Roman. Well, he thought, he and Gaulus didn't need conversation; they only needed their packs carried in this hot sun.

Without the weight of his pack, Marcus swung into his usual long strides. He knew it was hard for the Jewish boys to keep up, but Gaulus winked and matched him stride for stride.

The marker in the road showing the end of the mile came quickly—

too quickly. Gaulus spit at it. Under no circumstances were the soldiers allowed to order their packs carried by these men for another mile.

"There, Roman!" The older boy threw down Gaulus's pack and turned on his heel before Gaulus could reach for it.

Marcus waited for the other boy to throw down his pack too, but instead the younger boy said something to him in his own tongue. Marcus was not sure what all the words meant, but the intent was clear; the boy was offering to carry his pack another mile.

"No!" Marcus said. "No! Your mile is up!" He reached for his pack. If he were reported for making a Jew carry his load a second mile, he would be lashed severely.

The Jewish boy pulled the pack away from Marcus. "I'll take it another mile—for the Messiah."

"Messiah!" Marcus looked at Gaulus, who had lived here for several years.

His friend shrugged. "It's a long story. He means a Jew named Jesus who stirred up a lot of trouble. Pilate had to put Him to death. The Jews themselves demanded it, although Pilate never thought this Jesus was much of a criminal. Some of His followers were saying He was the Messiah—the King of the Jews—but He died on the cross like any other thief, except for not lasting as long and not swearing or cursing at us. In fact, I heard that He asked His God to forgive us."

"But if He's dead, why do they still think He's the Messiah?" Marcus asked. He knew only a little about the Jewish belief that someday a savior would come to them. "Isn't the Messiah supposed to rule over them? A dead man can't rule much!"

Gaulus laughed. "They believe the Messiah will get rid of us, but we're still here. When He was put into a tomb, His followers came at night and stole the body. Some of our troops that were guarding the tomb fell asleep. If I had been on duty, they wouldn't have taken the body! Now His followers are saying that He rose from the dead!"

"Rose from the dead after a Roman crucifixion?" Marcus was **incredulous**. "No one could do that! But what does that have to do with carrying my pack another mile?"

"Once, when He was talking to the people, this Jesus—He was from Nazareth and was a carpenter—told them that if we commanded them to carry our gear a mile, they should carry it another one," Gaulus answered. "No one I know has ever met one who did it though! Go on, let him take it. I'll swear you didn't force him!"

The older boy was back now, arguing with his brother. At last he turned to the soldiers. Marcus understood what he was saying. "My brother is crazy! He thinks Jesus rose from the dead and that because He commanded us to carry your packs an extra mile, he should do it. I will not! But my brother is crazy! He wants to carry it."

Marcus frowned. It could be a trick, something these two had thought up to get the Roman soldiers in trouble with their centurion. But the boy was starting to walk on now, carrying the pack, so there was nothing to do but walk.

"You're the lucky one," Gaulus grumbled. "Why couldn't I have gotten the one who wanted to go another mile? Wait'll we tell them in the barracks tonight about this! No one has ever had a Jew carry his pack a second mile."

Suddenly Marcus understood. "It is a trick! Not the usual kind though. Don't you see? If he carries it for me because he wants to, I have lost my power over him! My orders to carry it are no good; he's carrying it because he wants to!"

"All I know is you're getting yours carried and I'm not," Gaulus complained.

Marcus looked at the boy again. He was panting, and his face was red from the **exertion** in the hot sun.

"Halt!" Marcus ordered. He got his pack from the boy and took out the water bottle. He tilted it, letting the warm water run into his mouth, watching the boy all the time. The Jew's eyes were wide, and his tongue ran over dry lips as he heard the water gurgle in Marcus's throat.

Gaulus took out his own bottle, tipping it so that the water ran into the dust at his feet.

"Here!" Marcus suddenly thrust his water at the boy. He looked at Marcus with frightened eyes, and his older brother spoke quickly to him.

Marcus was not sure what was said, but the younger boy shook his head. Then he reached for the water, still watching Marcus **warily**. He held it so his lips did not touch the bottle, then let a little water run into his mouth. He swished it around, then spit it out.

"What's wrong with you," Gaulus demanded, "letting an **accursed** Jew drink your water?"

"He is carrying my pack for me," Marcus said. "I owe him something for that since I didn't order him to."

As they went on, Marcus looked back at the brothers. He wished he could talk to them, especially the younger one. He wondered about this man Jesus who had told them that they should carry a heavy Roman pack two miles.

"Come here!" he called to the one with the pack. The boy approached slowly and cautiously.

Marcus was not sure that the boy would understand his questions; but these Jews, he had been told, sometimes pretended ignorance even when they understood every word.

"Who is Jesus?" Marcus demanded.

"The Messiah," the boy said quickly. "He rose from the dead."

The older brother, who had overheard, began to argue loudly. Gaulus laughed and said, "I told you most of them don't believe it."

The boy with the pack said no more, so Marcus ordered them onward. But he still wanted to know more about Jesus.

"Here's the end of the second mile," Gaulus said. "Now you'll see him get rid of your gear fast enough!"

But the boy did not throw the pack to the ground, as his brother had done with Gaulus's. Instead, he handed it carefully to Marcus. "Shalom," he said.

As the boys walked away, Marcus stared at them. He was sure that no Jew had ever wished a Roman peace. But then, none had carried a pack longer than a mile, either. It was confusing.

"Let's go," Gaulus said.

Marcus nodded. He shouldered his pack thoughtfully. *I'll find that boy again—when his brother and Gaulus aren't around,* Marcus promised himself. *I'll make him tell me about this Jesus. I want to know his secret for myself.*

"Let another man praise thee, and not thine own mouth; a stranger, and not thine own lips." – Proverbs 27:2

The Rescue

J. Lincoln Steffens

Some of the best newspaper reporters cannot write a sentence correctly. They are not expected to do so. It is their business to collect the facts, which they relate to others who put them in form as a news story.

Something is lost, of course, by this method of secondhand reporting, for the writer cannot reproduce a scene from imagination so well as he could if he had seen it. But the assistants or "reporter's boys," as they are called, are not sent out alone on any incident that promises much importance. Their work is the small news of the day, which is intended only for short paragraphs. That their stories are often interesting enough for longer accounts is due in part to accident; but it is also, sometimes, due to the industry and native intelligence of some of these reporter's boys.

Isaac Hofstein, or Itzig as he was called for short, was such an assistant. He was a child of New York's East Side tenements, and his work was chiefly among his own people, the Jews of the New York Ghetto. Shrewd and accurate, Itzig was always to be trusted to fetch all the facts and to state them correctly. None of the other boys could beat him to a story, and none of the others was so accurate as Itzig. He never failed to get names and addresses, and he never got them wrong.

This devotion to completeness and accuracy made his accounts sometimes a bore, for he brought in details that were of no use. But it was an invaluable trait, of course, and very rare, except among the very best reporters. His work was **libel** proof, and no other paper could go over his investigation and add new particulars to his story. When he came back with a story, he was done. He would sit down with his notes and tell all about the fire, accident, or crime with swift ease and unhesitating confidence.

224

One day, however, there was an exception. He had been to a fire. To cover so commonplace an incident was child's play for him, and something he liked, because he rejoiced in description and the heroic. It was a never failing pleasure to him to discover and celebrate a bold rescue by a policeman, fireman, or neighbor.

"Say, it was great!" he would say, when he came to tell about such a deed. "William J. McGlory, number four truck, twenty-eight years old, Number 17 Cannon Street, he—" Then, laying down his notes, Itzig would reproduce with gestures, grimaces, and language a vivid picture. The **picturesque** details were always as complete as the names, initials, and addresses.

But on this day, while several of us reporters were waiting for his fire story, he was shuffling and hesitating. His sense of "the great" was evidently struggling with some other feeling, and it was impossible to figure out what was the matter.

"It wasn't much, only a two-alarm fire, and it didn't do no damage—to speak of," he said. " 'Twasn't in a good neighborhood either—just a tenement house. Number 16 Essex Street, five-story, red brick, full of families with young'uns—young'uns by the hundreds, eighty-seven of 'em. But you see there was a panic and a—had to—you know how it is when people get a scare trun into 'em!

"Just describe top floor families fleeing by way of the roof to the next house, third- and fourth-floor families cooped up in halls, some of 'em rushing to fire escapes, others too askeered to move, just shriekin' and 'rending their garments,' as the Bible says.

"Across the street," he hurried on, "other 'Motzes' out on fire escapes raised their hands and faces to the sky, crying, *Ei wei! Ei wei!* You know how it is. You can describe it, and I'll give you the names. But the firemen was late, on account of no one knowing how to ring in an alarm. Samuel Bernstein, forty-two years old, Number 16 Essex Street, next door to the fire, tried it first, then—"

"Oh, come to the point!" I interrupted. "What about it?"

"Well, there was a fire rescue. It wasn't very hard either. You see—"

"Give us the name of the rescuer, while you're at it."

"Oh, it was just a fellow passing by ran in and saved some people, mostly children."

"Didn't you get his name?"

"I got the names of them he saved, which was the most important."

"Well, go on."

"The fire," resumed Itzig, "started in the basement, shoemaker shop, Abram Koswingky, thirty-six years old, married, three children, oldest four—do you want names and ages?"

"If they did or suffered anything."

"No, they got out by the rear window, through the area to Number 22, in back. But the flames were just climbing up the stairways. Escape by the front door was cut off when I got there. I happened to be over that way on a crime call and heard the wails, you know. If somebody hadn't helped, we'd have had a big story with a dozen roasted to death. Put in, *Scared, white faces looked out of the windows each second, then disappearing back in the smoke.* It was tough, I tell you. There was a way to get to the third story by the next house. You could climb from one fire escape to the other and get in the window. Inside the flames was cutting the floor in half. A man and woman and two children in the front room were passed out by the time the man came. Their names were—"

"Keep them till afterwards."

"The thing to do was get to the rear rooms, where there was more of 'em. The man—the fellow that had come up to save the whole crew—had to get down and crawl along the floor under the flames, and they licked his back hair off and set his coat on fire. But he got there. And he found two men, three women, and five young'uns huddled in one corner, one woman and two babies unconscious from smoke. The others were getting air by breathing low down on the floor.

"The men had to be made to go down the rear fire escape with the women and jump. This took time, and the flames burst out of the rear, cutting off that way out. So there was the five young'uns. I think the man grabbed two and was going to throw them out to the old people, but they had run away. So he had to go out front.

"He started to run for it; but he was set fire to and had to lie down and roll the flames out and crawl again. The firemen had come, and they caught the young'uns all right. The fireman who caught 'em was Jerry Sullivan, truck eleven, the first there, and—"

"Give us that later."

226

"The fellow sneaked back the same way and got two more. The firemen had a ladder up to take the children. One was left. As he went back for that, he seen the game was up. He had to shake his coat, which was burned, so he whacked it against a wall till it was out, and wrapped the last young'un in it."

"Then came the fun. The flames covered the back of the house and was coming in the window. House full of smoke, floors hot, hallway ablaze, solid, you know. *Hemmed in by fire, babe in arms!* That's the feature of the story! The stairways fell, the hall floor curved, the whole building shook. The fellow thought of a lot of things, but they didn't have anything to do with getting out of that hole. There was an awful crash, then he just sank in a heap."

Itzig wiped his face. The perspiration dampened his handkerchief.

"The next thing the man knew, he was in a drugstore and the fire was out."

"But how did he escape?" asked one of the reporters. "Didn't he go down with the walls when the crash came?"

"No, that part of the house didn't fall, and you see, the firemen knew him. When he didn't show up, they crossed the air well from next door, got through a window, and battered down the door to the room where he was.

"They found him asleep and—a feature of the story is they couldn't get the young'un out of his arms to save the two separately. They had to carry them out together."

The reporters laughed at Itzig. "What's the hero's name?" asked one.

"Oh, he wasn't a hero. He wouldn't have done it if he hadn't started to, being there first. Besides, he didn't save the last child, but had to be rescued himself!"

"Did you interview him?" asked Chapman, who was writing the story.

"No, not much; he didn't want to talk."

"Not even to tell his name?"

Joseph Lincoln Steffens (1866-1936) was born in San Francisco. After studying in Europe, he returned to New York and took up journalism. He edited various magazines and was one of the first "muckrakers," writers who exposed government and business corruption.

"He didn't want to."

"But the firemen, you said they knew him."

"Not very well—only his first name."

"What was that?"

"I didn't ask."

"Didn't ask! You didn't get the most important detail of the whole story! Are you losing your mind?" cried Chapman in amazement.

One of the other men spoke up. "Was his name Isaac?"

Itzig flushed.

"Itzig," said a reporter who had gone behind him, "your hair is all burned off, and your neck is blistered."

"Yes, and you've got your Sunday coat on!"

"Oh, get out!" cried Itzig. "It's so disgusting when you reporters go sticking your noses into other people's affairs!"

"Let us therefore follow after the things which make for peace." – Romans 14:19

Faint Heart

Author Unknown

In 1677 and '78, William Penn helped about eight hundred Quakers escape persecution in England by moving to New Jersey in North America. Then in 1681, Penn obtained a large portion of land in North America as a grant from King Charles II. King Charles named the huge wooded area "Pennsylvania." Many more Quakers left England and moved to Pennsylvania. Some of them, like the brothers in this story, pioneered the way into the wilderness for other Quakers.

Unlike the Scotch Presbyterians, who were also moving to the new land of America, Quakers refused to take up arms and fight. We can imagine the brothers in this story clearing a place in the forest and planting crops in preparation for the Quaker families who would soon join them and form a new "Society of Friends," as the Quakers called themselves.

Candlelight flickered across the faces of the two men talking in the one-room log cabin. Although the brothers were dressed alike in the plain clothes of the Society of Friends and had a strong family resemblance, they nevertheless presented a marked contrast. Miles was only a little older than Henry, but his face already bore lines of care and anxiety. His shoulders drooped slightly. Restlessness mingled with grim determination in his **demeanor**. Henry, though no less determined, still **retained** the eagerness of adventure with which they had set out from England many months ago to seek freedom in a new world.

"We must rise before light tomorrow," Miles was saying, "and go to the upland clearing. Our corn is certainly ready for its first hoeing. That was splendid seed Arrow-in-the-Dark gave thee."

"A fine stand of corn, Miles, and the rain last week came just right for it. But there's a long day's work ahead. Shall we take our dinner with us? We can eat it under the pines by the brook."

"Aye, that is well planned. As the crow flies, it cannot be more than two miles from here, but the way we poor mortals must travel, it seems a long journey indeed. It's a lonely spot. From the bare knoll to the west, one faces a whole new world. Thou know'st the place I mean, Henry?"

"Indian Rock? Aye, 'tis there the braves hold their War Council. Night before last they met, some say a hundred strong, all in war paint and feathers. The village nearby has posted **sentries**, and this morning the men were at work strengthening the stockade, bringing in supplies to stand a **siege**, if necessary. I wish that they might see their mistake in season. Fear breeds fear. If the settlers shared our conviction against violence, the Indians would trust them, as they trust us."

"Thy faith never falters, does it, Henry?"

"Why should it falter? Our dealings with the natives have been acts of friendship, and in return they have given us assistance and helpful advice. Arrow-in-the-Dark told me about planting corn on the ridge above the frost, and what time of moon to plant, after the oak buds opened."

Miles shook his head solemnly and cast a glance toward the open doorway before he replied in a low voice, "Thomas Vinton in the village cautioned me only yesterday against going unarmed to work in the upland. He said that Arrow-in-the-Dark is old in craft and gave us that plot of ground so far from the village to lay a trap for us.

" 'Next moon your scalps may be dangling from Arrow-in-the-Dark's belt, and squaws will take over a corn patch planted and hoed by two white men whose bones the crows are picking. Better go armed,' warned Thomas."

"Cheerful advice, that, but I don't believe a word of it. Arrow-in-the-Dark is a man of honor. I'd trust him as I'd trust thee, Miles. The villagers' problem is that they do not follow the way of peace, as we do."

Before daylight the next morning, the two brothers set out, carrying in a light basket of birchbark enough simple food for their dinner. For drink they counted on sparkling brook water. Henry hoped to find the sunny slope south of Indian Rock red with wild strawberries. Arrow-in-the-Dark had showed him the white blossoms a few weeks ago.

"The Great Spirit," the old chief had told him, "causes the fruit to ripen, a gift to all his children without toil or payment. The Indian shows his white brother where to look for them. Take what you wish. There is peace between us."

230

At noon, after a hard morning's hoeing, Miles and Henry sat down by the brook to eat, rested a bit, and then went to see whether the wild strawberries were ripening. They found the berries just commencing to crimson beneath the leaves.

"In another week there will be quantities. Dost thou not find their taste delicious, Miles?"

Henry clambered up the steep face of Indian Rock. Miles watched him but stayed below, still hunting for berries and rather soberly wondering if Indians were watching them.

During the afternoon, Miles was absorbed, and they hoed silently, side by side, anxious to finish the last rows before sunset. But hard as they toiled, they presently saw that they must return in the morning.

On their way home they heard rustling in the hazel brush along the trail, and the eerie cry of the whip-poor-will across the dusk of the lowland.

"The Indians can imitate every bird and every wild creature of the forest," Miles worried. "One never knows whether what one hears is the true or the false. But methinks never were whip-poor-wills so plentiful as this evening. Birds they may be, but more likely signals to surround the village."

"Miles, pray thee frighten not thyself nor me by thy talk. If the Indians rise against us, they rise. But to my thinking, a show of resistance on the part of the village will cause them to rise all the sooner."

At the edge of the settlement an armed party of villagers came out to meet the brothers.

"You've returned safely! Bad news arrived by messenger within the hour. Not far from here to the eastward, the savages are on the warpath. Many settlers have been massacred, for they were unwarned. We have word in season. Tonight we will all gather within the stockade. It's our only security. Though we be but a handful, every man is well-armed, and every man will be needed for defense."

"We do not fear the Indians," Henry said stoutly. "Arrow-in-the-Dark has always been friendly. If we arm, they will arm. Nor can we blame an Indian if he takes a leaf from our book."

"Well enough to practice peace in peacetimes, neighbor, but war is a grim fact. There are our women and children to think of."

"I do think of them, especially," replied Henry. "Their chances are far better without resistance on your part."

The armed villagers laughed aloud at Henry's simplemindedness.

"What would be your defense, then?"

"We will proceed as usual. Miles and I always sleep in our cabin with the latchstring out. Tomorrow we go back to finish hoeing our corn patch. And a fine stand of corn we have. If it harvests well, there will be plenty for all our people whom we expect before harvest and plenty to share with you."

"Do you hoe under the shadow of Indian Rock without arms?" sneered one man.

"Assuredly. Why should we not?"

"You'll never live to see your corn in tassel. Braves on the warpath spare none. The more scalps, the more glory."

That evening the brothers talked again in the darkness, and the fear which prevailed in the village kept them alert for sounds of danger. But no harm came during the night, and at dawn they made ready for work again.

"We can finish ere noon, methinks," said Miles. "No need to carry food with us. But hark thee, Henry. I lay till long after midnight, pondering on this situation. It may be sheer foolhardiness to go to a lonely place unarmed. When we go to the forest for game, we carry muskets. Today if we take along powderhorns and muskets, the Indians will see that we are armed and fear to attack us. I would never shoot a man, red or white, being, as thou knowest, a stout believer in peace. But just bearing a weapon may serve to keep the warriors at a distance. In sooth, Henry, I like my scalp where God put it, as well as any man. So I go forth this morning, hoe on one shoulder and musket on the other. And so I intend to return, the hoe having performed an active service and the musket a passive one."

"I think thee art wrong, Miles. The Indians will see your gun and conclude that we no longer trust in their good faith. Arrow-in-the-Dark is our friend."

"These hostile Indians may be none of his tribe. Nay, Henry, I am older than thou. Be guided by my counsel. 'Tis folly to throw our lives away. Our strength and our usefulness we owe to the coming community."

So in the fair pink sunrise, the two brothers set out to hoe their corn. In silhouette against the morning sky, their tall figures strode on, Henry with a hoe and Miles ahead with a musket over one shoulder and a hoe over the other. The younger man was sullen and sick at heart. The elder was a prey to fears he had not known when he still believed in good faith between Indians and settlers. He was a little ashamed of his **defection** and felt that he had fallen in Henry's estimation. They went on in silent discomfort, unhappy at not being in their customary accord.

The path they took skirted the knoll called Indian Rock. Suddenly from behind thickets of hazel and alder came a rain of arrows. Miles was struck, and then Henry. Side by side they lay, not a hundred yards from their growing corn. They lay still, mercifully pierced to the heart by the sure aim of the warriors.

Later in the day, Arrow-in-the-Dark came to the cornfield to see if the brothers were safe. He found them lying in the path.

"Those were my friends you have slain," he said sternly to his tribesmen.

"Friends do not bring muskets when they work in the fields, O Chief!" replied the warriors. "They came against our Council Rock with a musket. Behold beside their bodies, the musket loaded to kill. So we killed first. Yesterday we watched also. They brought only hoes and food. They ate berries and drank water. We let them live. Today they are dead. Peace had gone from their hearts."

"Look not every man on his own things, but every man also on the things of others." – Philippians 2:4

The Silver King

E. G. Perrault

"You eat too fast," she called as he moved away from the table.

"I eat that way in the city too, Aunt Ruth," said Herbie. "I thought maybe I'd ride Mike awhile before the sun goes down."

"Don't get into mischief. Have the pony in before dark."

"Yes, Auntie." The screen door slammed, and he was gone.

"Time he gets home to his folks he'll be a regular savage," said Aunt Ruth as she began to clear the dishes.

Herbie rounded the corner of the house and ran across to the barn. Sandy was sitting on a three-legged stool in front of Mike's stall. The ground around him was littered with harness straps; the **aura** of sweet hay and old leather hung over him like a specially blended perfume. He was past sixty, gnarled as a juniper, with a stubble-salted lantern jaw.

"Goin' ridin', Herbie?"

"I thought I'd take Mike out for a little while. He must be getting lonesome for me."

"He don't bother bein' lonesome for no one these days. He's gettin' so much pasturin', he looks like a rain barrel with legs." The old man cast a scornful glance at the fat white pony dozing in the stall. "A little exercise would do him good. Where you aimin' to take him?"

Herbie pretended carelessness. "Just riding."

"Down by the river, maybe?"

"Maybe." The old man was always curious.

"Goin' to watch the Indians fish, maybe?"

"No!" The boy's voice was sharp, almost angry. "I'm not going anywhere near there."

Sandy regarded him, half amused. "You got it in for those fellows, haven't you? There's worse sights than an Indian with a fish spear, boy. There's an art to it. I can remember when—"

"Auntie says I should be back before dark. I'd better go now." He wasn't usually this abrupt, but Sandy could keep him for hours with his story-telling. There were important things to be done this night.

The old man led Mike out and helped to saddle him. "Keep away from the cliffs if you're going the river way. The edge ain't too safe." Herbie didn't answer. He lifted a coil of rope from the barn wall and sent Mike through the yard at a nimble-hoofed trot.

On the road he wheeled the pony sharply to the left, away from the river, and moved off without a backward glance. Mike's sleek girth upset the ramrod posture he tried to maintain. He could feel Sandy's eyes boring two cool holes in the back of his neck and could picture the little half smile on his whiskery face as he **shambled** back to the harness straps in the barn. Sandy was a nice old fellow, but he could be exasperating at times. He had ways of knowing things, of finding out things. Secrets weren't safe when he was around.

Herbie maintained the trot till he reached a bend in the road, then cut into the scrub and broke a path to the river trail. He glanced back several times as he walked Mike on the carpet of pine needles. Nothing moved. A hundred yards from the river, he led the pony off the trail and tethered him to a clump of huckleberry. It would be necessary to go from here on foot; not down the river trail, but through the undergrowth, brushing aside the clinging lace of reindeer moss, pressing down the spring-steel whips of vine maples. He dug his heels into the leaf-matted side of a gully and descended like a mountain goat, leaping with feet together down the glade. Gold and crimson maple leaves tumbled after him in a rustling avalanche.

At the bottom of the gully, a small creek battled its way through the warp of fallen snags and boulders, like a variegated silver thread. Herbie stopped with his feet sucking the wet clay on the water's edge. He took off his shoes and clambered down onto the rocks in midstream, leaping from one stone to the next, with his small flexible toes curling on the slippery surfaces. Ahead of him spread the polished surface of a pool.

It was the creek's most ambitious creation, a deep quiet basin shadowed on one side by overhanging maples. He peered anxiously into the depths.

The bottom was a tawny, pebbled screen flickering with minnows as they flashed to the surface in pursuit of water spiders.

Herbie examined the barrier on the river side of the pool. It was still intact: a fence made of cedar saplings rising up from a rampart of stones, a task that had occupied most of his afternoon. On the other side of the pool, a sieve of rocks and shallow water prevented escape. He scrambled back to the fence to search for a possible exit, and as he did, a movement in the maple shadows caught his eye. Deep down in the water, a part of the bank detached itself: a submerged log, it seemed, drifting on the bottom of the pool, but Herbie knew it was no log.

He watched, with fingers clenched in the mossy bank, invisible hands lacing his breath in as the salmon came out of the darkness into a dream world of ruby light. Each scale glittered silver and scarlet, alternating as it glided through the bars of light. It was a fish of silver, and a fish of fiery gold, dreaming on the bottom of the pool; and then a ventral fin flickered impatiently to end the dream. The great shape slanted to the surface and cut the water with a square dorsal. Circles of darkening water spread from the fracture and were destroyed suddenly as the fish whipped around in a metallic arc and hurled itself across the pool at the fence. Almost on the rocks it nosed up and broke the water in a shower of spray, tail flailing, jaws agape, straining to clear the barrier.

Herbie cried, "No!" in an anguished voice; then sank back with a sigh of relief as the salmon rebounded from the saplings. The surface heaved in a miniature storm as the fish vented its rage in a series of dashes across the pool. Finally it cruised to a stop, suspended almost beneath the boy's eyes, fins undulating angrily. It was a mighty fish. "Silver King," he whispered. "I'll call you Silver King!"

He was aware suddenly that the water was fading from bronze to gray. "I'll be back tomorrow," he promised. The salmon hung sullenly, like a dark submarine, above the floor of the pool.

He clambered upstream again and put on his shoes. This was a secret that could be shared by no one, not even Sandy. Just up the river, beyond the gorge, the reserve Indians were spearing fish by the hundreds. If ever they heard of the Silver King . . . The thought of a spear piercing that gleaming body filled him with horror and cold anger. He would have to guard his secret from everyone.

The Silver King had taken on a strange significance in his mind. He had watched the salmon run in other years, on similar visits with his aunt, and no human situation could compare with the drama of that homecoming; struggling fish running a gauntlet of seine nets, fish spears, and rapids to reach their spawning grounds in the lakes. The Silver King was a symbol— Herbie had captured the spirit of the upriver migration.

His mind was busy now as he struggled up the steep slope. The fence might not stand repeated batterings from the powerful body. Silver King's escape to the river would be hard to endure, but there was a more unbearable possibility than that to be considered. The Indians were waiting beyond the gorge, the last spearing camp before the lakes and freedom. Silver King would have to pass those cruel, probing shafts feeling out the breadth of the stream.

He could picture the Silver King skewered on a drying rack, silver scales pierced and smoked to a dull gray, prey to a buzzing swarm of black flies. He drove the picture out of his mind with a little shiver and scrambled the final steps of the incline with increasing determination.

Mike was waiting for him, a portly white ghost in the closing dusk. He whinnied impatiently as Herbie unfastened the reins and led him onto the river trail once more. The Indians would be up at the camp now; they rarely fished beyond sunset. It would be possible to approach the scaffold behind the shield of darkness and the river thunder. Herbie's scheme was comparatively simple, and yet as he approached the fishing aerie, his heart became a salmon, leaping on the rampart of his ribs.

Mike's hooves rang sharply on the flinty edge of the gorge as they reached the trail's end and turned up toward the scaffold; the sound was lost in the river noises, but to Herbie it was louder than the fall of a mountain. He halted the pony a few yards past the frail lattice of poles and uncoiled the rope, securing one end to the pommel of the saddle and the other to the framework of the platform. Then he remounted and took a deep, shaky breath. They would be gone before anyone could stop the plunge of the framework. He tried to tell himself there was no danger, and the thought of the Silver King in the pool below renewed his strength of purpose.

As he brought his hand down hard on Mike's side and tightened his hold on the reins, the pony reared and leaped ahead. Behind them the scaffold tottered and tore loose. He peered back through the dark to watch the timbers go, and as he did, the rope tightened with a jerk that stopped Mike dead.

The saddle twisted and tore away, spinning Herbie to the ground. Thousands of bright bubbles danced out of the darkness as he fought for breath. He called "Mike! Mike!" in a tight-lipped whisper and heard the pound of hooves fading away in the night. Behind him an angry babble of voices rose in crescendo. He stumbled to his feet, still gasping for breath, and ran wildly toward the scrub. A dark shape crashed in his direction, and he swerved to dodge it.

Someone called out, "There he is. Get him!"; and a hand clamped on his shoulder. He wriggled free and lunged ahead. The hand returned heavily, twisting strong fingers into his shirt collar. A man's voice, breathless and angry, was shouting in his ear, "Stop! You wanta get yourself killed?"

He put all his strength into one great heave that carried him ahead, feet straining for a grip on the flint-littered bank; and then, with horrible suddenness, there was no foothold. His legs flailed in terrifying space, and the cry of fear that gathered on his lips was engulfed in a cold torrent of water that caught at him and sucked him down. The river roared in the channels of his ears. Liquid fire trickled into his lungs. His arms, windmilling to gain the surface, were thrust awry by the angry current. He knew he would drown, and a strangely sane vision of his aunt flashed through the cold flutter of panic.

She was talking to Mom and Dad: "Herbie drowned today. Herbie drowned today. Drowned today!" the words repeated themselves endlessly. In the midst of this impossible dream, he felt a firm grip under his armpits. A powerful thrust shot him upwards into the delicious night air. He clutched wildly at his savior. Rough hands broke the grip and transferred themselves to his hair with a scalp-ripping force that shocked him agonizingly back to reality.

The current was carrying him and his unknown companion at great speed toward a cluster of flickering lights on the riverbank. Unbelievably soon they were level with the torches. A rope burned his face; another tangled between his legs. The rough hands were busy again, looping a strand about his waist. He felt himself moving back against the current in surges as the rescuers pulled the line in rhythm. Beside him the dark shape of his companion was visible at intervals, outlined in the luminous foam. Herbie tried to speak, but the strange noises that left his throat were lost in the torrent.

They were landed, like dripping water monsters, on the riverbank, and Herbie had no strength to resist as they carried him up to the camp. The relief that filled his whole being left no room for fear or apprehension; he was alive and wildly grateful for it.

They put him down, without ceremony, beside a crackling wood fire in the encampment clearing, where he lay blinking up at the hostile faces that surrounded him. Across from him in the glow, he could make out the sodden figure of a man, slumped with his head bowed limply on his chest, breathing in great hoarse gasps. A woman had stripped the shirt from his back, and Herbie could see an angry red weal across the bronze corrugation of ribs, where the rocks had scraped him.

He sat up and called over, "Mister, I want to thank you for—" His word were cut short as an old woman broke from the circle and rained stinging blows on his head and shoulders with small knuckled fists. Some of the younger women secured her and led her away. Herbie said, "I'm sorry. I'm sorry for everything." And in his heart he was genuinely sorry. He wished that he might have been hurt in the river. It might have made them feel better if he had been hurt, just a little bit.

There was a stir in the darkness beyond the fire, and the crowd parted to admit Sandy, bristling with excitement and concern. "What's happened here? Your aunt is in a terrible state, Herbie. When I saw Mike coming back on the road with his saddle gone, I thought you was done for certain."

He saw the dripping clothes. "You look like a drowned rat, boy!"

Herbie said, "I fell in the river. He helped me out." He pointed to his rescuer.

"Johnny George hauled you out of the river?" When the tired Indian made no effort to speak, Sandy turned to the others for an explanation. It was the signal for a great hubbub. He was barraged on every side with angry accounts, punctuated with gestures in Herbie's direction. Sandy pieced a story out of the chaos and waited for comparative silence to return before he spoke to Herbie.

"They say you pulled their fishing platform into the river. Is that right, son?" His voice held an incredulous note.

Herbie said, "Yes. I'm sorry I did it." There was nothing else he could say. Extra words seemed foolish. He looked at Sandy with an expression that pleaded for understanding.

Sandy crossed over to Johnny George. "You all right, Johnny?" Johnny nodded briefly. "You want us to send over a doctor?" The Indian shook his head in a manner that dismissed further conversation. The woman was stroking an ointment into the **abrasion**; he winced as the fingers touched his skin. Sandy stood undecided for a moment, then turned back to the crowd.

"The boy says he's sorry. Tomorrow we'll come over and pay for the damages. If Johnny has any trouble tonight, we'll get a doctor for him." The crowd talked among themselves in an undertone while Sandy helped Herbie to his feet. "We'd better get you home before your aunt has a fit of **hysterics**. I brought Mike back. You can ride him." He took off his coat and put it around the boy's shoulders.

Herbie limped painfully through the muttering assembly, following close on Sandy's heels. Apologies seemed so foolish. Property had been ruined, and a man had been hurt. You couldn't make that right with apologies. He climbed onto Mike, and they moved out of the pale light, with the murmur of angry voices swelling into angry discussion behind them.

They moved along in silence for some time. Crickets chirruped merrily in the darkness, oblivious of the unhappy thoughts that filled the boy's mind. "I got a spring salmon down in the creek, Sandy," he said finally. "It's a beauty, over fifty pounds."

The silence hung as heavy as ever. He continued desperately. "It's the nicest salmon you ever saw, Sandy, kind of special. I—I fixed him up in a big pool with a fence across to keep him safe. I figured if he did get out, he'd have to go past the Indians, and maybe get speared. If you could see him, Sandy, you wouldn't want that to happen. The Indians have lots of fish now. I—I tore down the platform so they wouldn't get Silver King—I thought it was the best way." Sandy's silence made him uneasy. He stopped speaking and waited for a reply.

The old man held his words back till they had Mike in his stall and the barn door closed behind them. "You made a lot of mistakes today, Herbie. Looks to me like man and beast have taken punishment from you. Your folks can pay for a broken scaffold, but they can't make up for the fish the Indians are goin' to miss while they're buildin' another one. They need every bit of food they can get for the winter. As for the salmon you got down in the creek—that's downright cruelty. You're standin' in the way of nature, keepin' a fish from its spawnin' ground. It's like keepin' a thirsty man from water."

Herbie was bewildered. "But it seems just as cruel to let them get netted and speared and bruised in the river. It's good to keep a person from killing himself, isn't it? I thought I was doing right, Sandy."

Sandy appraised him in the lantern light. "I don't doubt but what you meant well, son, but you just didn't reason things out. Your salmon knows he's heading for a bruisin'; he knows the risks he's takin'; he's got a goal to gain, come fair or foul. I guess life is a lot like that. Once folks has set their sights, they can't stand to be nudged out of the line of fire."

He squeezed Herbie's shoulder with a leathery hand. "You run along in the back way and get into bed. I'll talk with your aunt tonight, and you can tell your story in the morning. I think maybe that's best."

Herbie cast him a grateful look as he started up the path to the house. Halfway up he stopped. "What should I do about the Silver King?"

The old man grated a stub of a finger on his whiskered jaw. "Well, son, if a feller don't deserve prison, there's only one thing to do. You gotta set him free."

Herbie went to his room and took off his wet clothes. He fought the sleep that waited for him in the warm, dry blankets. *Only one thing to do— set him free.* There was another way though, a harder way. In the midst of planning, he fell asleep. He didn't hear Aunt Ruth come into the room, nor feel the heated blanket tucked in around him. In the darkness he couldn't have seen that her eyes were red with crying.

He awoke shortly after sunrise the next morning, wincing as his sore muscles tortured him for more sleep. Aunt Ruth wouldn't be up for an hour yet. He scribbled a note and left it on his pillow. "Don't worry. I'm down at the Indian camp. I'll be back soon." Then he made his way downstairs and out of the yard. He left Mike in his stall for fear of making a noise.

He closed the gate behind him, crossed the road, and started down the river trail.

The encampment was astir with life. A flat veil of smoke hung over the cooking fires where the women were busy clearing away the breakfast remains. A group of men on the riverbank worked on the frame of a new platform, straining as they lifted a main pole into place. Johnny George was helping to direct operations. Herbie could see the bulky shape of a rough bandage beneath his shirt.

Several women called after him angrily as he walked down to the river, and the men watched his approach with scowls. They had a right to be angry. He tried not to let it bother him but walked straight to Johnny George. "I'm sorry about last night. I—I want to thank you for saving my life."

Johnny's face was expressionless. "If you was a man, I'd have let the river take you." Herbie felt a cold menace in the words.

He tried another approach. "I'm sorry about what happened. I'll help my dad pay the damages."

Johnny swung around impatiently. "Maybe you could hold the fish back till we're ready to spear again. We should be fishing now."

Herbie said, "I know," in a small voice and groped for other words. He didn't want to say what was in his mind. He had hoped that an apology would be enough, and that Johnny would understand that he hadn't meant any harm. An apology wasn't enough though; it couldn't possibly have been enough. The words built up from a dry whisper. "I—I came here for another reason this morning—I've got something to show you, something that might help you out."

"You've made enough trouble," growled Johnny. "Go home."

"It won't take long. You won't be sorry."

The Indian was coldly suspicious. "I got no reason to trust you."

"You've got to believe me," begged Herbie. "I have to pay you back in some way." He saw Johnny wavering. "It's a—it's a fish—a big one."

"Where?"

"Down in the ravine pool. It's bigger than six ordinary ones." The words were bitter in his mouth. "Come with me and I'll show you."

Johnny eyed him stonily, weighing the words. Finally he turned to a cluster of fish spears jutting barb-upwards from the turf. He stroked a wet thumb over several of the points before he selected a shaft and turned to Herbie. "Show me," he said.

Herbie knew what it felt like to be a traitor. All the way down to the pool, he could feel his heart shriveling within him. Branches whipped his face as he led Johnny through the underbrush to the lip of the ravine, but he barely felt the sting. The Silver King was down there imprisoned, waiting for execution, and it was too late to change his mind—too late to try some other way to pay his debt. Johnny walked grimly behind him with the spear clenched firmly in his strong brown hand. Herbie made little effort to check his pace as they plunged down the slope. He was carried ankle-deep into the creek by the force of his descent. Cold water rippled icily over his boot tops as he stared downstream.

"I—I'm not going any farther," he said. "You'll find him in the big pool—a salmon, a big silver salmon." He felt his voice getting lost in his tightening throat. Johnny shifted his grip on the spear and started down the creek. Ahead of them there was the sudden sound of rending wood and shifting granite. Herbie started after Johnny with an incredulous cry. "The fence! The fence is going down!"

Johnny grunted angrily and raised the spear for casting as he leaped the last few yards to the pool.

Sandy was there lifting the last of the stones from the pool exit. He stood up as Johnny leaped to **intercept** him. "Easy, Johnny. There's a big fish in this pool, right enough—but I've got a couple sides of good bacon up in the smokehouse that'll feed you longer than he will."

"He promised me the fish." Johnny's grip on the spear hadn't relaxed.

There was a calming note in Sandy's voice. "Sure, he did. He had to make good some way, but that salmon means a lot more to him than it does to us. I think maybe he's learned a lesson." They turned to look at Herbie standing knee-deep in the creek eddies. Johnny's barb lowered into the mossy carpet on the bank.

Herbie was blind to both of them. He stood with his legs braced in the bubbling current and watched the Silver King wriggle through the breach. The broad tail flickered briefly as it disappeared in the foam of the creek, and the great fish was gone, speeding down to the freedom of the river.

"So built we the wall; and all the wall was joined together unto the half thereof: for the people had a mind to work." – Nehemiah 4:6

The Jonah Pie

Ruby Holmes Martyn

It was Lorena, setting the table in the dining room, who saw him first. "Here comes Reuben Thorpe!"

Agnes was standing by the range, frying pies in a kettle of boiling grease. The fried ones were on a platter on the large shelf, and she had just begun to turn the last batch. "Oh, Mother!" she cried. "Which is the Jonah pie?"

The girls heard their mother laugh merrily from somewhere in the depths of the pantry. "Put an extra plate on the table between your place and mine, Rena. You know quite well I myself couldn't tell which is the Jonah pie now, Agnes. Frying changes all the marks of a pie completely."

Agnes's answering voice was tragic. "What if Cousin Thorpe should happen to get the Jonah? I shall try the bottom of every pie with a fork."

"No such thing!" declared Mother, coming out of the pantry. "Wearing overalls for an hour would do Reuben Thorpe a sight of—"

Mother broke off her sentence abruptly as a quick step sounded on the back porch. The next minute Reuben Thorpe Johnston stood in the kitchen. Good nature shone in every line of his handsome face, and he greeted his aunt and cousins heartily.

"Hello, Aunt Martha! I see you've got the extra plate on already, Rena. I tell you, Aggie, those pies look good enough to eat."

Just then another young man came into the kitchen, and he was a fellow so similar to Reuben Thorpe that they might have been taken for brothers. But the newcomer was heavier limbed; the sleeves of his loose-necked shirt were rolled snugly above his elbows, showing a pair of work-trained arms. His patched overalls were splotched with the good red earth of a forenoon's following of the plow, and his hands were hardened with years of gripping plow handle, hoe, and scythe.

"I was pretty sure that was you I saw coming up the road five minutes ago, Thorpie," he said, welcoming his cousin with an outstretched hand.

"Heard you geeing-up the horses, Reub," was the laughing answer.

Both cousins had been named Reuben, after their paternal grandfather, and the middle "Thorpe" of the city-bred cousin was habitually used by the family to distinguish the one from the other. Young Reuben was glad to follow his lifework on the Johnston farm, living in the big farmhouse with his widowed mother, two sisters, and young brother Jimmy.

While the boys talked, Agnes made a **surreptitious** attempt to hunt for the Jonah pie with her long-tined frying fork, but Jimmy's bright eyes spied her.

"No fair, Aggie!" he protested. "Mother said Reuben Thorpe was to fare like the rest of us, Aggie."

"I hope so," declared Reuben Thorpe as he followed Agnes and the platter of hot brown pies into the dining room. "What's the doings I'm to share particularly?"

Reuben, in his father's place at the head of the table, explained. "It's a kind of drawing lots proposition that's always run in the Johnston blood, Thorpie. We have a Jonah pie made up in the batch of fried ones when there's some particular piece of work that no one is hankering to do."

"Or when one is so desirable we all want to do it," added Lorena.

"I'm in the game today," cried Jimmy.

"What's a Jonah pie?" asked Reuben Thorpe.

"It's filled with sawdust," his cousin answered. "Mother makes them, but one of the girls does the frying so that Mother herself loses track of the Jonah, so the game's perfectly fair for all of us."

Rueben lifted the platter of pies, and they went from one pair of hands to another around the table amid a babble of jolly talk. Each one chose a pie, and at a signal from Reuben, each took a bite. Apple and mince and cranberry were found, but no sawdust Jonah for which **forfeit** must be paid.

"Escape number one," said Lorena with a laugh.

"I wouldn't mind getting it," declared Jimmy bravely.

"Make you feel like a grown-up to do the little stunt at the end, eh?" asked Reuben Thorpe.

Jimmy nodded. "I'll help you on the job if you get it," he volunteered.

"Same here. Is the forfeit picked out?"

"Yes."

Reuben looked down the table at his city cousin and cocked an eyebrow. "Office work slack with you, Thorpie?" he asked.

Reuben Thorpe shrugged. "Sure isn't. But this morning looked so fine, I telephoned Uncle Dan for a day off. The office gets to be an awful grind sometimes."

Reuben raised his eyebrows, but Reuben Thorpe had already dismissed the subject of his absence from their uncle's office. He really did consider office work a grind—something to be shifted to other fellows' shoulders as much as possible; moreover, he knew that this morning a particularly disagreeable piece of work was to be done. Surely, being a nephew to the head of the firm gave him some privileges! True, he always had to make his peace with Uncle Dan afterwards, but from continued successes he had grown confident.

"You know, Uncle Dan is planning to come out to the farm someday soon," said Mother thoughtfully.

"Oh, well, I didn't tell him I had a notion to come today," said Reuben Thorpe with a laugh.

"Is everybody ready for another pie?" asked Jimmy.

"I am."

"And I."

Again the platter made the round of the table.

"One! Two! Three! Bite!" said Reuben.

Jimmy, half hoping for the honor of a grown-up duty, found red cranberry inside his crust; Mother's was cranberry too. Lorena bit into apple, and Reuben's was mince. Agnes, opposite Reuben Thorpe and fearing the Jonah pie for her **fastidious** cousin, saw his face change as he bit through the crust. For a moment, she read disgust at the taste; then he rallied as he realized the joke was on him.

"I'm the Jonah," he announced with good humor.

Lorena laughed merrily. "Oh, I'm so glad you came, Reuben Thorpe. It's such a messy job to clean the cupola," she cried.

"What about cleaning the cupola?"

Mother answered. "That's the job of the one who got the sawdust pit today. Once each spring one of us goes up in the barn cupola to clean out the year's accumulation of cobwebs and flies and wasps. Then it has to be broomed out and the windows washed."

"And it's up to me to do it?" jested Reuben Thorpe, trying to keep his distaste for the job out of his voice. "Well, I'm game," and he accepted an edible pie in place of the sawdust Jonah.

After the meal, Reuben Thorpe went up to his cousin's room and changed his own faultless clothes for a farmer's outfit. He rolled the coarse shirtsleeves over arms that struck him suddenly as disgustingly pale for a strong man. The blue overalls were patched even more than those his cousin wore, and they hung loosely on his more slender frame.

As he dressed, his brain was busy: Had Agnes expected him to decline to play the Jonah game to its finish? Had she really marked him for a quitter? He went soberly down the stairs.

His aunt had a broom ready for him to use. "Kill all the blue flies and drive out the wasps and broom the place clean of webs," she directed. "Then come down for cloths and a bucket of hot soapsuds to wash the windows."

"I'm going too," said Jimmy, who was carrying a hand brush.

In the barn, they climbed the ladder to the haymow, then to a higher loft. From that loft a rickety stairway led to the cupola above the tiptop of the barn roof. It was a tiny room some four feet square, with windows on every side.

A network of cobwebs was festooned from the dark rafters overhead. A dozen blue flies buzzed angrily against the dirty windows with a score of noisy wasps. And the smell was a stuffy, warm, cowy odor.

Jimmy, who had gone up ahead, was already busy catching flies. Reuben Thorpe set to work at another window with disastrous results—the wasps resented the unskilled human interference. Reuben Thorpe did not succeed in evading them as he hunted flies. There were angry stabs at two fingers, and a bolder wasp ran a big stinger into his forehead.

"The wasps are an awful nuisance," said Jimmy sympathetically.

And Reuben Thorpe agreed right heartily. He felt again that flush of determination that had swept over him at Agnes's words. Discomforts would not **oust** him from a game he had undertaken with good faith to play.

By the time they had opened the windows, cleared the cupola of its undesirable tenants, and swept down the cobwebs, Reuben Thorpe's appearance was grotesque. Grimy streaks ran in all directions across his handsome face; dark broken bits of cobwebs ornamented his blond hair; and his sweaty arms had gathered a thick coating of grime.

"Soap and water takes all this off, I suppose," he said dryly to Jimmy.

"Sure," said Jimmy, undisturbed by his own disheveled appearance.

When he went into the kitchen for the bucket of hot water, Reuben Thorpe saw Lorena tittering over the dishpan.

"Didn't you think I could clean the cupola, Rena?" he asked.

"I didn't think you'd like to."

Reuben Thorpe did not answer as he took up the heavy bucket of steaming suds and an armful of soft cloths. For the third time within a morning he was roused from his habitual easygoingness: Agnes had suggested that he be left out of the game; the wasps had given him physical pain; and Lorena had told him quite frankly that she didn't expect him to do something he disliked.

Up in the cupola, he and Jimmy washed and wiped and polished. The windows on one side after another took on a brilliance that did credit to the workers.

"You 'most wouldn't know the glass was there at all!" cried Jimmy, standing back to admire the result. "Hey, look! See that automobile coming way down at Will's Corner?"

Reuben Thorpe could see the car coming rapidly along the turnpike. It had a familiar look to him, but he dismissed it—coincidence, surely. But when the gray roadster turned in at the farmyard gate, he knew who it was. "That's Uncle Dan."

"Hurry up and finish this last window so we can go down and see him," cried Jimmy.

Reuben Thorpe's mouth twisted in a grim smile. "I'm not in the least bit of a hurry to see Uncle Dan," he said under his breath.

They washed and polished the last window. When it was finished, Jimmy slid off down the narrow stairs, fireman fashion, without a parting word.

Reuben Thorpe did not follow. Instead he leaned against a window jamb and looked over the hills to where the green of the pines met the sap-colored patches of the leafless trees. Nearer, he could see the field where his cousin Reuben was following the plow as it turned under furrow after furrow of sod. And everywhere the sunshine was chasing the shadows toward the east.

Unaccustomed to such bodily exercise as the last hours had held, his muscles ached; and the pain of the wasp stings was still sharp. His hands were painfully blistered too, and he was alertly conscious that his appearance would not stand critical inspection. He tried to figure out by what detour he could reach the house and his own clothes, unobserved by Uncle Dan.

"What a mess I got into playing that Jonah pie game!" he groaned.

Suddenly he heard voices in the barn below, Jimmy's and a man's heavy bass—undoubtedly Uncle Dan. They seemed to come nearer and nearer, and Reuben Thorpe caught words that made him groan again.

"The windows shine so I can see through them?"

"Yes, sir," came Jimmy's triumphant treble. "I tell you, Reuben Thorpe polished them fine. He's got the muscle when he gets in practice."

Reuben Thorpe was filled with a momentary panic. Uncle Dan and Jimmy were coming up the last ladder to the cupola. The only escape he could think of was to crawl from one of the open windows and hang to the ridgepole by his fingers. But there was no time to put the **preposterous** scheme into operation. He sighed; and turning, he faced Uncle Dan's twinkling eyes as nonchalantly as he could.

"Hello!"

"Hello, Thorpie," replied Uncle Daniel, laughing. He had grown so portly with sixty years of living that he had to pause and catch his breath from the unaccustomed exertion of the climb. "I like the way you and Jimmy have done your sky-parlor job."

Reuben Thorpe grinned as sheepishly as a youngster caught at mischief. "I got the Jonah pie, and this was the job," he explained.

Uncle Daniel laughed again. "That Jonah pie is part and parcel of the old homeplace. Your grandmother used to put in a Jonah sometimes when we were boys, and I've had to do some strange stunts on that proposition before now."

"It really wasn't so bad as you might think," said Reuben Thorpe.

His uncle drummed on a shining windowpane. "See here, Thorpie," he said abruptly. "I've put another man in your place at the office. Couldn't stand your shirking when you took the fancy. And now I'm trying to think whether to give you a chance at that shipping room job Fred's promotion will leave vacant."

Reuben Thorpe's jaw dropped. His job had really been taken from him! He knew there was to be some vacancy in the shipping room, but he wasn't hankering after that job.

"It would be a sort of Jonah pie drawing to you, I know, but I need someone of about the caliber of you at your best in that place just now, and there'd be a chance to develop your muscle." Uncle Dan paused an appreciable instant. "Will you try it?"

Reuben Thorpe watched the sunshine chase the cloud shadows across the Johnston fields. For the first time in his life, he had finished a piece of work that looked distasteful to him; and there had proved to be a keen satisfaction in doing it well. He had put up a fight, and he had won.

Would this shipping room job also be one to rouse his mettle? If loyalty to a game compelled him to rise to an emergency, what must not a task of life accomplish? A glimpse of the truth came to him—that a fellow who picks here and there at the things that seem pleasant is going to fail of the best expression of himself.

He threw back his head and smiled. "I'll take the job, Uncle Dan," he said.

Glossary

The root word of every word in boldface type in *The Road Less Traveled* is in this glossary. With each word is the dictionary pronunciation and a definition for the way the word is used in this book. Many of these words have other definitions. The example sentence in italics shows how to use the word correctly. The page number following the sentence indicates where the word is found in the reader.

abhor (əb hȯr′) *v* : to regard with horror and disgust. *After a nearly fatal fight with a beaver, the dog abhorred them and would not go anywhere near one.* 217

abject (ab′ jekt′) *adj* : of the lowest degree; wretched. *Samuel was shocked to see the abject poverty in the large city.* 126

abrasion (ə brā′ zhən) *n* : an injury caused by a wearing, grinding, or rubbing away. *Kyle had a painful abrasion on his arm as a result of his bicycle wreck.* 240

acclamation (a′ klə mā′ shən) *n* : praise or enthusiastic approval. *The acclamations of my teammates motivated me to improve as a player.* 90

accursed (ə kərst′) *adj* : being under a curse; despised. *Brother Dan referred to the story of Achan, who hid the accursed things he had taken.* 223

agility (ə ji′ lə tē) *n* : the ability to move quickly and easily. *Mountain goats leap and climb with amazing agility and skill.* 10

alloy (a′ lȯi′) *n* : a blend of two or more substances into one, usually of a poor ingredient with a good one. *Pure aluminum is often mixed with small amounts of other elements to form a strong alloy.* 153

amendment (ə mend′ mənt) *n* : a change to a decision or document. *The Thirteenth Amendment to the United States Constitution made slavery illegal.* 90

apparent (ə per′ ənt) *adj* : appearing to be true. *Despite his apparent lack of attention, Zachary had actually absorbed the teacher's words.* 60

ardor (är′ dər) *n* : a strong feeling, especially of devotion. *The boys' ardor for swimming cooled when the first September frost hit.* 109

attorney (ə tər′ nē) *n* : a lawyer; one who represents a client in court proceedings. *The Jones family considered several attorneys before deciding which one to hire.* 71

aura (òr′ ə) *n* : an atmosphere or impression surrounding something. *Mrs. Sanchez radiated an aura of joy and contentment as she cheerfully went about her work.* 234

benevolence (bə nev′ ləns) *n* : an inclination toward doing acts of kindness. *The millionaire was well-known for his benevolence.* 176

blasphemy (blas′ fə mē) *n* : words or actions that show disrespect for God or sacred things. *By God's mercy, John Newton repented of his blasphemy and served the Lord.* 129

blunt (blənt) *adj* : straight to the point; abrupt and direct. *Fred bluntly told his friends that it was wrong for them to pressure him to disobey his father.* 142

boisterous (bòi′ strəs) *adj* : full of energy and noisy enthusiasm. *"That was the most boisterous group of customers we've ever had in here," the waitress declared.* 114

brusque (brəsk) *adj* : blunt or abrupt in manner or speech. *Kevin apologized for being brusque when I asked him to help me get the cat out of the tree.* 211

calamity (kə la′ mə tē) *n* : an event that causes misery and suffering. *The Arizona fire was the worst calamity in that state's history.* 175

capacity (kə pa′ sə tē) *n* : duty, position, or role. *William offered to serve in any capacity that would be useful to Mr. Doane.* 97

Pronunciation Key ———————————————————————
/a/ bat; /ā/ acorn; /är/ star; /e/ pet; /ē/ eagle; /er/ bear; /ər/ her; /i/ bit; /ī/ ivy; /ir/ deer; /ä/ top; /ō/ go; /ò/ lost; /òi/ coin; /aù/ out; /òr/ corn; /ə/ but; /ü/ boot; /yü/ use; /ù/ foot; /th/ thick; /th/ this; /ŋ/ bang; /zh/ measure

captor (kap′ tər) *n* : one who has captured or who takes captives. *The bobcat pressed himself to the ground as he heard his captor's footsteps approaching the trap.* 29

complacent (kəm plā′ sənt) *adj* : self-satisfied and unaware of possible dangers. *The students spoke complacently of the upcoming exam.* 150

confinement (kən fīn′ mənt) *n* : the state of being confined or kept within limits. *Henry doesn't like to talk about his three-hour confinement in the old cellar.* 170

contemptuous (kən temp′ chə wəs) *adj* : full of contempt; showing strong dislike or disrespect. *Tim answered contemptuously when the officer cited him for speeding, resulting in a heavier fine.* 128

contribute (kən tri′ byət) *v* : to give to a common fund or for a specific purpose. *By contributing a dollar each, we were able to buy Miss Swenson a new Bible for her birthday.* 79

contrive (kən trīv′) *v* : to plan to accomplish in a clever way. *My uncle contrived a way to run his car on propane instead of gasoline.* 88

convulsive (kən vəl′ siv) *adj* : jerky or sudden; uncontrollable. *The boys laughed convulsively at the young goats' antics.* 93

coordination (kō ȯr′ də nā′ shən) *n* : the harmonious working together of parts. *Driving a car requires good eye, hand, and foot coordination.* 19

cordial (kȯr′ jəl) *adj* : friendly and courteous. *Aunt Marcia is a cordial hostess, making sure all her guests are comfortable.* 39

credible (kre′ də bəl) *adj* : reasonable to believe or trust. *Terry gave his father a credible explanation for being late for supper.* 67

cynic (si′ nik) *n* : one who finds fault or is critical of others' motives. *"Justin gave that beggar money just because he wants us to think well of him!" scoffed the cynic.* 109

damsel (dam′ zəl) *n* : a girl or young woman. *Jesus took the girl by the hand and said, "Damsel, I say unto thee, arise."* 167

decimate (de′ sə māt′) *v* : to kill off in large numbers or destroy a large part. *The army decimated the population of their enemies' cities.* 114

decline (di klīn′) *v* : to turn down or refuse. *Jack declined my offer of a puppy; his father said he had enough dogs already.* 76

defection (di fek′ shən) *n* : abandonment of one's group or a belief once held. *Sanford's defection from his earlier nonresistance confused his friends.* 233

defile (di fīl′) *v* : to make unclean, impure, or unholy. *Crude oil and refined fuel spills from tanker ship accidents sometimes occur in coastal waters, defiling the waters and destroying fish.* 220

delirious (di lir′ ē əs) *adj* : disturbed or confused as a result of fever or illness. *Because he was delirious, the sick child's words did not make any sense.* 115

demeanor (di mē′ nər) *n* : outward manner or behavior toward others. *The writer had a brilliant mind, but her humble demeanor meant that no one felt any condescension from her.* 229

derisive (di rī′ siv) *adj* : mockingly scornful. *The king sneered derisively at the prophet's warning.* 90

desolate (de′ sə lət) *adj* : lacking signs of life; deserted and barren. *The travelers felt anxious as they drove through a desolate part of the country.* 92

destitute (des′ tə tüt′) *adj* : completely lacking what is necessary or desired. *The destitute old woman begged at the street corner.* 167

deteriorate (di tir′ ē ə rāt′) *v* : to become worse in quality or value. *After buying the property, Mr. Wilson began to renovate the deteriorating log cabin.* 178

disastrous (di zas′ trəs) *adj* : leading to disaster or great ruin. *A hailstorm in June is disastrous for the barley crop.* 81

discreet (di skrēt′) *adj* : not attracting attention; not readily noticeable. *Rebecca discreetly exited the auditorium and went downstairs for a drink.* 17

disposition (dis′ pə zi′ shən) *n* : one's usual mood or attitude. *The Broadwater family is fun to be around; all the children have such cheerful dispositions.* 12

dominion (də mi′ nyən) *n* : a kingdom over which someone rules. *The dominion of the Roman Empire was one of the most extensive in history.* 169

eavesdrop (ēvz′ dräp′) *v* : to listen secretly to a private conversation. *Merle leaned against the door to eavesdrop but was startled when the door flew open.* 163

elation (i lā′ shən) *n* : a feeling of great happiness or pride. *With a thrill of elation, Beverly paged through her nearly perfect math test.* 23

eligible (e′ lə jə bəl) *adj* : qualified to be chosen for a position, privilege, or office. *Jerry was eligible to become a member of the debate team because of his A average.* 184

embody (im bä′ dē) *v* : to represent a quality or idea in visible form. *When Jesus came to earth, He perfectly embodied God's nature.* 135

emphatic (im fa′ tik) *adj* : forceful and definite. *Insisting that the skates were a gift, June emphatically refused to accept payment for them.* 146

endorse (in dȯrs′) *v* : to support or approve. *Jenny's pastor endorses her decision to serve as a teacher in Liberia next year.* 10

essential (i sen′ shəl) *adj* : of great importance; necessary. *In order to resolve conflict, it is essential for both sides to respect each other.* 100

estranged (i strānjd′) *adj* : separated in bonds of friendship or loyalty. *After years of being estranged from his family, Tobias returned home and made peace with his father.* 108

excess (ek′ ses′) *n* : an amount that is more than necessary or usual. *After serving everyone ice cream, Herman found he had an excess of two cones.* 30

exertion (ig zər′ shən) *n* : mental or physical effort. *After much exertion, the boys finally got the cement bags unloaded from the truck.* 222

expanse (ik spans′) *n* : a wide, open area. *When standing on the plains, the expanse of the sky seems especially vast.* 18

expectant (ik spek′ tənt) *adj* : being in a state of eager anticipation. *The crowd hushed expectantly as the speaker stood and strode toward the platform.* 106

famished (fa′ misht) *adj* : extremely hungry. *The famished farmers must have food very soon, or they will die.* 176

fastidious (fa sti′ dē əs) *adj* : being excessively neat or fussy. *Caroline was too fastidious to work in the garden lest it make her hands dirty.* 246

flint (flint) *n* : a hard type of stone that produces a spark when struck against steel. *Lacking matches, Jonas started a campfire by striking flint and steel together.* 169

forfeit (fòr′ fət) *n* : something lost or given up as punishment or because of a rule. *Tom's team had to pay a forfeit because of the mistake they had made in the game.* 245

foundry (faùn′ drē) *n* : a factory where metal is melted and shaped. *Riley read an article about a large semiconductor foundry located in Santa Clara, California.* 161

gaunt (gònt) *adj* : very thin, often because of suffering or illness. *After being lost in the forest for two weeks, the men returned home gaunt and weary.* 28

girth (gərth) *n* : the measure or distance around a body or object. *General Sherman, the largest living sequoia tree, has a girth of over one hundred feet.* 44

heedless (hēd′ ləs) *adj* : not paying careful attention. *Heedless of the dark clouds, we spread our picnic blanket and prepared to enjoy our lunch.* 14

Pronunciation Key

/a/ bat; /ā/ acorn; /är/ star; /e/ pet; /ē/ eagle; /er/ bear; /ər/ her; /i/ bit; /ī/ ivy; /ir/ deer; /ä/ top; /ō/ go; /ò/ lost; /òi/ coin; /aù/ out; /òr/ corn; /ə/ but; /ü/ boot; /yü/ use; /ù/ foot; /th/ thick; /th/ this; /ŋ/ bang; /zh/ measure

hermit (hər′ mət) *n* : a person who lives in seclusion. *During the Middle Ages, some monks chose to live in the deserts as hermits, neither seeing nor speaking to others for years at a time.* 101

hypocrite (hi′ pə krit′) *n* : someone who pretends to be what he is not. *The man who is kind and gentle in public but behaves differently at home is a hypocrite.* 129

hysterics (his ter′ iks) *n* : an outburst of uncontrollable emotions. *The distraught mother went into hysterics when her toddler disappeared.* 240

immortal (i mȯr′ təl) *adj* : going on forever; never dying. *Although we have mortal bodies, God has given each of us an immortal soul.* 138

impart (im pärt′) *v* : to give, share, or tell. *With his years of experience, Mr. Jenkins was happy to impart helpful tips to his employees.* 153

impassable (im pa′ sə bəl) *adj* : impossible to travel over or around. *The mountains of Tibet are impassable during the winter months.* 72

impish (im′ pish) *adj* : playful and mischievous. *With an impish grin, Josh described his sister's reaction to the frog in her bed.* 38

import (im pȯrt′) *v* : to bring goods into a country, usually to be sold. *Each year, people in the United States buy thousands of imported cars from Japan and Europe.* 213

incredulous (in kre′ jə ləs) *adj* : unable or unwilling to believe a claim. *Dave's announcement was greeted with a burst of incredulous laughter.* 221

infest (in fest′) *v* : to swarm or spread over in a harmful or unpleasant manner. *An Indian meal moth infests food such as flour, cereal, seeds, and spices.* 205

inimitable (i ni′ mə tə bəl) *adj* : impossible to imitate. *Josey's inimitable laughter identified her even though she was outside the room.* 11

initiate (i ni′ shē āt′) *v* : to begin a process or activity. *Dale initiated his seventh grade studies at Bent Creek School on Monday.* 18

intercept (in′ tər sept′) *v* : to stop, seize, or interrupt in progress. *Mother tried to intercept the rumor before it spread throughout the community.* 243

interval (in′ tər vəl) *n* : a space of time between events. *The program was divided into three parts, with short intervals between each segment.* 16

intimate (in′ tə māt′) *v* : to hint indirectly. *Cliff intimated that he would like a job with my father, a carpenter.* 96

iridescent (ir′ ə de′ sənt) *adj* : shining with different colors when seen from different angles. *A male mallard's head is iridescent green.* 20

isolation (ī′ sə lā′ shən) *n* : separation from other people. *Certain types of diseases require isolation so they do not spread to others.* 171

justify (jəs′ tə fī′) *v* : to prove to be just, reasonable, or right. *To justify his client, the lawyer used photographs that showed Mr. Carter in France on the day of the crime.* 202

lavish (la′ vish) *adj* : giving more than needed. *Mom gave me a lavish helping of ice cream after I dug the postholes.* 176

legion (lē′ jən) *n* : a large group. *In the Roman army, a legion consisted of three to six thousand soldiers.* 69

libel (lī′ bəl) *n* : a false statement that is published with the intent of damaging a person's reputation. *In an effort to prevent accusations of libel, newspapers try to have all their facts accurate.* 224

listless (list′ ləs) *adj* : without effort or energy. *Melissa sighed and turned listlessly to gaze out the window.* 146

luster (ləs′ tər) *n* : a glow of reflected light; brightness. *Karla polished the silver to restore its luster.* 153

Pronunciation Key
/a/ bat; /ā/ acorn; /är/ star; /e/ pet; /ē/ eagle; /er/ bear; /ər/ her; /i/ bit; /ī/ ivy; /ir/ deer; /ä/ top; /ō/ go; /ò/ lost; /òi/ coin; /aù/ out; /òr/ corn; /ə/ but; /ü/ boot; /yü/ use; /ù/ foot; /th/ thick; /th/ this; /ŋ/ bang; /zh/ measure

malice (ma′ ləs) *n* : a desire to see another suffer. *Although Elizabeth had suffered terribly at the hands of her persecutors, she bore no malice toward them.* 130

maul (mȯl) *v* : to attack and injure by tearing or beating. *David Livingstone, a missionary in the Congo, was attacked by a mauling lion.* 112

meager (mē′ gər) *adj* : lacking in quality or quantity. *The meager harvest cast a cloud of gloom over the whole community.* 161

meander (mē an′ dər) *v* : to wander aimlessly. *Aubrey likes to meander along the seashore looking for shells and pebbles.* 39

meditate (me′ də tāt′) *v* : to consider deeply and carefully. *Pastor Joseph meditated on the Scripture and prayed for wisdom as he prepared his sermon.* 47

mellow (me′ lō) *adj* : (1) fully ripe and sweet. *Paul brought a basket of mellow peaches to the shop, and we ate them all at lunch.* 54   (2) pleasantly rich or full. *Grandfather's mellow voice added a beautiful harmony to the song.* 55

misgiving (mis′ gi′ viŋ) *n* : a feeling of doubt or confusion. *Beatrice had misgivings about entering a business contract with her neighbor, whom she did not know well.* 134

monitor (mä′ nə tər) *v* : to look after and regulate. *In their teacher's absence, Shannon is monitoring the children's activities.* 195

objectionable (əb jek′ shə nə bəl) *adj* : offensive; worthy of disapproval. *I have never heard Mr. Hyatt use objectionable language.* 147

obtain (əb tān′) *v* : to gain something, usually by effort. *Patty filled out the forms and mailed them, hoping to obtain her passport by the end of the month.* 47

oust (au̇st) *v* : to remove by force. *When an investigation proved his corruption, the mayor feared the townspeople would oust him from office.* 248

pacify (pa′ sə fī′) *v* : to calm or soothe. *Ida did everything she could to pacify the crying baby.* 87

pageant (pa′ jənt) *n* : an elaborate or colorful display. *Last fall Katura saw the northern lights, a beautiful pageant of red and green that filled the sky.* 27

parasite (per′ ə sīt′) *n* : a living thing that lives in or on an animal or plant. *Our science class taught us the difference between an internal and external parasite.* 210

passion (pa′ shən) *n* : strong, focused emotion or desire. *Jacob's passion for the Word led him to memorize the Gospel of John.* 202

perception (pər sep′ shən) *n* : a view or opinion resulting from observation. *Ole's perception of the accident was the most reliable, since he had been standing on the curb when the cars collided.* 144

picturesque (pik′ chə resk′) *adj* : creating a clear mental picture. *The picturesque details Charity includes in her letters make me feel I'm really in that little Romanian village with her.* 225

posse (pä′ sē) *n* : a group of people temporarily organized by a law officer to help with law enforcement. *In the old West it was often necessary to gather a posse to search for a thief.* 92

premises (pre′ mə səz) *n* : a building and its surrounding area of land. *The first Saturday in August is scheduled for cleaning the school and maintaining the premises.* 10

preposterous (pri päs′ trəs) *adj* : going against what is sensible or reasonable. *Marcus's excuse for being late was preposterous, and no one believed him.* 249

provender (prä′ vən dər) *n* : dry food for livestock. *The pioneer settlers hoped to find provender along the way for their teams.* 167

providential (prä′ və den′ shəl) *adj* : occurring as if by the leading of God. *Our car broke down on the loneliest stretch of the highway; it was providential that another vehicle came by within only a few minutes.* 56

Pronunciation Key

/a/ bat; /ā/ acorn; /är/ star; /e/ pet; /ē/ eagle; /er/ bear; /ər/ her; /i/ bit; /ī/ ivy; /ir/ deer; /ä/ top; /ō/ go; /ò/ lost; /òi/ coin; /aủ/ out; /òr/ corn; /ə/ but; /ü/ boot; /yü/ use; /ủ/ foot; /th/ thick; /<u>th</u>/ this; /ŋ/ bang; /zh/ measure

raving (rā′ viŋ) *n* : wild, senseless talking. *The man's ravings caused his accusers to suspect that he was guilty.* 202

rebellious (ri bel′ yəs) *adj* : defying authority or opposing normal standards of behavior. *The rebellious prodigal returned to his father and repented of his sin.* 141

reinforce (rē′ ən fȯrs′) *v* : to strengthen by adding more material for support. *The concrete driveway needs reinforcing so that it will not crack when trucks drive over it.* 22

relent (ri lent′) *v* : to soften in attitude; to give way. *Father might have relented had the twins asked respectfully instead of begging and whining.* 105

remorseful (ri mȯrs′ fəl) *adj* : marked by feelings of regret. *Shane apologized remorsefully for the trouble he had caused on the playground.* 147

rend (rend) *v* : to tear apart, especially with force or by violence. *A tiger uses its sharp teeth to rend its prey.* 183

render (ren′ dər) *v* : to give what is due. *Nathan was the first person from the community to render his service as a firefighter.* 67

reprove (ri prüv′) *v* : to scold or correct. *When reproved for doing wrong, a wise person will respond humbly.* 202

repulsive (ri pəl′ siv) *adj* : causing strong dislike or disgust. *Frances screamed, brushing the repulsive-looking beetle from her arm.* 24

resort (ri zȯrt′) *n* : a source of help or refuge. *A Christian's first resort in any difficult situation should be prayer.* 111

retain (ri tān′) *v* : to continue to have or keep. *Daniel retained his custom of praying to God even when it went against the king's decree.* 229

retract (ri trakt′) *v* : to pull or draw back. *After taking off, the pilot retracted the plane's landing gear.* 21

rigid (ri′ jəd) *adj* : stiff and inflexible. *A person who is too rigid in his opinions will often be embarrassed when the truth is revealed.* 202

rime (rīm) *n* : a buildup of ice or frost on an object. *Mike scraped a heavy coating of rime from the windshield.* 19

rogue (rōg) *n* : a mischievous person. *Uncle Robert's rumpled appearance gave him a roguish look, but in reality he was a true gentleman.* 215

rout (raůt) *n* : a wild retreat from a fight; a complete defeat. *The battle ended in the utter rout of the invaders and the flight of their leader.* 69

ruddy (rə' dē) *adj* : a healthy red color. *A person who works outside often has a ruddy complexion.* 38

sanctuary (saŋ' chə wer' ē) *n* : a holy place; a place of worship. *God told Moses exactly what kind of furniture should be made for the tabernacle's sanctuary.* 169

scheme (skēm) *n* : a plan of action, often a secret one. *Our scheme to surprise Mrs. Snyder on her birthday worked out beautifully.* 191

scoundrel (skaůn' drəl) *n* : a person who is dishonest or not respectable. *King Ahab probably heads the list of Old Testament scoundrels.* 67

scrimp (skrimp) *v* : to spend as little money as possible. *Grandpa's stories of growing up during the Depression made scrimping and saving seem attractive to us children.* 186

sentry (sen' trē) *n* : a guard, especially one who controls entrance or access. *Sentries positioned at each gate were prepared to stop anyone who approached the walled city.* 230

severe (sə vir') *adj* : causing hardship or discomfort; harsh. *Southern India experiences severity of heat and drought in April and May before the monsoon rains come.* 10

shamble (sham' bəl) *v* : to walk awkwardly with dragging feet. *The old man shambled to his seat by the door of the general store.* 235

Pronunciation Key

/a/ **bat**; /ā/ **acorn**; /är/ **star**; /e/ **pet**; /ē/ **eagle**; /er/ **bear**; /ər/ **her**; /i/ **bit**; /ī/ **ivy**; /ir/ **deer**; /ä/ **top**; /ō/ **go**; /ò/ **lost**; /òi/ **coin**; /aů/ **out**; /òr/ **corn**; /ə/ **but**; /ü/ **boot**; /yü/ **use**; /ů/ **foot**; /th/ **thick**; /<u>th</u>/ **this**; /ŋ/ **bang**; /zh/ **measure**

siege (sēj) *n* : the surrounding and blocking off of a city or fortress by an enemy. *The Babylonian siege of Jerusalem lasted many months.* 230

slough (slü) *n* : a place of deep mud or mire. *Trying to hurry across the sloughs, Trevor lost both his shoes in the mud.* 38

solitary (sä′ lə ter′ ē) *adj* : being alone or apart from others. *After a solitary walk through the woods, Shawn rejoined his family around the campfire.* 170

solitude (sä′ lə tüd′) *n* : the state of being alone. *Stephen enjoyed a time of solitude after a busy day of serving customers.* 123

solution (sə lü′ shən) *n* : a mixture formed by dissolving something in a liquid. *Gargling with a saltwater solution is soothing to a sore throat.* 192

sparse (spärs) *adj* : spread thinly; not plentiful. *Grandpa rubbed his hand over the sparse hairs on his head.* 62

spasm (spa′ zəm) *n* : (1) a sudden tightening of muscles. *Grandfather grimaced as a spasm gripped his leg.* (2) a sudden strong burst of action or emotion. *Dwight woke up during the night because of a spasm of coughing.* 108

stagnant (stag′ nənt) *adj* : not moving or flowing. *Bacteria breeds quickly in a stagnant pool of water.* 52

stature (sta′ chər) *n* : the natural height of a person. *In spite of his small stature, Wilfred was a valuable member of the team.* 23

staunch (stȯnch) *adj* : steadfastly loyal. *Canada and the United States have been staunch allies for years.* 5

sterilize (ster′ ə līz′) *v* : to clean by destroying germs or bacteria. *You can sterilize a needle by pouring alcohol over it.* 82

stipple (sti′ pəl) *v* : to speckle or fleck. *Many fish, such as rainbow trout, are stippled with gray or brown spots.* 17

submerge (səb mərj′) *v* : to sink under water. *The submerged car created a perfect hideout for the fish.* 117

supervise (sü′ pər vīz′) *v* : to oversee and direct others. *Miss Wilson joined the class on the playground, supervising activities and making sure everyone had a good time.* 79

suppress (sə pres′) *v* : to hold back or put an end to. *The dictator attempted to suppress the news about a rebellion in a nearby country.* 72

surreptitious (sər′ əp ti′ shəs) *adj* : done in secret to avoid notice. *Johnny made a surreptitious attempt to hide his library book inside his textbook.* 245

tantalizing (tan′ tə lī′ ziŋ) *adj* : tempting; very appealing. *Timmon's store has a tantalizing array of candy.* 81

tariff (ter′ əf) *n* : a tax placed on goods as they cross national borders. *On Tuesday, the President announced a new tariff on steel imported from Europe.* 206

threadbare (thred′ ber′) *adj* : worn thin from much use. *Although nearly threadbare, the old blue chair remained Granny's favorite.* 179

transfix (trans fiks′) *v* : to hold motionless, as though fastened in place. *The sermon held Joey transfixed, and he felt a surge of hope in his heart.* 11

transmitter (trans mi′ tər) *n* : a device that generates and sends out radio waves. *The ship's transmitter sent its location at regular intervals.* 195

tumult (tü′ məlt′) *n* : noisy uproar, often caused by a crowd of people. *The marketplace in a big city is often a tumult of voices with the noises of buying and selling.* 5

untainted (ən tān′ təd) *adj* : not corrupted or dirtied. *The water of the lakes high in the Cascade Mountains is untainted by pollution.* 120

vengeance (ven′ jəns) *n* : punishment inflicted in return for a wrong. *God does not want us to take vengeance on our enemies, but to leave vengeance to Him.* 67

/a/ **bat**; /ā/ **acorn**; /är/ **star**; /e/ **pet**; /ē/ **eagle**; /er/ **bear**; /ər/ **her**; /i/ **bit**; /ī/ **ivy**; /ir/ **deer**; /ä/ **top**; /ō/ **go**; /ò/ **lost**; /òi/ **coin**; /aú/ **out**; /òr/ **corn**; /ə/ **but**; /ü/ **boot**; /yü/ **use**; /ú/ **foot**; /th/ **thick**; /<u>th</u>/ **this**; /ŋ/ **bang**; /zh/ **measure**

verdict (ver′ dikt) *n* : a decision or judgment. *The jury took four hours to reach a verdict in the trial of the man who stole bread to feed his starving children.* 52

verge (vərj) *n* : the edge or boundary. *Bill was on the verge of quitting his job because of the late hours it required.* 142

veteran (ve′ tə rən) *n* : one who has had much experience in a particular field. *Miss Lewis is a veteran science teacher; her classes have inspired many a budding scientist at Harmony School.* 3

vibrant (vī′ brənt) *adj* : full of life or energy. *The lark soared into the air with a high, vibrant song.* 8

wage (wāj) *v* : to take part in; to carry on. *Finland and Russia were enemies during World War II, waging war against each other twice.* 69

warden (wȯr′ dən) *n* : a jailer or guard in a prison. *Neither smiling nor frowning, the warden simply did his job without showing any emotion.* 172

wary (wer′ ē) *adj* : cautious and alert for danger. *Donning his beekeeper's suit, Wendell warily approached the buzzing hive.* 222

wheedle (hwē′ dəl) *v* : to persuade or coax by using flattery or deceit. *Ben tried to wheedle his brother into doing an extra share of the chores.* 64

wrought (rȯt) *v* : worked. *The blacksmith wrought a pair of complicated gate hinges.* 191

zenith (zē′ nəth) *n* : (1) the highest point. *The discovery of gold brought the town to the zenith of its fame.* (2) the point in the sky directly overhead. *Your shadow is shortest when the sun is directly at the zenith.* 26

Acknowledgements

Artist: David W. Miller

Cover artist and design: David W. Miller

Some reference material from Getty Images and iStockphoto.com.

Editorial Committee: Jennifer Crider, Keith Crider, Ruth Hobbs, Mark Kardel, Jonas Sauder, Ava Shank, Shana Strite

"A Cry in the Night," from *Wood-Folk at School,* by William J. Long.

"A Time to Talk," by Robert Frost.

"All Things Are Thine," by John Greenleaf Whittier.

"Betsy's Sewing Society," from *Understood Betsy,* by Dorothy Canfield Fisher.

"Bless Them That Curse You," from *The Price of Peace,* by Mary Zook. Used by permission of Rod and Staff Publishers, Crockett, KY.

"Buffalo Dusk," from *Smoke and Steel,* by Carl Sandburg, copyright 1920 by Harcourt, Inc. and renewed 1948 by Carl Sandburg, reprinted by permission of the publisher.

"Deer," by Clive Sansom.

"Desert Miracle," by Agnes Ranney.

"Dots and Dashes," adapted from "The Cripple of Husavik," by Lois Trimble Benedict.

"Eliezer's Prayer," from the KJV Bible.

"Escape From Slavery," from *The Narrative of the Life of Frederick Douglass,* by Frederick Douglass.

"Even Uncle Henry," by Miriam Sieber Lind.

"Faint Heart," from "Faint Heart Failed." Author unknown.

"First Hunt," from *Through Many Windows,* by Arthur Gordon. ©1983 Fleming H. Revell Company, a division of Baker Book House Company. All rights reserved. Used by permission.

"Flor Silin's Gift," adapted from "The Generous Russian Peasant," by Nikolai Karamzin.

"If I Can Live," Author unknown.

"If I Can Stop One Heart," by Emily Dickinson.

"Journey by Night," by Norah Burke.

"Mother to Son," from *The Collected Poems of Langston Hughes,* by Langston Hughes, edited by Arnold Rampersad with David Roessel, Associate Editor, copyright ©1994 by the Estate of Langston Hughes. Used by permission of Alfred A. Knopf, a division of Random House, Inc.

"My Prairies," by Hamlin Garland.

"Oh, Father, in My Testing Hour," by Leonard Sommer.

"Our Heroes," by Phoebe Cary.

"Pioneering in Canada," from *Wild Goose Jack*, by Jack Miner. Used by permission of the Jack Miner Migratory Bird Foundation, Kingsville, Ontario, Canada.

"Seek-No-Further," from *Better Known as Johnny Appleseed*, by Mabel Leigh Hunt. Text copyright © Mabel Leigh Hunt. Used by permission of HarperCollins Publishers.

"Shade," by Theodosia Garrison.

"Standing Bear's Vision," from *Indian Journal*.

"Stoop!" adapted from *The Fourth Reader*. Adaptation ©2004 Christian Light Publications, Inc., Harrisonburg, VA. All rights reserved.

"Stopping by Woods on a Snowy Evening," by Robert Frost.

"The Boy Judge," from *Arabian Nights*.

"The Chickens and the Mush," by William E. Barton.

"The Cloak," by Patricia St. John. ©1977 Patricia St. John, first published by Scripture Union, 207-209 Queensway, Bletchley, Milton Keynes MK2 2EB England in 1977 and used with permission.

"The Day I Made Bread," by Sem C. Sutter, from *On the Line*, June 27, 1976, Mennonite Publishing House, Scottdale, PA. Used by permission.

"The Family," by Savannah Lee.

"The Farmer's Treasure," by Aesop.

"The Fox," by John Burroughs.

"The God of the Exodus," from the KJV Bible.

"The Hippie," adapted from "He Had a Heart." Adaptation ©2004 Christian Light Publications, Inc., Harrisonburg, VA. All rights reserved.

"The House by the Side of the Road," by Sam Walter Foss.

"The Jonah Pie," by Ruby H. Martyn.

"The Judge's Sentence," by Archibald Rutledge.

"The King's Questions," adapted from "The Three Questions," by Leo Tolstoy. Adaptation © 2004 Christian Light Publications, Inc., Harrisonburg, VA. All rights reserved.

"The Mahogany Fox," by Samuel Scoville, Jr.

"The Peanut Man and the Peanut Men," adapted from *George Washington Carver, the Man Who Overcame*, ©1966 by Lawrence Elliot.

"The Plowing," from *A Son of the Middle Border*, by Hamlin Garland.

"The Rescue," by J. L. Steffens.

"The Rich Family in Our Church," by Eddie Ogan.

"The Richest Prisoner," from *Let the Waters Roar*, by Pyotr Rumachik, as told to Georgi Vins. ©1989 Baker Book House, Grand Rapids, Michigan. All rights reserved. Used by permission of Baker Book House and Natasha Vins.

"The Road Not Taken," by Robert Frost.

"The Second Mile," by Betty Steele Everett. ©1975 Betty Steele Everett, Defiance, OH. All rights reserved. Used by permission.

"The Sense of Smell," by Tim Kennedy. Used by permission of the author.

"The Silver King," by E. G. Perrault.

"The Sweater," adapted from "The Red Sweater," by Mark Hager. Originally published in *Collier's Magazine*.

"The Way It Is," by John Ruth.

"There Is a Season," from the KJV Bible.

"Thou Art Coming to a King," by John Newton.

"Trees," by Bliss Carman.

"When Tata Prays," reprinted with permission from *God Knows My Size!* by Harvey Yoder. ©1999 TGS International, PO Box 355, Berlin, Ohio 44610. All rights reserved.

"Woof," adapted from "The Bear That Thought He Was a Dog," by Charles G. D. Roberts. Adaptation ©2004 Christian Light Publications, Inc., Harrisonburg, VA. All rights reserved.

"Your Place," by John Oxenham.